ACQUISITIONS, DIVESTITURES, AND CORPORATE JOINT VENTURES

ACQUISITIONS, DIVESTITURES, AND CORPORATE JOINT VENTURES

An Accounting, Tax, and Systems Guide for the Financial Professional

JOSEPH M. MORRIS, CPA

Contributing Authors
CHARLES A. HAWES, MA, JD, LLM
RONALD J. MARINO
EDWARD J. PILOT, CPA
CHARLES W. SEITZ II, CPA

A RONALD PRESS PUBLICATION
JOHN WILEY & SONS
New York • Chichester • Brisbane • Toronto • Singapore

Library of Congress Cataloging in Publication Data:

Morris, Joseph M., 1949–
    Acquisitions, divestitures, and corporate joint ventures.

    "A Ronald Press publication."
    Includes index.
    1. Corporations—Finance—Handbooks, manuals, etc.
2. Consolidation and merger of corporations—Handbooks,
manuals, etc.   3. Corporate divestiture—Handbooks,
manuals, etc.   4. Joint ventures—Handbooks, manuals, etc.
I. Hawes, Charles A.   II. Title.

HG4026.M67   1984   658.1'5   84-11991
ISBN 0-471-88848-6

Printed in the United States of America

10 9 8 7 6 5 4 3 2 1

This book is dedicated to
Cindy,
whose help and support in its
preparation was invaluable,
and to
Joseph, Heather, Tara, and Lindsay

PREFACE

The financial professional will find that the many roles required to function in changing business entities present some of the most significant career challenges. Great amounts of expertise and creativity are needed to perform the financial management role as companies acquire other businesses, joint ventures come together and are taken apart, and as companies carry out divestitures.

Different kinds of financial professionals find themselves working as financial managers, chief financial officers, controllers, management accountants, business consultants, independent certified public accountants, tax professionals and internal auditors. This book has been prepared to help all business professionals perform their roles in this changing business environment.

Portions of the book deal with technical accounting and tax requirements that are not necessarily relevant to all. All financial professionals, however, even those not directly concerned with accounting and taxes, will benefit from reading or referring to these sections to at least develop an awareness of the complexities involved.

Chapter 1 covers the acquisition process from beginning to end, and touches upon some areas not covered elsewhere in the book. The purpose of Chapter 1 is to provide an appreciation for the arena of the acquisition situation in which the financial professional works.

The sections dealing with the more general business considerations, such as preacquisition reviews, will help the financial profes-

sional fulfill his or her role in rendering advice and carrying out partic-
ipative roles in a business combination, joint venture, or divestiture.
Here, the financial professional must be doubly alert, in dealing with
diverse real-life business decisions that can seriously impact either
the employer or client.

The major thrust of this book is to approach business combinations
from the point of view of an acquirer. Many of the concepts in the
chapters that discuss material solely from the point of view of an
acquirer also have applicability to the chapters on corporate joint ventures and divestitures.

I have had the pleasure of working at one time or another with each
of my coauthors in various aspects of acquisitions, joint ventures, and
divestitures. We have endeavored to present in this book a nuts-and-
bolts approach to the financial professional's need in the areas of business combinations, joint ventures, and divestitures. Particular mention should be made of the work of Ronald J. Marino in the computer
systems transition area, Charles A. Hawes in the federal taxation area,
Edward J. Pilot in the divestitures area, and Charles W. Seitz in the
area of SEC and regulatory requirements.

We all have commented that we wish a book like this had been
available when we started working in these areas, and we hope that it
will be of use to its readers.

JOSEPH M. MORRIS

Denver, Colorado
September 1984

ACKNOWLEDGMENTS

Various references and brief quotations are made in this book to materials contained in pronouncements on accounting and auditing that have been issued through July 31, 1984. These are as follows:

Copyright by Financial Accounting Standards Board:

Statements of Financial Accounting Standards
FASB Interpretations
FASB Technical Bulletins

The references to, and quotations from, the above pronouncements are contained herein with the permission of the Financial Accounting Standards Board. Complete copies of the pronouncements are available from the Financial Accounting Standards Board, High Ridge Park, Stamford, Connecticut 06905.

Copyright by American Institute of Certified Public Accountants:

Opinions of the Accounting Principles Board
Accounting Interpretations of APB Opinions
Codification of Statements on Auditing Standards
Numbers 1 to 47
Statements on Standards for Accounting and Review Services

The references to, and quotations from, the above pronouncements are contained herein with permission from the American Institute of Certified Public Accountants. Complete copies of the pronouncements are available from the American Institute of Certified Public Accountants, 1211 Avenue of the Americas, New York, New York 10036.

J. M. M.

CONTENTS

1

ACQUISITIONS—A GENERAL BUSINESS PERSPECTIVE

WHY COMPANIES ACQUIRE OR MERGE

Mergers and acquisitions are a common and important aspect of modern business. A company may be motivated to acquire or combine with other business entities for various reasons, including the ones which are discussed in the following paragraphs.

Although the following comments cannot by any means be considered all-inclusive, they give a representative cross section of the kinds of goals and objectives that motivate companies to grow and diversify through combining with and acquiring other companies, in working toward such overall objectives as maximizing growth, return on investment, and protection of invested capital.

These motivations are often directly or indirectly part of the carrying out of a corporate plan, and are best managed when performed as stepping stones in fulfilling short-, medium-, and long-term goals.

Growth and expansion, and shifting of corporate emphasis will often involve dealing with the question of whether to acquire an existing operation or to start a new business from nothing. New businesses or entry into new industries through start-up always seems to involve numerous difficulties, including the discouragement of a long initial investment cycle where the new business absorbs large amounts of cash while revenues and gross profits are still growing. A successful acquisition of an existing operation will enable the acquirer to bypass much of the initial start-up aggravation, and achieve its short- and medium-term goals sooner.

Faster Growth

Mergers and acquisitions make it possible to achieve growth at a rate higher than possible through solely internal means. Furthermore, by creating a larger organization through acquisition, economies of scale can be achieved more rapidly, particularly where operations similar to the company's existing businesses are acquired.

Vertical Integration

Companies may wish to expand operations into new activities where a company's existing resources and activities provide a base for successful performance, resulting in improvement in the efficiency of the overall organization. Important motivations for vertical integration are the achieving of more stable outlet markets and greater profits through elimination of the "middle-man," and more cost efficient and stable sources of supply. Vertical integration is, for example, where a manufacturer selling on a wholesale basis acquires an existing retail distribution operation in the same industry, or acquires a company that supplies its raw materials.

Acquiring Market Share

Through acquiring other entities, an acquirer can strengthen market shares in geographic areas where the acquiring company already operates, or achieve instantaneous geographic expansion by acquiring operations in new locations. Acquisition of existing market share is often easier than starting up a new operation to compete with another entity which already has a share of the market.

Portfolio Investment

Some companies function as holding companies, by acquiring entities in unrelated industries for the purpose of investment. Ownership of a controlling interest is considered more desirable by some than acquiring small percentages of ownership because of the ability to influence the policies and activities of an investee. This approach is used by certain larger conglomerates, where the parent company functions substantially as a holding company and evaluates performance of subsidiary companies primarily from an investment analysis standpoint. The parent company may not be committed to any particular industry or industries and may acquire and dispose of the controlling interests in other companies the way an investor manages a securities investment portfolio.

In recent years, many of the aggressive conglomerates have, however, found that the acquisition of unrelated businesses sometimes creates an inefficient, unwieldy organization, and many of these conglomerates have narrowed their field of operations by divesting some of the operations previously acquired.

Changing Industries

By acquiring companies in different industries, an acquirer can shift its emphasis to industries believed to have better outlooks for the future. Sometimes an acquisition program motivated for this reason will be combined with a divestiture program, thereby resulting in a redeployment of capital.

Diversification for Counter-Cyclicality

Diversification is sometimes made by acquiring entities in industries expected to produce results counter-cyclical to those of the acquirer's present activities. That is, when seasonal or economic conditions normally cause unfavorable results in one line of business, results in the counter-cyclical business will typically improve. This can produce a more consistent earnings stream for a consolidated entity, both within fiscal years in the case of seasonally counter-cyclical businesses, and from year to year in the case of combining businesses that are counter-cyclical based on longer-term economic trends.

Diversification to Reduce Risk

Diversification into unrelated industries can reduce overall risks of the acquirer by limiting the potential total impact of negative economic trends important to individual industries.

THE ACQUISITION PROCESS

The following sections of this chapter present a discussion of the acquisition process. Although the financial professional's involvement in the process can take many different shapes, an understanding of the overall process is essential to carry out the financial and administrative support role effectively.

The discussion is divided into the following sections:

The Acquisition Team

Overall Acquisition Strategy and Criteria

Structuring Acquisitions

Establishing Price

Financing Acquisitions

Formalizing the Deal and Due Diligence

Consummation of the Acquisition

After the Acquisition—Financial and Organizational Concerns

The Acquisition Team

The process of carrying out an acquisition can require contributions from personnel in virtually every significant area of expertise within the acquirer organization, and usually will require assistance from outside specialists. There should be a single individual assigned responsibility as team leader to coordinate the work of all personnel involved and to be sure that proper steps are taken in every area of importance. The leader may be someone with financial or legal orientation, but often it will be someone in a general management line position, such as the acquirer's chief executive officer or executive vice president, or someone in a business development capacity. The person having overall responsibility should delegate to someone with a financial or legal orientation responsibility for coordination of all items of an accounting, financial, and systems nature. This person might also be given responsibility to coordinate the legal side of the acquisition process, or to serve as the liaison between the financial side and legal side of the acquisition, as well as with marketing, production, and other areas.

At a minimum, personnel having the required expertise and ability to perform in the following areas should be included on the acquisition team from the accounting, financial, and systems side.

1. Preacquisition review of the acquisition candidate.
2. Accounting for the acquisition and review of accounting principles and policies followed by the acquisition candidate.
3. Accounting systems review and transition and setting up initial reporting mechanisms for monthly operating results.
4. Systems evaluation and transition from a data processing standpoint.
5. Liaison for continuing matters requiring coordination with the seller's financial personnel.
6. Tax aspects of the acquisition, including evaluating structure of the acquisition, evaluating possible exposure to past tax liabilities and transitional tax matters (new registrations, etc.), and planning procedures for future tax compliance.

In respect to the legal area, specialized legal counsel should be available for matters dealing with the following areas:

1. Negotiation, contract preparation, and corporate structure.
2. Legal compliance with regulatory laws applicable to acquisitions, such as Blue Sky laws and Federal Trade Commission regulations.
3. Review of contractual and other legal commitments of the acquisition candidate.
4. Securities and Exchange Commission and stock exchange requirements.

Periodic meetings should be held with the people assigned responsibility in each of the above areas. It is wise for the "core" of the team, which would include those individuals whose tasks overlap and require more coordination, to attend all general meetings and to hold specialized meetings involving other personnel. The results of all meetings, including action plans and timetables, should be recorded in written memorandums, but distribution may be restricted depending on the sensitivity and confidentiality of the subject matter.

Outside experts who may also be part of the acquisition team include:

1. Outside appraisers.
2. Outside attorneys.
3. Certified Public Accountants.
4. Financial and other types of merger and acquisition consultants.

In some cases, these outside specialists may function as integral members of the team, in addition to performing specific professional services as outsiders.

The actual discussions and negotiations surrounding an acquisition can be handled any number of ways, and by different types of personnel representing the buyer and seller organizations. Depending on the size of the respective organizations and magnitude of the transaction, there may be significant involvement from the highest managerial levels, or the responsibility may be delegated to middle management levels. Normally, one would expect that each side will have an individual assigned primary responsibility for handling the transaction. This individual will draw on the support of internal and external experts from many disciplines in evaluating the acquisition candidate and developing and negotiating the terms of the acquisition. Lawyers will often handle the actual negotiations.

Overall Acquisition Strategy and Criteria

Acquisition strategies and procedures will vary widely from company to company. For some companies, an acquisition may be an isolated event. For others, acquisitions may be an integral part of the overall corporate plan, and on an ongoing basis significant resources may be allocated to developing strategies, identifying and evaluating acquisition candidates, and carrying out the acquisition process.

Some companies are so involved in acquisitions that they employ specialists in this area and have organized acquisition guideline and screening criteria which are followed in identifying and evaluating acquisition candidates. Whether a company makes acquisitions frequently or infrequently, it is a good idea to compare each acquisition candidate with predetermined criteria which have been carefully developed, based on a company's goals, capabilities, and style. Following are some general criteria that should be included in any organized acquisition guideline and screening program:

1. Kinds of industries, and company characteristics and size.
2. Size of markets and expected market growth.
3. Share of market held by the candidate.
4. Ease with which competitors can enter the market.
5. Stage of the technology—for example, still in the development stage or a mature technology.
6. Competitive advantages of the acquisition candidate's product or service.
7. Amount of investment required and anticipated return rates.
8. Existence of skilled in-place management.

The process of searching for and identifying acquisition candidates can be multifaceted, involving extensive use of internal and external resources. A search may consist of analysis of all companies in an industry with volume or assets in specified ranges of size, or using other criteria to develop the initial listing of companies to submit to the screening process. The Standard Industrial Classification (SIC) codes developed by the federal government can often be used as a source for identifying companies in a particular industry.

Outside sources, including commercial and investment bankers and business brokers, can be asked for advice and assistance in identifying acquisition candidates. However, many large corporations will try to avoid using business brokers because of the large fees that may be involved. Of course, the acquirer would not be concerned where the seller has contracted with a business broker and agreed to pay any fees.

Acquisition discussions are sometimes initiated when a company desiring to be acquired establishes a contact with a potential acquirer or is put into contact with a potential acquirer by a broker or another third party. Companies may wish to be acquired for such reasons as financial difficulties or a desire of major stockholder/officers to retire or sell at a good price, and they may seek out potential acquirers. A divestiture of an individual line of business by a larger company might also be a reason for the initial contact between acquirer and seller.

In practice, a small percentage of acquisition investigations result in consummation of a business combination, because there will usually be one or more circumstances that will eliminate the candidate from consideration. Additionally, the parties may be unable to negotiate an agreeable transaction from the standpoint of purchase price, form of consideration, or for other reasons.

An acquiring company will want to acquire at the lowest price, and for that reason the most attractive acquisition candidates are often those whose potential value is greater than current fair market value, whether based on stock market prices or negotiable purchase price. An acquirer may believe an acquisition candidate has been underutilizing its resources, and that with changes the acquirer has in mind, the operating results of the acquisition candidate can be improved. It sometimes works to the seller's advantage to create the impression that the seller, for whatever reason, hasn't done a quality job in managing the entity being sold, even though most of the fundamentals of a successful business are present.

Structuring Acquisitions

In conducting negotiations, extending and accepting offers, and working out the terms of an acquisition, two fundamental issues are always present:

1. The identification of what is to be purchased (e.g., which assets, stock, or business).
2. The structure of the transaction and the form and amount of consideration to be paid, including treatment of liabilities of the entity to be acquired.

The acquirer and seller, in negotiating and developing the structure of an acquisition transaction, may be influenced by many factors, including tax ramifications. The tax aspects of acquisitions are covered in detail in Chapter 6. Two primary forms of structuring acquisitions are for the acquirer to purchase (a) assets, together with an associated business, or (b) stock of a corporation that owns assets and operates an associated business.

Asset Purchases. A major advantage to the acquirer commonly envisioned with a transaction structured as an asset purchase is the opportunity for the acquirer to eliminate uncertainty as to liabilities being assumed. In respect to the agreement with the seller, it may be that the acquirer assumes no liabilities, making the transaction "clean" from the acquirer's standpoint. Responsibility for unidentified claims from creditors related to prior transactions will usually remain with the seller. It has been said that "the acquirer always wants to purchase assets, and the seller always wants to sell stock." Although this may be an oversimplification, many people do concur.

However, there are pitfalls that should be taken into consideration by the acquirer in an asset purchase, including statutory responsibilities which impact an acquirer of assets in certain cases. The Bulk Transfer Act as included in Article 6 of the Uniform Commercial Code requires that notice of an intended sale of assets be given to the creditors of a business where the principal business of the seller is the sale of inventory from stock. To be subject to the bulk transfer disclosure requirements, a major portion of the inventory must be sold. The transfer of a substantial portion of the fixed assets of a business is a bulk transfer for purposes of the Bulk Transfer Act only if in connection with a bulk transfer of inventory. There is no clear definition in Article 6 of what is precisely meant by a "major" portion of the inventory or a "substantial" portion of fixed assets. The Bulk Transfer Act requires that for covered transactions, specific information about the assets being transferred and the debts of the seller be given to all creditors and claimants against the seller at least 10 days before the transfer or payment for the goods. This supposedly gives the creditor ample time to take any action considered necessary. If the required notices are not given, the acquirer may be exposed for claims with respect to the assets purchased. These are some of the general concerns of the Bulk Transfer Act; a more detailed legal treatment is beyond the scope of this book. Legal counsel should be sought where this law seems to apply.

Other areas to consider are possible exposure for product liability where a consumer previously dealt with the business now operated by the acquirer, and possible exposure to unpaid taxes and workmen's compensation claims associated with the acquired business. Again, legal counsel should be sought in these areas.

These types of liabilities would normally initially result in claims against the seller, but in the seller's inability to pay, they could lead to claims against the acquirer. This gives great importance to proper compliance with statutes, to the indemnifications normally requested from a seller with respect to liabilities, and also to the insurance coverages maintained by the seller and acquirer both before and after the acquisition.

Another perceived major advantage of an asset purchase is that the acquirer will achieve a stepped-up basis on the assets for tax purposes through allocation of the purchase price to the assets acquired. Although stepped-up basis can sometimes also be achieved after a stock purchase, the process of stepping-up basis after a purchase of stock is somewhat more complex, sometimes involving liquidation of the acquired corporation.

The tax aspects of a sale of assets are often not favorable to the seller, because this can result in a tax gain at the corporate level on the sale of the assets, followed by a tax on gain to the shareholders of a selling corporation upon payment of dividends or liquidation of the selling corporation. Careful tax planning and proper tax elections by a selling corporation are required to avoid or minimize this double taxation.

Stock Purchases.   Stock purchases are often structured as tax-free reorganizations, which have stringent requirements as to the forms of consideration that may be given (generally an exchange of stock of the acquirer for the stock of the acquired company). This has the obvious advantage to the seller of deferring any tax gains, and may often be an important point in negotiation to the seller. The tax disadvantage to the acquirer is that it is not as easy to obtain a stepped-up basis of the assets for tax purposes.

Whether the transaction is a tax-free exchange or a purchase of stock for cash or other consideration (resulting in a tax gain to the seller), the tax attributes of the acquired corporation in a stock purchase are normally carried forward into the consolidated tax return of the acquirer, including the carrying forward of the tax losses for offset against future taxable income. Restrictions exist, however, regarding the extent to which these losses can be offset against future income, based on the nature of the business of the acquired corporation before and after the acquisition, and on the percentages of ownership changes.

Some stock acquisitions are made through the use of tender offers, where an offer is made to the stockholders of another company to exchange cash or other consideration for their shares of the target company. "Friendly" tender offers involve cooperation between the acquirer and directors and management of the target company before the tender offer is made. In an "unfriendly" tender offer, directors and management of the target company may be opposed to the tender offer, and may fight to convince the stockholders not to convey their shares to the company extending the tender offer. Occasionally, several competing acquirers will attempt to obtain control of the same company through competing tender offers.

Establishing Price

The potential acquirer may use traditional valuation techniques in developing estimates of purchase prices to propose in negotiation, and in estimating maximum purchase prices it might agree to. Five general valuation approaches used in estimating the value of an acquisition candidate (and the selling price to be asked for by the seller, for that matter) are discussed in the following sections.

Discounted Cash Flow.   Because an acquisition is an investment decision, use of the discounted cash flow return on investment concept (frequently referred to as *DCF-ROI*) is an important step for the potential acquirer to employ in evaluating most acquisitions. This approach is based on a fundamental concept that as a result of the acquisition of the new entity, two things will happen: (1) cash goes out for the purchase, and (2) cash comes in from positive cash flow from operations. In performing a DCF-ROI evaluation, the cash outflows (presumably early in the cycle) are related to the cash inflows provided by the earning of the acquired entity, plus a final cash inflow provided by the assumed sale of the entity at the end of the holding period (frequently referred to as *residual value*). In many cases the residual value will be assumed to be far in the future, and will have less impact on the results of the DCF-ROI computation than the positive cash flows expected for the years closer to the acquisition.

One way that the DCF-ROI concept can be used in developing an opinion as to the estimated value of an acquisition candidate is to determine the present value of the estimated future cash inflows which would be provided by the acquisition candidate, using an assumed rate. In theory, the present value obtained by using the minimum rate of return that the acquirer considers acceptable should produce a present value which is equal to the highest amount that the acquirer should be willing to pay for the acquisition candidate. Many alternative computations using different estimates of future cash inflows and different assumed discount rates, or required rates of return, can be made in analyzing the effects of potential future events and developing ranges of potential present values of the acquisition candidate.

Another use of the DCF-ROI approach is to determine the discount rate, or rate of return implicit in the relationship between the asking price for an acquisition candidate and the acquirer's estimate of future cash inflows, or even for future cash inflows projected by the seller. If this rate is below the rate of return required by the acquirer, then the acquirer might consider the asking price too high.

Price Earnings (P/E) Multiples. Simply stated, a price earnings multiple of an acquisition candidate is its purchase price divided by its net income after income taxes for a one year period. The one year period will normally be the current year, although another way to do the calculation is to take the present quarter's net income and annualize it. If the calculation is done this way, seasonality should be considered. As can be noted for some publically traded securities, the P/E ratio of an entity on a rapid earnings growth trend can become quite high (e.g., 40 times earnings) in that investors are paying a higher price in the belief that future earnings will be much greater.

P/E ratio statistics are often compared, and available for major companies in a particular industry in trade publications. Sometimes, recent purchase prices paid for similar businesses can be used for a guideline comparison by applying the P/E ratio implicit in the comparative business acquisitions to the earnings of the acquisition candidate to arrive at an estimate of comparative value. Businesses in the same industry, or with similar risk and reward characteristics should be used.

Percentage of Gross. In some situations, particularly where much smaller businesses are involved, an acquirer may compare the possible purchase price with the gross sales of the entity, and express the purchase price as, for example, 50% of gross. Undeniably, a prudent acquirer will also look at the acquisition candidate's assets, and also examine the costs and expenses of the acquisition candidate to determine if there is anything that would prevent the acquirer from realizing the normal profit margins expected in a particular industry.

Value of Assets.   Most acquisitions involve the purchase of net tangible assets with a premium arising from the ongoing value of the business as a going concern. Therefore, the fair market value of the net tangible assets of an acquisition will in most cases be a useful item of information to the acquirer in establishing a minimum (and probably below minimum) value for the acquisition candidate. If a seller cannot sell a business as a whole for at least the fair market value of the tangible assets, then the seller is usually better advised to liquidate the entity by selling the assets individually. The seller may not do this, however, because of the comparative difficulty of taking apart an ongoing business for individual sale of assets, or for tax reasons.

To the acquirer, the "bargain" purchase of assets bears some value in that if the acquisition turns sour from the standpoint of continued operations as a going concern, the assets can always be disposed of to recover a good percentage of the acquirer's investment.

Market Value of Stock.   Market value of recent transactions in stock of an acquisition candidate will give an overall indicated market value of the stockholder's equity of the acquisition candidate. This will be most determinable where public companies are involved, but may also be determinable in some cases for the shares of privately owned companies where such have recently changed hands.

The fair market value of an acquisition candidate's shares of stock will be of particular concern to an acquirer who is attempting a tender offer; normally a higher price than the present market will be offered to induce stockholders to sell. However, one should note that the acquirer, in arriving at the price to be offered in a tender offer, has probably evaluated the acquisition candidate's tangible asset value and future earnings and cash flow potential in comparison with the market value of stock, and the price that must be paid to make the tender offer successful.

Summary of Establishing Price. Although quantitative evaluations such as the preceding can provide guidelines in developing a proposed purchased price, there are many other factors that affect purchase prices, and a purely mathematical approach to pricing an acquisition will rarely be the sole determinant. For example, market values of stock sometimes do not reflect the fair market value of a company's assets, so the market price of stock at some point may not be an adequate measure of the value of a company or its assets on a liquidation basis. The market value of shares of stock owned by many shareholders can take on a significantly higher value in the context of a single acquirer owning a majority of the shares and therefore controlling the acquired company.

In many acquisitions, the effects of the structuring of the transaction on future taxes can be an important negotiation point in determining the price. Furthermore, and perhaps most significant, the dynamics of negotiation, economic considerations, and other motivations of the acquirer and seller can affect a negotiated purchase price substantially.

An important procedure for an acquirer is to evaluate carefully the pro forma projections of future operating results and the financial position of its consolidated entity, assuming the acquisition is consummated. This information can be used to measure the ramifications of consummating an acquisition at various purchase prices, or consummating a transaction at all. The effects of a proposed acquisition on projected earnings per share may have a bearing on the total purchase price and form of consideration an acquirer can afford to offer. For example, where new shares of stock are issued to consummate a business combination, earnings per share of the acquiring company (or issuing company in the case of a pooling of interests) can decline if the increased earnings of the combined operation are not sufficient to offset the effect of the increased outstanding shares in the computation of earnings per share. This is why the market prices of public companies sometimes decline immediately after the announcement of the intent to acquire another company in exchange for newly issued common stock. The implications of any impact such as this should be carefully evaluated.

Financing Acquisitions

Many major corporate acquisitions are carried out with the purchase price being paid in cash, or by an exchange of shares of stock. However, many smaller acquirers, and even some large corporations will attempt to finance a portion of the purchase price. This may be in the form of the seller holding notes for a part of the purchase price on a short-, medium-, or long-term basis, or outside financing from banks or other lenders. Acquisitions will typically be easier to finance from outside sources where the company being acquired has a strong asset base that can be pledged as collateral.

Senior lenders, usually banks, other financial institutions, and other asset-based lenders (including commercial finance companies) function solely as creditors of the acquirer. Often, the assets of the acquired entity will be pledged as collateral for funds borrowed from these senior lenders with the amount that may be borrowed limited to percentages of the different kinds of assets. The best interest rates from this group will be obtained from banks.

Subordinated lenders, which include insurance companies and pension funds, take a subordinated position in liquidation to the senior lenders. Frequently, for his subordinated position, a lender will have some equity participation, either through the right to convert his or her debt instruments into common stock, or through a bargain purchase of stock at the time of lending funds pursuant to the subordinated debt instrument.

A third layer of funding for financing acquisitions involves those entities that provide funds on the basis of heavy equity participation. Although subordinated debt may also be involved, the entities which provide financing of this sort will normally receive significant equity positions in the acquired company. This form of financing would not have much applicability to major corporate acquisitions. The types of entities providing this kind of funding include venture capital firms and some insurance companies.

Many smaller acquisitions, particularly those made by individuals or small groups of investors, do not involve the complicated financing considerations implied by the dealings that would be required with the various types of lenders previously mentioned. In fact, in a typical smaller acquisition made by these types of acquirers, one might expect to see a down payment for a portion of the purchase price, perhaps a bank loan for working capital needs or a little more of the down payment, and the seller holding a term note over 5 to 10 years for over 50% of the purchase price at a favorable interest rate.

A detailed presentation of how to raise funds for an acquisition or leveraged buyout, where the use of leverage plays a significant part in the character of the transaction, would be very complex, involving many special technical and promotional areas, and is beyond the scope of this book. The foregoing is provided to give an overview of some of the major considerations, and to point out the importance of financing in the acquisition process for some transactions.

Formalizing the Deal and Due Diligence

Letters of Intent. At a point where the parties have arrived at an understanding that an acceptable transaction can be consummated, the parties may exchange a document referred to as a letter of intent. Letters of intent are used to define the major terms of the proposed transaction. They are normally not legally binding, but serve as a working document signed by both parties to ensure that their understandings are consistent, and to provide a guide for the preparation of the formal contracts. Some or all of the following items are typically covered in letters of intent:

1. The nature of the transaction, including the assets or stock to be sold, and treatment of liabilities.
2. The form and amount of consideration, and structure.
3. Definition of what procedures the acquirer and seller must carry out before the final determination to go ahead with the transaction, including verification of assets, financial records, and examination of contracts and other legal documents.
4. A proposed timetable for carrying out the above procedures, preparing the formal agreements, and consummating the transaction.
5. A statement that although the letter of intent accurately sets forth the intent of the parties, it is not legally binding.

Also, either as part of a letter of intent or as the subject of a separate agreement, it is advisable for the parties to enter into a confidentiality agreement in which each party agrees to keep confidential any business information or trade secrets learned during the discussions of the possible acquisition.

Due Diligence.   Due diligence is a term used to refer to the process of reviewing and verifying information about the company being acquired. It often is carried out after the parties have arrived at a preliminary understanding that an acquisition is likely, and may even take place after a letter of intent has been exchanged.

Due diligence procedures may be performed by internal personnel from an acquirer's organization, outside lawyers, CPAs, or other specialists. The depth and intensity of due diligence procedures can vary from cursory inquiry and investigation of only the most general and obvious areas, such as corporate documentation matters, to in-depth audit and verification of asset ownership, reviews or audits of financial records, and due diligence procedures that are less financial and legal in nature. For example, if a major item of value is an apparent technological development, due diligence procedures might include an evaluation of the technology by qualified scientists or experts, including developing an estimate of how defensible patents with respect to technology of the acquisition candidate would be.

The term *preacquisition reviews* has been used in this book to describe the due diligence procedures typically performed by a financial professional. This area is covered in detail in Chapter 2.

Consummation of the Acquisition

Somewhere along the line, most acquisitions under investigation fall off the track for one reason or another. For those that pass all the tests and survive the investigations, evaluations, and negotiations, the actual consummation can sometimes seem anticlimactic in relation to the excitement and uncertainty of all the events that lead up to the actual closing. Lawyers for either the purchaser or seller will prepare a draft of the pertinent contracts, and it is common for many details requiring further negotiation to arise as the formal contract is developed and agreed upon.

If all goes well, the day for closing will finally arrive. At a closing, various kinds of documents are executed by lawyers and officers of the buyer and seller.

Following is a general list of major documents executed or provided at the closing of an acquisition transaction. Of course, the documents needed for any one transaction will depend on the nature of the specific transaction.

Stock Purchases

1. Stock Purchase Agreement.
2. Opinion of counsel as to legality of transaction.
3. Stock power conveying control of corporation.
4. Promissory notes and security instruments.
5. Resolutions of boards of directors.
6. Assignments and required consents from third parties.

Asset Purchases

1. Asset Sale and Purchase Agreement.
2. Opinion of counsel as to legality of the transaction.
3. Bills of sale and deeds.
4. Promissory notes, mortgages, and security instruments.
5. Assignments and required consents from third parties.

AFTER THE ACQUISITION—FINANCIAL AND ORGANIZATIONAL CONCERNS

After consummation of the business combination, a new combined business entity comes into existence. From the accountant's standpoint, if the combination qualifies for accounting under the pooling of interests method, the existing balances of assets and liabilities are carried forward. If the combination does not satisfy all the conditions for pooling of interests accounting, the purchase accounting method is used, and the assets and liabilities of the acquired entity are revalued to current market values. Usually this will result in increasing the carrying values of assets, and the recording of goodwill. The acquirer must go through the mechanical process of determining these revaluations and establishing record keeping for these changes. This often involves the engagement of a professional independent appraisal firm to appraise the value of the individual assets. The acquirer must also prepare for tax compliance with respect to the acquired entity.

There is an immediate need for systems and financial reporting methods to be reviewed and integrated with the acquirer's operations, for processing of transactions, and continued financial and operational reporting. All of these areas are covered in detail in Chapters 3, 4, and 5.

2

PREACQUISITION REVIEWS

A financial professional may be called upon to perform specific procedures, or to investigate an acquisition candidate using general guidelines as to the conduct and types of matters to be investigated, with the financial professional planning the specific procedures. Such assignments are frequently referred to as preacquisition reviews. Preacquisition reviews can be performed by financial personnel from an acquirer organization, by outside consultants, or outside CPAs in conjunction with an audit, review or compilation of financial statements, or as a separate special service. The term *accountant* will be used in this chapter to refer to financial personnel employed by the acquirer, or to outside CPAs, or other business consultants who might perform a preacquisition review.

A preacquisition review should enable accountants to comment on all significant accounting and business matters coming to their attention as a result of the procedures from their perspective as financial experts and businesspersons.

The following sections discuss different aspects of preacquisition reviews that are important to the accountant. The topics parallel the detailed preacquisition review program set forth in Appendix 2-1.

GENERAL BUSINESS CONSIDERATIONS

An understanding of the industry environment in which the acquisition candidate operates is important for properly carrying out a preacquisition review. Where the acquisition candidate is engaged in more than one industry or line of business, each should be considered separately, if significant. The study should include analyzing the industries in which the principal customers and suppliers operate, and also identifying and analyzing the major competitors of the acquisition candidate. Recent and expected future trends in the availability and cost of key materials and services are important.

Trends and growth of the market with respect to the industry as a whole and the individual companies in the industry, and the potential of the acquisition candidate to maintain or increase market share in light of the indicated trends can be important and indicative of the future potential of the acquisition candidate.

The relative financial, operational, and technological strengths of the companies in the industry should be compared, together with the relative acceptance and demand for each competitor's products or services.

The possibility of customers or suppliers further integrating their operations, thereby increasing competition, should be evaluated. This may depend to some degree on the complexity of the industry's technology, or the amount of investment required to enter the industry.

The potential for technological obsolescence through technological advances, creating a need to invest heavily in research and development, is an important consideration.

The company's activities and commitment to research and development activities should be noted, as well as the results of past efforts. In this area in particular, the accountant may not be qualified to evaluate the implications of research and development activities, but inquiries may provide additional information of interest to persons in the acquirer organization who are qualified to evaluate this area.

The overall stability and seasonal and cyclical aspects of the industry should be focused on, as should the extent to which government regulation may influence the business.

ORGANIZATIONAL INFORMATION

The review of the organization of the acquisition candidate should include identifying key management personnel in each area of needed expertise and reviewing the background and present responsibilities of each. The management team should be considered in light of anticipated needs to provide continuity of competent management after the acquisition. Where the successful management of the company is dependent on the abilities of one or a few individuals, that fact should be identified and carefully evaluated.

The compensation of management in relation to compensation of officials at comparable levels of responsibility in the acquirer organization should be noted, as should any employment contracts that may have been entered into. Frequently, companies expecting to be acquired enter into employment contracts with key management, especially where members of management are also significant stockholders.

Review and discussion of organization charts and procedures manuals can provide extensive insight into the business and operations of the acquisition candidate and identify areas where efficiency may be improved. This type of information can assist the acquirer in measuring the profit potential in the future through better utilization of resources or the ability to reduce staff.

Major plants, assets, facilities, and productive capacity in relation to actual capacity utilized should be identified, together with remaining estimated useful lives of the assets and facilities.

Company records, such as minutes of board meetings, articles of incorporation, corporate bylaws, stockholder agreements, and listings of all legal and corporate entities controlled by or affiliated with the acquisition candidate should be reviewed.

Employee benefit plans, particularly pension plans, should be carefully reviewed, including the funding status of pension funds. Review of this information can provide the acquirer with insight into important matters that should be negotiated in the terms of the purchase agreement in situations such as where the vested benefits under a pension plan exceed the balance of the pension fund assets. These possible "hidden" liabilities related to employee benefit plans can be of great concern.

The insurance program and policies of the acquisition candidate should be analyzed to determine major risks that are present as well as adequacy of coverage. Any self-insurance practices should be particularly noted. Even though in the circumstances self-insurance may be a prudent decision, the potential for financial exposure from self-insured losses from events both before and after the acquisition should be focused on by the acquirer. The review of product liability insurance policies can point out a product line which might be more susceptible to liability claims than the acquirer may consider acceptable. The acquirer may also note possible reductions in premiums available by combining insurance policies of the acquisition candidate with those of the acquirer.

EVALUATING PURCHASE AGREEMENTS

Any preacquisition review should include a careful review of the purchase agreement to ensure that the procedures are planned with an understanding of all significant aspects of the proposed transaction. In addition, the review of the purchase contract will enable the accountant to make suggestions on how to better structure the transaction, or to provide advice on implications of an accounting, business, or operational nature.

The accountant should carefully examine any sections that include terms dependent on accounting measurements. These types of terms can impact determination or adjustment of the purchase price, or representations made by the seller regarding the financial condition of the business being sold.

An area of particular concern for the accountant to focus on is the accounting basis upon which the acquisition candidate's financial statements and data referred to in the purchase agreement are based. Frequently, "usual and customary accounting practices" will be mentioned and reference made to an attached set of financial statements. A typical passage from a purchase agreement will read "consistent with the company's usual and customary accounting practices used in preparing the attached financial statements in accordance with generally accepted accounting principles." A problem could develop in interpretation of the agreement at a later date if any of the accounting practices of the acquisition candidate are believed not to be in accordance with generally accepted accounting principles, and the accountant should be alert for any problems that could result from interpretation of such a definition. The possibility of a problem in this area will be reduced significantly if the financial statements have been audited and reported upon by an outside CPA. However, differences of opinion on matters of generally accepted accounting principles can exist which cause one accountant to disagree with another as to the preferability or correctness of accounting practices and principles used in preparing financial statements.

Following are some specific areas that the accountant should be particularly alert for in reviewing a purchase agreement:

1. Guarantees of net realizable values of accounts receivable and inventories, where the purchase price will be adjusted depending on amounts realized.

2. Provisions dealing with the assumption of liabilities which may be handled any number of ways in purchase agreements, ranging from the buyer indemnifying the seller completely from all past liabilities associated with the business, to the seller assuming all liabilities, whether or not they have been recorded in the balance sheet at the purchase date.

3. The accountant should ensure that the acquirer understands the accounting and business ramifications of any contingencies that it will be assuming exposure for in the purchase agreement. The resolution of a preacquisition contingency can ordinarily be treated as an increase of the acquisition cost for accounting purposes in a purchase method acquisition, thereby avoiding an immediate reduction in reported earnings from an unfavorable resolution of a preacquisition contingency. However, the economic effect of a cash outlay which could be caused by an unfavorable contingency resolution should be discussed with the acquirer for consideration in negotiation.

4. The seller may represent in the agreement that the net worth of the company being acquired is at least equal to a specified minimum amount. The existence of this type of provision normally requires ascertaining that operating results and other factors between the date the agreement was drafted and the transaction date do not cause the net worth to decline below the minimum required amount.

5. Provisions that would prevent pooling of interests treatment, if such is the intent of the parties, or any provisions that might cause a problem with the desired tax structure of the transaction.

6. Aspects of the agreement that the accountant believes should be considered for legality, such as possible antitrust violations.

7. Covenants or representations which the accountant believes may not be accurate, or which either the acquirer or seller may have difficulty complying with.

8. Contracts or obligations being assumed by the acquirer which may be unfavorable or which could be at other than current market rates.

9. Terms regarding employee benefit and pension plans, and the disposition of existing pension and other employee benefit funds.

10. Maintenance of prior years' accounting and tax records and changeover of accounting and data processing systems.

REVIEW OF PROPOSED TRANSACTION

A key area to be considered in reviewing a proposed acquisition is whether the terms of the transaction are consistent with the desired tax and accounting effects. In particular, the accountant or a tax specialist should ascertain that if a tax-free transaction is desired, none of the terms of the agreement would prevent the transaction from being tax-free. Similar considerations would result in confirming that pooling of interests accounting will be applicable, if the parties so desire.

It may be appropriate, in reviewing the proposed transaction, to review or prepare pro forma financial statements on a historical and projected basis to provide a clear, forward-looking view of the impact of the transaction. Part of the evaluation of a proposed acquisition should include evaluating the expected financial impact on reported earnings after the acquisition. With the pooling of interests method, pro forma combination of data of the previously separate companies will be a more simple process than where a purchase acquisition is involved. Projecting the future earnings impact of a purchase acquisition will often require estimating higher depreciation charges from the written-up value of acquired fixed assets and the amortization of goodwill.

Furthermore, the initial period after an acquisition may include in cost of sales a higher charge for acquired inventories stated at a higher than normal amount. In view of the normal expectations of an acquirer that its accountants will provide advice on the accounting aspects of an acquisition, it is important that the accountant anticipate the post-acquisition financial reporting implications of a proposed acquisition and that he or she advises the acquirer accordingly.

Besides projected reported earnings, projected cash flow after the acquisition should be carefully reviewed. Often, an acquired operation can require supplemental working capital or other investments by the acquirer soon after the acquisition, and this should not come as a surprise.

Computation of pro forma financial ratios may provide additional insight into the economic effects of the proposed transaction.

ACCOUNTING AND FINANCIAL CONSIDERATIONS

The analysis and review of historical financial data should include identifying any unusual or nonrecurring items that distort reported earnings. Inquiry should be made regarding any significant adjustments made at year-ends which may give indication of the kinds of items that could cause distortion of current interim period data. Funds flows should be scrutinized carefully through reviewing the statements of changes in financial position, and cash flow statements. Prior years' budget to actual comparisons should be reviewed. Balance sheets and components of financial position should be analyzed and related to the proposed purchase price where possible, on a historical and current cost replacement basis.

Forecasted and projected balance sheet and income statement data provided by the acquisition candidate should be reviewed and critically analyzed. A forecast refers to what is believed to be the most likely outcome based on the most probable future conditions, and may also include the effects of certain strategies planned by management. The assumptions upon which the forecasted or projected data are based should be reviewed for reasonableness, and the accountant should consider to what degree the assumptions may be motivational or overly optimistic. Where major assumptions have a significant effect, ranges should be computed to indicate the effects of possible variations in the future outcomes that would be caused by different assumptions. Prior forecasts or projections should be compared with subsequent actual results to ascertain how accurate these have been in the past.

One should expect that a company trying to sell itself will present an optimistic impression of its future potential, and there is always a risk that projections and forecasts of future financial results provided by an acquisition candidate are unrealistic. This is particularly noticeable where an acquisition candidate is young in its growth cycle or is introducing a new technology. In a preacquisition review, the accountant should have an open mind to recognize the potential of an acquisition candidate, but should be prepared to adopt a posture of professional skepticism should the circumstances require.

Historical, forecasted, and projected data should be analyzed on the basis of product lines, by facility, or any other breakdown that depicts results in separately identifiable segments. Firm order backlogs should be reviewed on this basis also, and compared with sales trends and firm order backlogs existing in prior periods to identify any trends which should be investigated further.

APPENDIX 2-1: CHECKLIST FOR A PREACQUISITION REVIEW

GENERAL BUSINESS CONSIDERATIONS

1. Develop an understanding of the major business factors in the industry in which the acquisition candidate operates.
   a. Identify the major companies, market share, and distinctive features and ways of doing business (production, marketing, etc.) of the acquisition candidate and major competitors. Determine if there are features that make the acquisition candidate more attractive than its competitors.

b. Determine trends in market share, revenues, unit quantities and volumes, and profitability for the acquisition candidate and major competitors.

c. Determine what the important technological aspects of the industry are and if there have been any significant recent developments, and how this would appear to influence the business of the acquisition candidate.

d. Evaluate the significance of government regulation and regulatory requirements, including any new or proposed regulatory requirements which may not have yet affected the acquisition candidate's reported results.

e. Determine how difficult it is for a new competitor to enter the industry, and to what degree competitors or suppliers might try to integrate their operations forward or backward.

2. Analyze the major materials and productive resources used in producing the acquisition candidate's product, the status of relationships with major vendors and suppliers, including information on recent years' volumes and prices for purchases from the vendors and suppliers.

3. Review listings of major customers, and ascertain the amount and types of business done with each. Consider the risk factors present where a high percentage of the acquisition candidate's business is done with one or a few customers.

4. Determine to what degree the business of the acquisition candidate is seasonal, and how this impacts the compatibility of the acquisition candidate with the acquirer's business trends.

5. Evaluate labor relations in the industry, including the extent to which the labor force of the industry and the acquisition candidate are unionized. If the labor force of the acquisition candidate is not unionized, evaluate the likelihood that this will become a concern in the future, and evaluate the additional costs that might result.

ORGANIZATIONAL INFORMATION

1. Obtain the history and background of the acquisition candidate, from the time it was founded to the present.

2. Obtain details of the current capital structure of the company, including any contingently issuable shares from conversions or stock options.

3. Review organization charts, procedures manuals, and information on key management personnel, including compensation, age, position, and background. Review management compensation for several preceding years.

4. Obtain and review a list of all current contracts. Note all important aspects, including transferability clauses in the event of change of ownership of the acquisition candidate. Ensure that the following kinds of contracts have been specifically requested and reviewed.

   a. Employment contracts.

   b. Stockholder agreements.

   c. Sales and purchase agreements.

   d. Union agreements.

   e. Pension and other employee benefit plans and agreements.

   f. Leases.

   g. Loan and banking agreements.

5. Identify all related parties and analyze the details of all intercompany transactions, including dealings with unconsolidated related parties.

6. Review procedures for preventing illegal acts or payments.

7. If the acquisition candidate is a subsidiary, consider what services provided by the parent may need to be replaced after acquisition.

8. Obtain and review credit agency reports on the acquisition candidate.

9. Read minutes of meetings of board of directors and committees for several years, articles of incorporation, corporate bylaws, and all other legal instruments related to the corporate activities of the acquisition candidate.

10. Obtain geographical information on location of markets, facilities, and employees.

11. Obtain a listing of all employee benefit plans. Review pension fund financial statements, the status of pension funding in

relation to prior service and vested benefits, and compliance with ERISA and IRS requirements.

12. Obtain copies of all insurance policies, and analyze major coverage and exposures, including any self-insurance practices, and details of major insurance claims in the last few years.

13. Obtain an understanding of the acquisition candidate's research and development activities—including an analysis of funds and resources committed and results of past research and development activities.

14. Review the acquisition candidate's major assets and operational facilities, and estimate their remaining useful lives and productive capacity in relation to capacity utilized in recent years.

15. Determine the adequacy of the system of internal control.

REVIEW OF PROPOSED TRANSACTION

1. Ascertain the following:
   a. The reason the company is for sale.
   b. If any previous proposed transactions have been terminated by the prospective buyers and why.
   c. If any cosmetic actions have been taken by the seller to make the acquisition candidate look more attractive than it really is.

2. Review the purchase agreement and any other documents related to the transaction.

3. Review the prospectus or offering memorandum and correspondence related to the proposed acquisition.

4. Determine the desired tax structure and accounting method (purchase or pooling of interests) to be used, and determine if the terms of the transaction are consistent with the desired effects.

5. Consider any filings with the SEC or other regulatory authorities that may be required as a result of the acquisition.

6. Ascertain and consider the role of intermediaries and other professionals in the transaction, and inquire as to the amounts of fees payable to each.

7. Consider whether any potential antitrust considerations could exist and if any pretransaction filings or approvals are necessary.

ACCOUNTING AND FINANCIAL

1. Develop an understanding of significant industry and company accounting practices and policies.
2. Review financial statements, annual reports, and SEC registration statements for several preceding fiscal years, and the most recent interim financial data available.
3. Review income statement, balance sheet, and cash flow forecasts for current and future years, including product line and business segment breakdowns.
4. Determine carrying values of major facilities owned, and identify any assets pledged as collateral or as to which liens exist.
5. Review copies of recent years' tax returns and information on status of tax examinations for open years, and copies of recent reports on tax examinations.
6. Ascertain details of pending or threatened litigation.
7. If possible, review auditors' work papers and letters of recommendation.
8. Review current backlog information by product line and business segment, and comparative backlog data for prior periods.
9. Review the detailed accounting records to the extent deemed appropriate in the circumstances, comparing such to trial balances used in preparing the financial statements. Be alert for adjusting entries made in consolidation for judgmental adjustments to the financial statements.

3

SYSTEMS TRANSITION

Once an acquisition has been completed, the transition phase begins. Actually, the well-organized acquisition team will have begun to study the situation well in advance of the actual closing of the transaction and will have already begun to make its plans for transitioning the systems of the entity being acquired.

Overall responsibility for coordinating the accounting and systems transition will usually rest with someone in the controller's department of the acquirer. This team leader, with the support of specialists in the accounting and data processing areas, must develop a priority list of the most critical areas to get under immediate control.

In all cases, the most critical area will be to ensure that systems will be in place to handle the ongoing processing of transactions with minimal slowing down or loss of control over the normal flow of business. These areas include payroll, billing and collection, and recording purchases and making disbursements. The situation will be much simplified if the acquired operation has its own freestanding data processing capability—in fact, business may continue without missing a step. However, where the acquired operation has been a remote job entry site of a larger system with a central data processing organization, the transitional situation is more complex. In an extreme sense, one could picture the seller "pulling the plug" that connects the remote job entry site to the host computer, thereby bringing processing to a virtual stop. Sellers often view the support of a communications network which they no longer own as an unnecessary burden to their staff.

Often, an arrangement must be made with the seller to continue to process transactions and produce general ledgers and other systems products using the seller's data processing capabilities until the acquirer can establish independent systems for the acquired operation or integrate the acquired operation into its own systems. Sometimes, portions of some systems must be handled manually on a temporary basis until data processing capability can be increased.

After satisfying the need to continue processing business transactions, the acquirer should set up procedures for normal monthly and periodic operational and financial reporting. This will include establishing monthly closing schedules, procedures, and formats for providing balance sheets, income statements, and other data to the new parent company for consolidation. In addition, procedures should be put in place for monthly commentary by management of the acquired entity on the operating performance. In this respect, it is a great service to general management for the team leader to ask general management personnel responsible for the entity what kind of information they would like to receive to monitor the performance of the acquired entity.

On the accounting side, someone should be assigned responsibility for handling the acquisition accounting and reviewing the internal controls, accounting policies, and practices of the acquired entity for compatibility with those of the acquirer, and ensuring that any required reclassifications or adjustments are made in consolidation with the parent.

The personnel aspects of the accounting and systems areas are of great importance in the transition of the acquired entity. In some cases, it will be wise to transfer one or more supervisory or management people from the acquirer organization into the acquiree entity. An alternative is to assign someone in the parent organization as liaison to the newly acquired entity to assist and provide consultation regarding the new owner's requirements and policies. This will give the acquired entity access to someone familiar with the acquirer's systems and procedures, and will also give the acquirer some comfort in having some of its own management personnel on site "minding the store."

Each of these areas is discussed in more detail in the following sections.

PERSONNEL CONSIDERATIONS

The area of personnel matters and staffing will, as in all departments of the acquired company, be critical in the financial and systems areas. When an acquisition is in process, or has occurred, the obvious questions about possible organizational and personnel changes can cause employees great concern about job security. If not properly addressed, there could be losses of key employees, reducing the ability of the acquirer to carry forward the benefits of the existing work force of the acquired company. If at all possible, while management is working out the details of the acquisition, attempts should be made to obtain permission to visit the acquired company's financial and systems management personnel. For these initial meetings, it is wise to recognize the existing chain of command, in that there will be existing staff relationships and operating styles that should, at least in the early stages, remain in place.

In an acquisition environment, morale and productivity may decline, partly because of uncertainty about the future. Furthermore, there may even be negative feelings due to the prospect of new management control, because employees, having worked hard to gain recognition and credibility, may now have the task of proving themselves all over again to a new management group.

Effective communication is usually the best way to address this situation. In some cases, something as simple as a written communication from an officer of the acquiring company to all the employees of the acquired company welcoming them to the new organization can provide much comfort to the employees.

Employees on all levels will have questions about the future operation of the acquired entity which are important to them, but which are sometimes difficult to answer. It may be wise not to release too much information at one time, but to limit the first few meetings to discussions of general high-level facts. Management should accept all questions, however, and be prepared for pointed questions, some on a personal level. The staff of the acquired company will desire, and deserves, professional treatment in a trying, difficult time.

Despite its best efforts, an acquirer should be prepared to lose some employees from the acquired company because of the concerns about new management and possible termination. The positive impact of this is that when some employees resign, the remaining employees may see more potential for career advancement.

It is essential to understand the levels of professional expertise in each department. In the medium term, all key employees should be evaluated. A good starting point is review of individual personnel files to develop an understanding of the background, talents, and career progress of the individuals in the acquired company. Many failures in integrating acquisitions are caused by the acquirer not properly assessing the level of personnel skills and resources needed to continue operating and controlling the acquired company, and to integrate the acquired company into the acquirer's organization.

The important question will arise of whether to place managerial personnel from the acquirer organization in the lead roles in the accounting and systems departments of the acquired entity. Although some acquirers have specific policies in this area, based upon the relative qualifications of the management staff in place, sometimes it is best to have existing management continue in the role. This is an important area and should be reviewed carefully.

ACCOUNTING AND REPORTING

Commencing the accounting and reporting process for an acquired entity involves a combination of technical and administrative considerations. Things would be easy if the acquirer simply had to absorb the financial numbers as previously generated by the acquired entity, but this is rarely the case.

Chapters 4 and 5, which deal with the purchase and pooling of interests methods of accounting, demonstrate the complex accounting considerations for an acquisition. Nevertheless, those sections present the subject matter in terms of the correct technical treatments for information that is readily available. In the real world, there will be more time spent trying to assemble and comprehend the facts and circumstances related to an acquisition, and evaluating the accounts of an acquiree than time spent puzzling over the accounting rules.

Therefore it is important that someone qualified in this area be assigned responsibility for handling the acquisition accounting.

Recording the Opening Balance Sheet

The acquirer will need to book the acquisition into its balance sheet (in the sense of reporting the acquiree as a consolidated subsidiary) for the month in which the acquisition occurred, and this is frequently done using estimates. At this point, the process of compiling and analyzing the information may have only begun. A special effort to finalize these estimates should be made for a year-end balance sheet, or when financial data is first released to the public, such as at the end of a quarter.

These comments essentially relate to purchase method acquisitions, in that where the transaction has been accounted for as a pooling, the accounts of the separate entities are combined, with much less in the way of transitional adjustment to the accounting records.

Following every acquisition, with every month that goes by, an acquirer becomes aware of more and more information which gives greater clarity as to the correct opening balance sheet. The kinds of items that an acquirer may "discover" after an acquisition include:

1. Liabilities for items that relate to expenses properly allocable to prior periods. These should be recorded as liabilities in the opening balance sheet, unless the purchase agreement provides for recovery of such items from the seller.

2. Assets that do not have the value originally believed. This will include uncollectible receivables, obsolete or damaged inventories that must be written off or sold at a loss, or equipment or other fixed assets which do not have the usefulness or fair market value originally believed.

3. Extraordinary repairs and maintenance costs required to put machinery and equipment into normal operating condition.

4. Employee termination costs.

5. Rentals on facilities to be abandoned or otherwise not used.

Many of these items will fall under the category of resolution of preacquisition contingencies, for which adjustment to the opening balance sheet is required for an allocation period usually expected to last up to one year after the acquisition.

Although technically it would be acceptable to adjust the opening balance sheet continually as these preacquisition items become known and resolved, it is not desirable to have the estimated opening balance sheet changing every month for the first year of ownership. Consequently, the initial and subsequent estimates used become very important, and at some time the acquirer should freeze the estimates into a final opening balance sheet. Unless any significant adjustments are thereafter required, the acquirer should adopt a practical and sensible approach by running any smaller additional differences through postacquisition profit and loss.

Reporting Profit and Loss of the Acquiree

Frequently, in the initial months after an acquisition, there will not have been time to "push down" the opening balance sheet adjustments and the accounting practices of the acquirer into the records and the reporting cycle of the acquiree, and the results reported by the acquiree will be on the same basis as prior to the acquisition. These results must be adjusted for the acquisition accounting adjustments and accounting policy adjustments prior to consolidation with the parent.

The most apparent adjustments required to profit and loss on the basis of accounting previously used by the acquiree will be:

1. Providing goodwill amortization for goodwill to be included in the balance sheet at acquisition date.
2. Adjusting depreciation expense for any revaluations to the carrying value of fixed assets and new estimated remaining useful lives as of the acquisition date.
3. Reversing from reported postacquisition profit and loss items that may have been included as assets or liabilities in the balance sheet at acquisition date by reason of acquisition accounting adjustment by the acquirer, where such items have been included as profit-and-loss items in the postacquisition income statement of the acquiree on a separate company historical basis.

4. Adjustment of profit-and-loss items to conform to accounting policies of the acquirer, where such differ significantly from the policies previously used by the acquiree.

Keeping the Books of an Acquired Company

The purchase accounting section of this book discusses the "push-down" method of accounting for acquisition accounting, where the acquisition accounting adjustments are reflected in the separate financial statements of the acquiree. For an acquirer's review of financial data regarding the acquiree, and for external financial presentation, this up-to-date recognition of the fair market values of the assets and liabilities will be meaningful.

However, the practical question will arise of whether the actual books and records of the acquiree should be maintained on this basis or whether they should be maintained on a historical basis, with adjustments made after closing the historical books. The decision should be made based on the degree to which historical data will be required in the future. Two reasons for this may exist:

1. Tax returns of the separate legal entity, whether the entity is to file separate tax returns or to be included in the consolidated tax return of the acquirer, may have to be filed on a historical basis if a tax-free reorganization has occurred, or if the acquirer purchased the stock of the acquiree in a taxable transaction after which the basis of the acquiree's assets were not stepped up.

2. The existence of minority interests will require continuing data to be accounted for on a historical basis for the percentage of minority interest outstanding.

In some circumstances, it will be appropriate for the acquisition accounting adjustments to be made by the accounting staff of the acquiree prior to submission to the acquirer for consolidation. Where the acquisition accounting adjustments involve sensitive information that the acquirer wishes to keep confidential, it may be best for the acquirer to receive the financial reports from the acquiree on a historical basis, and for the acquirer to make the acquisition accounting adjustments.

TRANSITION OF SPECIFIC SYSTEMS

A project team consisting of accounting, data processing, and user department personnel should be formed for evaluating the degree and scope of transitional changes required, development of timetables, procedures, and carrying out the transition of specific systems.

An organized approach should be used in developing an action plan for dealing with each individual system, using the following in order of priority:

1. Ensure that ongoing business transactions can continue to be processed (payrolls, payables and disbursements, billing and collections) so that the company can continue to function on a short-term basis.

2. Ensure that adequate controls will be present and that data will be properly summarized through transaction listings and general ledgers to enable monthly closings and operational reporting.

3. Establish temporary procedures for screening all transactions over a specified dollar amount for review for proper cutoff and possible claim against the seller, where the purchase agreement indicates that the seller is responsible for any unrecorded liabilities or any recorded assets that are determined to have lower value than reflected on the books. The incidence of claims for overvalued assets will commonly include uncollectable receivables and obsolete or damaged inventories or machinery and equipment.

4. Develop plans for transition to the systems and procedures which will be used on a medium- and long-term basis.

The transition of individual operating and accounting systems after an acquisition can range from situations where most systems can be left essentially intact (as where an autonomous, freestanding corporation is acquired) to situations where substantial revamping, and modification or replacement of systems is required. To the extent that existing systems can be left intact, the task of transition is much easier. The first step in dealing with this area should be to evaluate the degree of modification required for each system.

The most critical short-range planning situations will exist where the acquiree's transactions have been processed through job entry sites communicating with a host computer at a central location, which is not part of the acquired operation. It is unlikely that the seller will agree to continue processing the acquiree's transactions (essentially functioning as a service bureau) for any great length of time. Furthermore, this kind of an arrangement would not be advisable for the acquirer on a long-term basis.

Usually, it will be best to try to arrange this service bureau-type relationship for some period of time to give the systems and staff support people adequate time to install and establish the acquirer's own hardware capability and establish the new system. In some cases, however, the seller cannot or will not provide this service, and "pulls the plug" on the existing systems on the effective date of sale. When this happens, if an outside service bureau or the acquirer's own data processing capabilities cannot pick up the processing load immediately, some hastily designed and implemented manual systems and procedures will have to be put in place for the short term.

An immediate area of concern for all systems is to determine if any new forms (e.g., invoices, purchase orders, checks) will have to be ordered because of changes in printed titles or legal terms. If so, this should be addressed immediately by compiling a comprehensive list of all forms used in each system and going through an evaluation process. Outside printers and job shoppers usually require approximately one month in an expedite mode at a premium price to deliver preprinted forms. Normal turnaround time for new forms is even longer.

The following sections will discuss some transitional considerations unique to specific systems. Major applications which will be discussed are:

1. Payroll
2. Purchasing and Disbursements
3. Billing and Accounts Receivable
4. Fixed Assets
5. Personnel Data Reporting
6. General Ledger
7. Automated IRS Reporting
8. Data and Master File Back-up Systems

There may be other systems that are unique to an individual company which require transition. They should be prioritized, researched, and dealt with in the same manner as the aforementioned systems.

Payroll

Continuing the payment of wages and salaries will be of immediate concern in the transition. If new bank accounts must be opened, an immediate determination of the time frame should be made for the first processing cycle. It is possible that the deadlines will make it impossible to have new forms (such as checks) printed and delivered on time, which will require alternate, intermediate steps.

Most printing shops have a supply of blank computer checks on hand. If supplied with the new bank account numbers, the print shop will print the account numbers on the blank checks. Although this will not be the final check format, they can suffice temporarily. With a few minor print program changes, these temporary checks and other special payroll forms can be utilized.

The exact date of acquisition may occur in the middle of a pay period. If so, it is normally best to have the seller run its payroll to the end of the pay period, or for the acquirer to pay the employees for the entire period and have the seller and acquirer reimburse each other for a pro rata portion of the payroll.

In the transition of a payroll system the following areas should be focused on:

1. The existence of proper payroll controls produced prior to printing the actual checks.
2. That the payroll report stream satisfies all the payroll department needs, such as:
   a. Credit union reporting
   b. Savings bonds
   c. Union reports
   d. Other miscellaneous withholdings
3. That the payroll is processed in a professional manner and in a secure location, with security precautions in place for check-signing plates.

4. That where there is a practice of producing computer payroll files for the IRS, continuation of proper procedures is arranged.

5. Validation that every printed payroll check is received by an active employee.

6. Many applications of payroll include the writing of manual checks for vacation, termination, or other special payments. Determination should be made that procedures are in place for proper update of individual employees' year-to-date payroll data when manual checks are issued. If improper processing is occurring for off-line manual payroll checks, significant problems can occur at year end in W-2 processing.

7. Review the recording and tracking of check numbers in the application, and ensure that all checks that have been voided are entered into the computer system and appear on a printed audit report.

8. All payroll subsystems should be considered. These will normally relate to processing needs such as employee bonds, union reporting, employee stock, and profit sharing calculation reporting. The key point to research will be where the data for the aforementioned reporting are obtained. If the payroll system is utilizing a data base approach where all necessary employee data fields are updated in a single processing cycle, the process will be relatively simple. On the other hand, if the updated payroll master is used to update separate files using separate processing routines, it is necessary to ascertain that a proper processing schedule and reconciliation procedures over the subsystems are in place.

Purchasing and Disbursements

Arrangements should be made immediately to facilitate a proper cutoff of purchasing activities where the seller is responsible for transactions prior to the acquisition date. This would include ensuring that meter readings are taken for utility services, cutoff and transfer of telephone billings, with final billings rendered to the seller, and continuation of service without interruption. Procedures should be put in place to screen all purchasing transactions and invoices received over a specified dollar amount for several months after the acquisition to determine if any are the responsibility of the seller. It is very desirable to communicate (by telephone or letter) with vendors to inform them of the change in ownership, and possibly to request that any billings for transactions prior to the acquisition date be sent to the seller.

Steps should be taken to ensure that the following important control points are covered:

1. It is especially important to ensure that proper invoice verification (e.g., matching to purchase orders and receiving reports) and/or approval procedures are in place. User department heads responsible for their individual budgets should establish and ensure correct invoice authorization by their respective staff members in accordance with company policy.

2. Correct input and output processing controls and audit trails should be present. Make sure procedures are in place to prevent duplicate payments.

3. Determine that bank reconciliations are up to date and prepared under a controlled environment.

4. Determine that the processing cycle allows for the taking of early payment discounts.

5. Ascertain that procedures for manual checks have been designed with adequate control.

6. Review the vendor master file for completeness and individual vendor activity. Many vendors may not have been used in recent years, or were used for one-time purchases, and should be deleted from the master file. This will result in better file usage and faster processing.

Billing and Accounts Receivable

The acquirer's credit personnel should immediately review and evaluate the credit and collection practices of the acquiree, and determine that adequate credit procedures will be in place. A review of overdue accounts should immediately be performed to ensure proper collection action is being taken, and for possible claim against the seller.

As with vendors, it is very desirable to communicate with customers advising them of the new ownership, and any changes in practices that will be implemented.

If necessary, a new lockbox for handling cash receipts should be opened.

The following additional points should be focused on in the billing and accounts receivable area:

1. Assurance that the procedures provide adequate customer credit limit control, including that the system enables credit personnel to know a customer's credit extension on a daily basis.

2. That procedures are in place to ensure that all shipments are billed.

3. Timely production of invoices to get them to customers as soon as possible to maximize cash flow.

4. That the invoice schedule meets with other departmental workloads, instead of a processing crisis arising every time invoices are produced.

5. That the type of accounts receivable system is acceptable to the new organization (e.g., "open item" or "balance forward").

6. The application of partial payments and freight; possibly requiring additional manual tasks by the billing department to apply cash correctly.

7. Processing of salesperson's commissions paid on the basis of sales.

Fixed Assets

After an acquisition that was accounted for as a purchase, maintaining fixed asset records can be somewhat tricky. Where the assets have been revalued to current fair market value for financial reporting purposes, and historical values must be retained for tax purposes, accountability must be maintained for each.

Sometimes, only one set of detailed fixed asset records will be maintained, which reflects the historical values, and the revalued amounts will be established in posttrial balance adjustments. Where value to be assigned to fixed assets is equal to the total appraised values of the fixed assets, the appraised values of the individual assets included in the appraiser's report can be used to assign values to the individual assets.

The individual appraised asset values may require adjustment on a pro rata basis if the total value to be assigned to fixed assets, based on allocation of the total purchase price, is less than the total appraised values. Additional pro rata adjustments may be required if there are adjustments to financial statement values for tax effects of differences in book and tax basis of the assets.

Where a formal appraisal by an outside appraiser has been performed, a detailed report will often be provided that lists each asset and the appraised fair market values. If, in assigning values to groups of assets (e.g., inventories, fixed assets, goodwill), the value to be assigned to fixed assets is equal to the total appraised value of the fixed assets, then the appraised values of the individual assets included in the appraiser's report can be used to assign values to the individual assets.

Depreciation accounts and record keeping is an additional area of concern. Upon an acquisition, estimated remaining useful lives from the acquisition date should be used for future depreciation charges. Both these remaining useful lives and the depreciation methods may differ from those used for historical accounting purposes and tax purposes. The acquirer will have to decide whether to maintain separate sets of depreciation records or whether to make summary entries to depreciation on a posttrial balance basis. If the latter approach is used, it is best to maintain the detailed records of the acquirer on a historical basis.

It is important to understand the background and makeup of the existing fixed asset accounting system. If the acquired company has an automated fixed asset system, determination should be made if the system was designed and programmed in-house or if the software was purchased from an outside firm. If the system was installed by an outside firm, it may have been part of a contract agreement where the outside firm, acting in a consulting capacity, performed the task of identifying the assets, assigning dollar values from purchase records and recording the data on the computer system.

Frequently, a computerized fixed asset system will have followed a ledger system that was manually maintained for years, or a manual ledger system may still be in use.

In any case, a complete asset count should be performed for comparison with the existing detailed records. After verifying the accuracy of the existing records, plans should be made for the medium- and long-range record keeping for fixed assets.

Fixed asset systems generally have a lower volume of input than other computer applications, and sometimes the maintenance of this system is given less priority than other systems. The acquirer should be aware of this in evaluating the condition of fixed asset systems of an acquired company.

Personnel Data Reporting

The increasing need to provide statistical information on hiring and employment practices to private and government agencies has forced many companies into a mad scramble to install a computer system that will help satisfy these requirements.

Some acquired companies will have a fairly recently installed integrated payroll/human resources computer system. Others will have a payroll system that was installed many years ago and a human resource reporting system that was recently installed. If the latter is the case, a review should be performed of the automated human resource reports, including comparison of the reported information to the current payroll master file. Much of the information on the human resource reports will not come from the payroll master file but from the personnel department via specifically prepared input forms. Determination should be made that there are adequate forms control and data reconciliation procedures in place.

In the long term, it should be noted that most older payroll systems were designed prior to current human resource reporting requirements, and do not have the capacity to store the additional personnel data. A search should be performed for existing integrated payroll/ human resource systems which may be presently installed in another company location. It will normally be more cost-effective to replace the existing systems rather than reprogramming.

General Ledger

Usually an acquirer will want to conform the chart of accounts structure to a standard chart used by the parent. An immediate transition may not be possible, however, requiring temporary use of the existing account and report structure.

If new account numbers can be added to the present chart of accounts without major computer changes, this will provide a stopgap measure until major revisions or installation of a new chart of accounts and general ledger structure can be accomplished.

A review should be performed to determine that the computerized general ledger produces all necessary reports and that the reports reflect the data correctly. In many computerized general ledger systems, reports are generated by programs that are driven by a table or matrix. This concept is excellent if the table and matrix are maintained properly. For example, a major account summary line in a report will contain an array of subaccounts. If the accounting needs are expanded to include additional subaccounts or if the array of accounts was modified, the table in the computer program should have been changed. If it was not, there will be improper reporting and summarization that will be difficult to trace. If there is an indication of this condition, data processing staff members should be directed to print out the internal program tables and matrix for review and analysis by accounting personnel.

An important area to examine is whether the acquired computer general ledger application is integrated with other computer systems and to what degree the data center is processing an integrated network.

When systems such as payroll or billing are not automatically creating entries for the general ledger, much accounting department time is required to prepare these entries. If possible, it would be advisable to add code to the existing computer programs.

In summary, the approach to the general ledger should be two-fold. Make the existing general ledger system acceptable with as few changes as possible, and second, decide if it should be replaced in the future with an existing computer system from the acquirer company.

A new general ledger system can be installed on a computer by data processing staff in a relatively short period; the heavy work is for the accounting staff to recode the account balances from the existing accounts to the new chart of accounts structure, and to design procedures for deriving data to be entered into the general ledger.

Automated IRS Reporting

In recent years, the IRS has requested companies with large data centers to provide employee wage and tax information in the form of magnetic tape rather than hard copy. Although this is not mandatory, many companies find it to their advantage to do so.

If the required company is performing this task of filing with the IRS using magnetic tape files, the IRS will have assigned an agent who is responsible to receive and accept files. Immediate contact should be made with the agent to set up future filing requirements.

Data and Master File Backup Systems

For all systems, it is essential to ensure that adequate file backup procedures are used. Data files that are updated by means of additions, deletions, and changes must be copied in a timely fashion as part of the system design.

The reason for having a backup file system is to enable a data center to restore data to a status level as it existed prior to a processing cycle. Many events can occur in a processing cycle of a computer application which cause loss of data, including power failure resulting in master file destruction, computer hardware malfunction, or incorrect update due to design error.

Exactly how many times and how often a master file should be backed up depends on the individual processing cycles in each system. If a master file is updated once a week and is used daily to produce user reports or inquiry information, it is a highly visible situation with low frequency updates. With a four cycle backup procedure, user personnel will have four weeks to detect any processing errors or improper data preparation.

On the other hand, if a master file is updated daily, the backup cycles should be much more comprehensive. The entire purpose is to be able to get the file back to a point where it was deemed correct and then reprocess data to correctly "re-update" the file.

Computer master files should be copied periodically and stored offsite. This procedure is important in case of a disaster at the data center such as fire or flooding. It is not practical to store all file backups offsite, but it is necessary to have a starting point after any data loss. The type of business and associated master files will dictate the scope of off-site storage procedures.

COMPUTER SYSTEMS TRANSITION

Companies of all sizes rely to a great extent on computers and data processing to accomplish financial and operational reporting and processing of business transactions, through an in-house data center staffed by data processing professionals. Proper coordination and integration of the data processing function of an acquired company is an important part of administering the acquisition process. This section will discuss guidelines for evaluating and integrating the data processing function in an acquisition.

Computer Hardware Acquisitions

Scoping the Hardware Environment. The person assigned responsibility for computer systems transition should contact the legal staff as early as possible and indicate the need to review and establish reliable information on data processing equipment, and related contracts and leases.

The legal staff, or other personnel administering the acquisition, should request a list of all computer hardware and all computer contracts and leases for review. In performing this review, one should consider the possibility of equipment in storage with active contracts.

In a complete review, each major vendor and lessor should be contacted for verification of the content of the contracts and comparison with data assembled in the review. Contracts are frequently revised or renewed, and, unfortunately, sometimes the revisions are misfiled, or not filed at all, and it is important to work with the most current documents and information. These procedures may be reduced where data processing management of the acquired company appears to have done a good job in maintaining up-to-date records.

A well-organized inventory of equipment is very important. A comprehensive list of all equipment should be prepared by equipment type, manufacturer, or lessor, indicating location and serial number. This information will be useful in the decision process of whether to utilize or dispose of the acquired computer hardware.

The hardware inventory should be divided into the following categories:

1. Central processing units and related input and output equipment.
2. Remote and local data entry devices.
3. Interactive input/output devices (CRT's).

Communications capabilities between the equipment is an important point to note. Modems and types of communications lines (for example, dedicated leased lines or dial-up lines) should be noted and evaluated as to their usage, necessity, and efficiency.

Reviewing Maintenance Records. At the time of compiling the list of hardware, it is wise to review the hardware maintenance records to ensure that the hardware has been maintained in conformity with the manufacturer's recommended schedule. A review of the equipment maintenance log book can establish whether the CPU has been in a downtime condition very often, which would give an indication of problem equipment. Normally, manufacturers' engineers maintain log books at the CPU locations.

Service Bureaus. As an alternative to owning or leasing computer hardware, service bureau processing is used in some companies. In the event that the acquired company is using an outside service bureau, it is important to contact the service bureau. Undoubtedly, their first concern will be whether you will continue to use their service. If the answer is affirmative, the only steps to be taken at this point will be to review the contract and reasonableness of charges for services, and to ascertain that quality and relevant service is being rendered. If the service bureau will not be used in the future, a transition plan will have to be developed. The following is a list of possible areas to address:

1. Scheduling a date to put the company on its own computer system, either on a stand-alone basis or on remote job entry to a host computer.
2. Determining whether the service bureau contracts extend to the scheduled new computer installation date.

3. If the dates in items 1 and 2 are not compatible, arranging to extend the service bureau contract at reasonable cost.

4. Arranging to obtain computer application master files from the service bureau to start up new master files such as payroll, accounts receivable, accounts payable, or any master file that carries a balance or contains names and addresses.

Review of Hardware Contracts.   The following types of contracts will typically be found in the data processing area of an acquired company:

1. Manufacturers' hardware contracts.
2. Third party leasing or hardware purchase contracts, such as from a bank or leasing company.
3. Hardware maintenance agreements.
4. Telephone lease line rental agreements.
5. Modem rental agreements.
6. Computer operating software contracts.

A good way to verify that all contracts have been identified is to review all charges to the data processing department included in the general ledger and accounts payable records. Although this is a good procedure, caution is called for because some companies, when a new computer application is installed, charge items such as printers or remote terminals to the user departments.

In contacting vendors, there is an opportunity to verify the details of active contracts and begin negotiation of new contracts. In many instances, hardware and software contracts are self-renewing.

Computer hardware contracts sometimes contain a clause stating that unless the supplier is notified in writing, perhaps 60 or 90 days prior to the contract expiration date, the contract will be automatically renewed on the terms of the original contractual agreement. These types of arrangements should be identified promptly. Also, in many contracts dealing with computer hardware, there will be a clause that will permit the buying out of the contract, which might be desirable if the contract is not consistent with future plans for the data center. These types of clauses should be noted.

All information derived from the preceding sources and procedures should be compared and used in developing the overall transition plan.

Capacity Utilization and Systems Adequacy. Reviewing an existing computer installation in an acquisition environment should be handled similar to a feasibility study of a possible new computer system. In both situations, it is important that the percentage of usage of the central processing unit and peripheral equipment be accurately estimated and evaluated.

Three major topics to be addressed in this capacity are:

1. Paper and data entry volumes.
2. Computer system efficiency.
3. Computer hardware capacity.

Paper and Data Entry Volumes. The general approach to addressing this area is to count every piece of paper that flows through a computer system, to identify peak processing periods, and to count the key strokes necessary to enter the data. It is imperative that every type of form in each application be identified and the key strokes properly counted. This enables estimation of data entry statistics which will assist in the evaluation of the data entry department's productivity as well as the efficiency of computer processing and scheduling.

An important part of this task is to identify the portions of input forms that may be duplicated for a series or group of records. For example, such information as names and addresses, invoice numbers, and purchase order numbers may be entered for duplicate input fields on different documents, causing needless consumption of capacity. Through discussion with data entry personnel and review of data entry documents, one can develop comprehensive data on the keystroke load, which will aid in the data center evaluation as a whole.

Computer System Efficiency. Discussions should be held with data processing and user department personnel, including the people who prepare the input data and supervisory and management personnel, to develop a clear understanding of how the system operates in practice. Determine whether for each application, edits come back to the user departments without a great deal of data entry errors.

The reasons for any inefficiencies noted in the review should be identified. These can include:

1. Improper data preparation in the user departments.
2. Incorrect data input by data entry operators.
3. Computer systems with inadequate edit functions.
4. Incorrect system processing by the computer operations staff.
5. Incomplete or misleading operation run books.

Computer Hardware Capacity. Occasionally, one will note in an acquired data center that capacity far exceeds the data actually being processed. It could be possible that, when the central processor was purchased, there was much greater usage, or perhaps more computer applications were intended to be installed than the company has installed to date.

Many data centers have devices that measure the central processing unit performance and capacity usage. With these tools, it is possible to monitor the hardware systems and evaluate usage in terms of current needs and growth potential without adding new hardware. Some of the more common devices that may be found are:

1. *CPU Workload Measurement Tool.* This monitors the job work load of the computer system by creating a log file of programs that were executed, indicating time of day, start and stop execute times, and actual elapsed time. This software device will also show what is the heaviest processing time of the day. The printed log can be used to determine if a computer application is taking an extraordinary amount of time to process data. The measurement tool lists all computer programs executed. Therefore, if a particular program is a problem, it will stand out.

2. *Disk Space Usage.* This will print or specify the capacity of the storage device, how much space is available, and the current content and data file organization. This information is used by technical personnel to ensure proper storage device usage and to keep abreast of the data center's storage capabilities for new computer applications.

3. *Tape Drive Usage.* This records by computer application the number of times a tape unit was accessed.

4. *Printer Monitoring Tool.* This will record printer elapsed time by computer system, and print programs within a given system. By knowing the long print jobs, the operations staff can properly set up the daily, weekly, and monthly processing schedules.

Computer Software Acquisitions

Computer Languages. If the data center has been in existence for a fair amount of time, one will probably find both Cobol and RPG programs in the computer applications. Cobol is the most frequently used language in medium-sized to large data centers. Managers particularly like Cobol due to its English language quality and self-documenting procedural techniques. It is not uncommon to use Cobol for system development, which will remain as part of the permanent applications library, and RPG for onetime reports, file conversions, and test data creation.

In smaller data centers with small hardware configuration, one will normally find RPG or the Basic language, with RPG being more common. Unlike Cobol, RPG runs very efficiently with a minimum of storage. Unfortunately, it does not have Cobol's documentative qualities. When dealing with a system written in RPG, the completeness and quality of documentation prepared by computer analysts and programmers are very important. This holds true for the Basic language also, although one is not likely to find many business systems written in this language.

If the data center is processing both batch mode and on line, additional languages may be noted that accommodate the on-line processing. These high-level languages are written expressly for the purpose of creating programs which allow data recordation and data retrieval by a user group without a lot of complicated code.

Personal computers are usually programmed in Basic or a particular vendor's own unique language. In a more scientific environment, one may find Fortran, PL1 and a host of other unique high-level languages.

Reviewing and Evaluating Code. Since the inception of computers it has become an established fact that no two programmers will write programming code to satisfy a business reporting need quite the same way, even where the same computer language is used. This difference factor can be carried into the full scope of an existing system design, making evaluation of code and existing software of an acquired company somewhat involved.

An example might be found in a payroll system, where under one approach, the system might contain 25 programs, and 100 programs under another approach. Either approach could be adequate in the circumstances, based on both achieving the upward flow of data through the operation of the system. Even though there is often increased overhead with more programs, of most importance is how efficiently the programs are written. Many systems analysts and project leaders prefer to design applications in small modules, believing that although it takes a few more seconds to execute and produce results, the systems are maintained more easily.

The task of evaluating software of an acquired company should be based on establishing the quality of the code that was produced. This, besides leading to a conclusion on the continuing value of the software, can tell an acquirer many things about the new staff.

Data processing personnel have individual styles in determining the quality of code written by computer programmers. However, most evaluations in an ongoing environment are based on knowledge of the systems and reliance on the staff's expertise. This approach may not work in an acquisition environment, where one is placed in the position of evaluating computerized business systems and program code written by staff programmers, past and present, who are unknown entities. For this reason, it is imperative that the method used for evaluation be methodical and concise.

For languages other than Cobol, including higher-level program languages and the RPG type code found in many applications, programming techniques usually involve a programmer preparing parameter specifications sheets. These sheets, when entered into the computer system, generate the program code necessary to process data as specified. For reviewing code in these languages, the following procedures should be followed:

1. Determine that program listings for every program in the system are accounted for and filed in a secure area.

2. Determine that the documentation reflects what the system is producing for the user department.

3. Review the program listings with a programmer other than the author, possibly one from the acquirer organization, and determine if proper data editing techniques have been utilized and that edit messages are meaningful.

4. Evaluate the data input format of the programs which create the input data file. Be sure that all necessary data fields for a record are consistent from program to program in the system.

5. Determine if any programs in a system have a history of creating problems at processing time.

6. Investigate excess usage of tape files as compared with disk storage media. Disk storage is faster to access and requires less or no computer operator intervention.

7. Talk to the user department personnel and get their opinions of the quality of the product provided by the computer system.

When dealing with computer applications written in Cobol, all of the aforementioned points apply with a few additions. With the Cobol language, one should research the following items:

1. Determine that each written program has a structural format consisting of input, process, and output, with notations explaining complicated calculations and routines.

2. If a particular program is processing several types of records, determine that one read and write routine is used, instead of a separate routine for each type of record.

3. Determine if there are edit criteria unnecessarily repeated in several different programs in the same system.

4. Determine that program coded routines are written in a way in which they can be easily changed if necessary.

There are basic areas that need to be addressed in an evaluation of code. If, as a result of the review, it is concluded that a data center has poorly written programs, with poor documentation, new programs should be considered instead of maintenance of the existing programs.

System Validation. To validate a computerized business system means evaluating two distinct and separate qualities: (1) The degree to which the system supplies the user with what is needed, and (2) the degree of smoothness with which the system processes.

A good first step is to compile a list of the people who receive output from the system. With reports in hand, discussions should be held with the users to establish whether reports are being utilized and to determine whether any necessary information is not being provided. The latter can be sometimes identified by reviewing user manually prepared reports.

Most computer operations will have a process control log. This log, if properly maintained, will indicate system stops and any reruns that have taken place during system processing, providing an indication of systems that do not run smoothly.

The actual format used for process control logs varies by data center. They are all basically designed with the same end purpose, which is to establish the system job steps and elapsed wall clock time necessary to process a computer application. Computerized systems are usually limited to three process stages: (1) edit, (2) process data, and (3) produce output.

The procedures used to record necessary data in processing control logs normally include the following:

1. Log-in of system start time.
2. Log-in of system completion time.
3. Log-in of job step time and stop time. A job step within a system could be a single program, or several programs, designed to accomplish a necessary system task.
4. Problems that may have occurred during processing are also recorded. If there was an input data error that was not detected by the edit program, or a human error caused by a computer operator, it is recorded on the log with the time that it occurred, and the elapsed time it took to correct the problem and restart the processing.
5. Reruns are indicated by referencing previous processing problems. This is the area most center managers look at to discover major problems in computer systems.

In a very sophisticated, complex data center, the log is expanded to record problem reporting data; for example, the time the programming staff was notified of a possible program problem, and the response time may be recorded. In more sophisticated environments, much of the data is actually captured by programs residing on the central computer.

Another step in validating systems should be to observe the operations staff and how they function while executing a system, and to note whether the system run books are being used and if computer logs and controls are properly maintained.

In the event that a computer application is noted with a high level of reruns, immediate steps should be taken to evaluate this further. Assign a programmer analyst the task of going through each program in the system. Doing an "input record walk-through" will point out individual program problems and any system design errors. If a computer system is noted which is inundated with both design and programming problems, a full evaluation should be performed.

It is possible, due to higher priorities or lack of cost justification, that a decision will be made to keep the acquired company's system intact at the present time, despite problems with the system. When this happens, more stringent manual controls should be put in place, including careful review of output from all problem systems by key data center and user department personnel.

Review of Systems Documentation. Preparation of complete systems documentation is usually done at the time new systems are created. Unfortunately, original system design and original programs often do not remain intact, as requirements and computer systems designs change. Only in the most thorough of computer centers will timely update of systems documentation faithfully occur.

If computer software of an acquired company is to be retained, it is important that systems documentation be compared with the actual applications. Any discrepancies noted should be written up in detail, and discussed with management and end users to ensure that the discrepancies are valid. If considered necessary, the original documentation should then be assigned to the programming staff members for rewriting of the systems documentation.

APPENDIX 3-1: CHECKLIST FOR SYSTEMS TRANSITION

GENERAL

1. Review the purchase agreement and make a list of all areas requiring accounting or systems follow-up and ensure procedures are in place to deal with these areas.

2. Review all forms and documents and determine if modifications must be made, depending on whether the acquired entity will be operated as a separate corporation, division of the acquirer, and so on. Arrange for new forms where required.

3. Determine whether an outside appraisal will be required to assign fair market values to individual assets acquired.

4. Arrange for any new permits, licenses, or registrations that may be required.

5. Evaluate management personnel in the acquired company and determine whether any replacements should be made, or whether anyone from the acquirer organization should be transferred to the acquiree.

6. Arrange for training and orientation of staff in the procedures and policies of the acquirer organization.

7. Review contracts and leases for any required notifications to lessors and other parties.

ACCOUNTING AND REPORTING

1. Assign a qualified person to handle accounting for the acquisition and for making acquisition accounting adjustments to profit and loss after the acquisition (goodwill amortization, etc.).

2. Review the accounting policies of the acquiree and arrange to conform these to policies of the acquirer, where applicable.

3. Prepare the opening balance sheet of the acquiree, giving effect to any required revaluations and other acquisition accounting adjustments.

4. Prepare a list of preacquisition contingencies, and ensure procedures are in place to monitor progress in their resolution and to make any required accounting adjustments.

5. Develop a long-range plan for record keeping for acquisition accounting adjustments (using the push-down method, posttrial balance adjustments, or consolidation adjustments).
6. Ensure that basic records provide the information that will be required for state, local, and federal tax returns.
7. Review the general ledger system and chart of accounts and plan any changes that will be required.

TAX COMPLIANCE

1. Arrange for filing of short period tax returns required as a result of change of ownership.
2. Ensure sales and use tax requirements are met, including filing of proper returns and payment of taxes payable as a result of the acquisition and related transfers of assets.
3. Review payroll tax implications, as to whether FICA, SUTA, and FUTA taxes must start over as if at the beginning of the year or if certain successor employer rules apply.

SYSTEMS

1. Review the systems configuration and determine if the systems in place are autonomous or a remote job entry site of a larger system.
2. Determine what processing and systems capabilities will disappear when the seller no longer supplies data processing support, and develop plans to replace this capability.
3. Evaluate and arrange to continue any outside service bureau arrangements, as appropriate.
4. If service bureaus are being used, determine how they will be used in the future.
5. Ensure that adequate backup file procedures are in place.
6. Take a complete physical inventory of all computer hardware.
7. Review maintenance records to ascertain that computer hardware has been properly maintained.

8. Review all computer-related contracts.

9. Determine to what extent computer capacity is being utilized and how much growth the existing system can absorb before system expansion is required.

10. Determine what languages the computer programs are written in.

11. Evaluate the quality of code present in the programs.

12. Validate the existing systems by determining to what extent the system supplies users with what is needed and that the programs function efficiently.

13. Ascertain the degree to which systems are documented, and the extent to which the documentation is current.

PERSONNEL AND PAYROLL

1. Arrange for payroll processing for the period in which the acquisition occurs, either by the seller continuing to pay until the end of the payroll period, or by the acquirer picking up payroll payments as of the beginning of the payroll period.

2. Arrange for proper filing of payroll taxes.

3. Determine that a human resource information system is in place which will provide information needed for reporting purposes.

4. Review IRS reporting requirements, and determine if such are to be made on magnetic tape.

5. Obtain new payroll deduction authorizations, if necessary.

PURCHASING AND DISBURSEMENTS

1. Arrange for proper cutoff of utility bills and placing accounts in name of acquirer.

2. Arrange to screen all payments made for possible charge-back to seller.

3. Consider communicating with vendors to inform them of the new ownership.

FIXED ASSETS

1. Develop record-keeping methods for revaluations of fixed assets and allocation of cost to individual assets.
2. Perform same procedures as in item 1 for depreciation records.
3. Compare book and tax basis of the assets to determine whether valuation adjustments for tax effects of differences between book and tax basis are required, and to determine whether separate records for book and tax will be required.

BILLING AND ACCOUNTS RECEIVABLE

1. Set up procedures for proper allocation of cash receipts to receivables that may have been retained by the seller.
2. Ensure that proper credit limit procedures are in effect.
3. Ensure that overdue accounts are being identified and pursued.

CASH

1. Arrange to open new general, disbursing and payroll bank accounts, as required.
2. Change check signers on bank accounts, if required.
3. Open any necessary lockbox accounts for customer remittances.

4

ACCOUNTING FOR BUSINESS COMBINATIONS—THE POOLING OF INTERESTS METHOD

Except for specific exceptions included in the *grandfather provisions* (see below), business combinations meeting certain conditions must be accounted for using the pooling of interests method; all other business combinations must be accounted for using the purchase method. The two methods both result in a basis of accounting designed to reflect the substance of the specific business combination.

The purchase accounting method accounts for a business combination as if one entity has acquired another, with a new basis of accounting established for the individual assets acquired and liabilities assumed in the acquisition based on their fair values at the date of acquisition. A business combination for which the pooling of interests method is required represents a combining of stockholder interests, and the separate recorded amounts for assets and liabilities of the combining companies are combined and carried forward. Because there is no adjustment of the carrying values of one of the combining companies to current fair value, and no recording of new goodwill (as there often is in a purchase method acquisition), the lower asset value usually carried forward in a pooling will result in lower future charges to expense for depreciation and goodwill amortization than would be present had purchase accounting been used. The pooling and purchase methods are never usable in accounting for the same acquisition, with two exceptions, referred to as the *grandfather clauses,* or *grandfather provisions.*

Most acquisitions are accounted for using the purchase method. This is because many conditions must be met for use of the pooling of interests method. Accounting Principles Board (APB) Opinion No. 16, issued in August 1970, sets forth the requirements, which are discussed in detail in this chapter.

It is interesting to note that prior to the issuance of APB Opinion No. 16, the principles followed by accountants and companies in accounting for business combinations were less well defined, leading to what many believed to be abuses in using the pooling of interests method for business combinations consummated by an exchange of stock. In fact, some business combinations that were consummated partly for cash and partly for stock were accounted for as part purchase and part pooling. The incentive to use the pooling of interests method was (and in many cases still is) the lower reported depreciation and amortization expenses in future periods. This is caused by the fact that the increases in carrying values of tangible assets to fair market values and recording of goodwill frequently noted in purchase acquisitions do not occur in poolings-of-interests. APB Opinion No. 16 set the record straight about which method to use based on very well-defined criteria.

THE "GRANDFATHER PROVISIONS"

Paragraph 99 of APB Opinion No. 16 and AICPA Accounting Interpretation No. 24 include provisions referred to as grandfather clauses or grandfather provisions, which provide exemptions from certain of the conditions used in the pooling of interests method.

Paragraph 99 of APB Opinion No. 16 provides that if as of October 31, 1970, a corporation owned 50% or less of the common stock of another company, a combination between the two companies initiated after October 31, 1970 may be accounted for as a pooling, provided that (a) the transaction meets all the conditions for pooling other than the restrictions on intercorporate investments prior to the combination, and (b) a modified requirement as to the required percentage of shares that must be issued in consummating the combination has been met. More specifically, these two conditions for pooling are modified as follows:

Normal Condition for Pooling	Exemption Under Grandfather Provision
The combining companies must hold as intercorporate investments no more than 10% in total of the outstanding voting common stock of any combining company (as described in APB Opinion No. 16, paragraph 46b).	Pooling may be used if intercorporate investments at October 31, 1970 were more than 10%, but not in excess of 50%.
The corporation that effects the combination must issue voting common stock for at least 90% of the voting common stock of the other combining company (as described in APB Opinion No. 16, paragraph 47b).	The 90% requirement will apply only to the total outstanding voting common stock of the combining company not already held on October 31, 1970.

A transaction qualifying for pooling under the grandfather provision of paragraph 99 of APB Opinion No. 16 may be accounted for in two ways:

1. The transaction may be completely accounted for as a purchase; or
2. A "part-purchase, part-pooling" treatment may be used. That is, the general principles of purchase accounting are applied to the intercorporate investment held at October 31, 1970, with pooling treatment used for the balance of the combination effected after October 31, 1970.

AICPA Accounting Interpretation No. 24 contains a second grandfather provision modifying the condition for pooling contained in APB Opinion No. 16, paragraph 46a, which requires that the combining companies be autonomous. This exception permits subsidiaries with significant (at least 20% of voting common stock) minority interests outstanding at October 31, 1970, to take part in a pooling combination provided the significant minority interest still exists at the initiation of the combination, provided that all other conditions for pooling are met.

These grandfather provisions were originally established to apply to combinations initiated within five years after October 31, 1970. FASB Statement No. 10, effective November 1, 1975, extended the grandfather provisions for an indefinite period.

CONDITIONS FOR USE OF THE POOLING OF INTERESTS METHOD

The conditions for use of the pooling of interests method contained in APB Opinion No. 16 are divided into three major categories:

1. Attributes of the combining companies (paragraphs 46a and 46b).
2. Manner of combining of interests (paragraphs 47a through 47g).
3. Absence of planned transactions (paragraphs 48a through 48c).

The specific conditions and a discussion of each follows.

Attributes of the Combining Companies

1. *Autonomy (paragraph 46a).*

   Each of the combining companies is autonomous and has not been a subsidiary or division of another corporation within two years before the plan of a combination is initiated.

A wholly owned subsidiary distributing voting common stock of its parent corporation will qualify under this condition if the parent would have met all the conditions for a pooling had it issued its stock directly. If a parent owns substantially all the voting common stock of a subsidiary, that subsidiary qualifies as wholly owned for this test. Less than 90%, in any event, will not be considered substantially all, and generally the percentage is expected to be higher. (See the previous discussion of grandfather provisions for an exception to this condition.)

The two-year autonomy requirement does not apply to a company newly incorporated within the two years prior to initiation of the combination, or to the portion of a company that may have been acquired in the two-year period in a business combination accounted for as a purchase. An established company may not "spin off" a subsidiary or a portion of its assets into a newly formed company and thereby escape the two-year autonomy rule. However, a subsidiary or a new company acquiring assets divested as a result of a regulatory or judicial decree is considered autonomous for this purpose. Personal holding companies and sole proprietorships are normally exempt from the autonomy requirement.

The date of initiation of a plan occurs when the issuing corporation has made an offer and is obligated to consummate the combination if the offer is accepted or any other specified conditions are met. The obligation to consummate the combination can be subject to required approvals from such parties as regulatory authorities or stockholders. The initiation date will be the earlier of when the major terms of the plan have been announced, as in a combination negotiated by the combining companies, or the date the stockholders of a combining company are notified in writing of an offer, as in the case of a tender offer. The ratio of exchange formula upon which the exchange of voting common stock is to be based must be announced as part of the initiation.

2. *Independence.*
   Each of the combining companies is independent of the other combining companies.

The combining companies may hold as intercorporate investments no more than 10% of the outstanding stock of any combining company. (See the previous discussion of grandfather provisions for an exception to this condition.)

Manner of Combining Interests

1. *Complete Transaction (paragraph 47a).*
   The combination is effected in a single transaction or is completed in accordance with a specific plan within one year after the plan is initiated.

The consummation date occurs when the assets are transferred to the issuing company, and ownership of the issuing company's stock has transferred to the stockholders of the other combining company. Consummation must occur within one year after the initiation date, unless there are delays beyond the control of the combining companies because of the proceedings of a governmental authority, such as deliberations by regulatory agencies on approval of the combination, or certain litigation, such as antitrust suits.

Modifying the terms of exchange of stock constitutes initiation of a new plan. If earlier exchanges of stock are adjusted to the modified terms, however, measurement of the one-year period for completion remains the same as under the original plan. If the earlier exchanges of stock are not adjusted to the new terms, previous exchanges under the original plan are treated as intercorporate investments at the date of initiation of the new plan. If a plan is formally terminated and later negotiations lead to initiation of a new plan, any shares previously exchanged are treated as intercorporate investments at the date of initiation of the new plan, even if the new plan is identical to the old one.

2. *Exchange of Voting Common Stock (paragraph 47b).*

A corporation offers and issues only common stock with rights identical to those of the majority of its outstanding voting common stock in exchange for substantially all the voting common stock interest of another company at the date the plan of combination is consummated.

In executing the plan, the issuing corporation must acquire, in exchange for shares of its own voting common stock, at least 90% of the voting common stock of the other combining company which is outstanding at the date of consummation. Excluded from this measurement are any shares held as intercorporate investments at the date the plan is initiated, any shares acquired other than in exchange for voting common stock of the issuing company, or shares outstanding after consummation of the plan.

In computing the number of shares exchanged for the 90% test, intercorporate investments are included in the number of shares outstanding, but are excluded from the number of shares exchanged to effect the combination. An adjustment must be made, reducing the number of shares exchanged by a factor for intercorporate investments in common stock of the issuing corporation held by the other combining company, whether acquired before or after initiation of the plan. This reduction is computed by adjusting the number of shares of the other combining company to the equivalent number of shares of the issuing company, based on the ratio of exchange. An example of this computation follows:

Outstanding shares of other combining company at consummation date	<u>100,000</u>
Shares of other combining company received by issuing company in exchange consummating the combination	95,000
Adjustment to state 1000 shares of issuing company held by other combining company into equivalent shares of other combining company based on an exchange ratio of:	
3 to 1 (1000 × 3)	<u>3,000</u>
Shares exchanged for purposes of 90% test	<u>92,000</u>
Percentage of shares exchanged for purposes of 90% test	<u>92%</u>

In the above example, the 90% test would be met. Had the other combining company held 2000 shares of the issuing company, the adjustment to the number of shares exchanged would have been 6000 equivalent shares, reducing the number of shares exchanged for purposes of the test to 89,000 shares, or 89% of the outstanding shares, which would not meet the 90% test.

As long as the issuing company receives at least 90% of the voting common stock in exchange for shares of its own voting common stock of the combining company in the combination, the fact that additional shares were acquired in exchange for cash, debt securities, warrants, or "tainted" treasury shares (discussed later) will not disqualify pooling. (See the previous discussion of grandfather provisions for an exception to the general 90% rule.)

A pooling of interests may be structured by the formation of a new company to issue stock to effect the combination of two or more companies. The 90% test must be met regarding the combining companies, and the above requirements for the exchange of voting common stock must have been met if any one of the combining companies issued its stock to effect the combination.

If the other combining company has outstanding debt securities or equity securities other than voting common stock, the issuing company has the following options that are acceptable for a pooling. The issuing company may:

1. Assume outstanding debt securities or allow debt securities or equity securities other than common stock to remain outstanding.
2. Exchange substantially identical securities or voting common stock for outstanding debt and equity securities other than common stock of the other combining company.
3. Retire the outstanding debt or securities other than common stock by paying cash if the securities are callable or redeemable.

The above notwithstanding, the issuing company may not exchange anything other than voting common stock for outstanding debt or equity securities other than common stock if such were issued in exchange for voting common stock during the two-year period prior to initiation of the business combination plan.

An issuing company may issue its voting common stock in exchange for the net assets of the other combining company. Some assets may be retained to settle liabilities of the other combining company provided any excess assets remaining after settlement are to be transferred to the issuing company. In this case, if the other combining company has equity securities other than common stock outstanding, the issuing company may issue only voting common stock, or voting common stock and other equity securities in the same proportions as outstanding with respect to the other combining company.

Where the common stock of the issuing corporation is exchanged for the net assets of the other combining company, and intercorporate investments in outstanding common stock are present, special computations to evaluate compliance with the 90% test are required. For illustration, assume that Company B has 100,000 common shares outstanding. Company A issues 40,000 common shares for all the net assets of Company B, 6000 shares of which are applicable to interests of preferred stockholders. Prior to consummation, Company A held 3000 shares of Company B and Company B held 1800 shares of Company A as intercorporate investments.

The computations required are expressed in shares of the issuing company and would be as follows:

Common shares issued in effecting business combination	40,000 (A)
Add, common shares of Company A held by Company B	1,800 (B)
Total shares of voting common stock of Company A issued for assets of Company B	41,800 (C)
Less, common shares of Company A issued applicable to preferred stock interests in Company B	(6,000) (D)
Shares of Company A issued for common stock interest of Company B	35,800 (E)

Reduction for intercorporate investments:
Company A shares held by Company B   (1,800)(F)
Company B shares held by Company A restated as equivalent shares of Company A based on ratio of shares of Company A issued for common stock interest of Company B to total outstanding shares of Company B

$$1800 \times \frac{35,800 \text{ (E)}}{100,000} =$$
(644)(G)   (2,444) (H)

Reduced number of shares for measurement of 90% test	33,356 (I)
Number of shares of Company A applicable to common stock interests of Company B	35,800 (J)
Percentage required	×90%
	32,220 (K)

Because item (I) is greater than item (K), the test would be met.

3. *No Changes in Common Equity Interest (paragraph 47c).*
   None of the combining companies changes the equity interest of the voting common stock in contemplation of effecting the combination

> *either within two years before the plan of combination is initiated or between the dates the combination is initiated and consummated; changes in contemplation of effecting the combination may include distributions to stockholders and additional issuances, exchanges, and retirements of securities.*

Dividends and other distributions to stockholders, which are equivalent to normal dividends, are not considered changes as defined above.

4. Limitations on Reacquisition of Stock (paragraph 47d).

> *Each of the combining companies reacquires shares of voting common stock only for purposes other than business combinations, and no company reacquires more than a normal number of shares between the dates the plan of combination is initiated and consummated.*

Acquisitions of the issuing company's shares by other combining companies after initiation of the plan are viewed as reacquisitions of stock, in addition to intercorporate investments affecting the 90% test.

Normal systematic acquisitions of treasury stock for such purposes as stock option plans are acceptable.

This condition prevents pooling accounting where excessive reacquisitions of stock have changed the character of an exchange of voting common stock of combining company to a transaction where, in essence, cash is used to effect the business combination, creating the substance of a purchase. This has been the subject of much discussion in the accounting profession and specifically addressed by the SEC, which has stated that for public companies, treasury stock reacquired within two years prior to initiation of the business combination, unless needed for normal reissuance under stock option and similar plans, are "tainted" for purposes of the business combination. An adjustment should be made for these "tainted" shares in applying the 90% test similar to the adjustment made for intercorporate investments. Therefore, up to 10% of the shares used in a pooling of interests can be "tainted shares" provided no other reductions to shares exchanged for such items as intercorporate investments are present in making the 90% test.

5. Same Ratio of Ownership Interest (paragraph 47e).

> *The ratio of the interest of an individual common stockholder to those of other common stockholders in a combining company remains the same as a result of the exchange of stock to effect the combination.*

This requirement states that in the new combined equity interest, each stockholder must retain the same percentage of ownership as previously held in the separate company before the combination.

6. **Voting Rights (paragraph 47f).**

   The voting rights to which the common stock ownership interests in the resulting combined corporations are entitled are exercisable by the stockholders; the stockholders are neither deprived of nor restricted in exercising those rights for a period.

In addition to requiring no restrictions on voting rights, the pooling requirements prohibit restriction as to stockholder discretion regarding the sale or holding of the stock, or the receipt of dividends. The stockholders of the previously separate companies must share equally in rights, risks, and rewards.

The issuance of unrestricted common stock in exchange for restricted stock of the other combining company does not disqualify the use of the pooling method.

Any restrictions imposed by legal requirements, such as the inability to sell shares because of SEC delays or requirements, will not disqualify use of the pooling method.

7. **Complete Resolution (paragraph 47g).**

   The combination is resolved at the date the plan is consummated and no provisions of the plan relating to the issue of securities or other consideration are pending.

There may be no consideration contingent on future events, such as additional issuance of shares based on future earnings or stock prices. However, an arrangement may be made for a future adjustment to the number of shares issued based on the resolution of unresolved contingencies at the consummation date, such as lawsuits, possible additional tax liabilities as a result of Internal Revenue Service examinations, or failure to meet general management or balance sheet warranties with respect to one of the combined companies.

Sometimes contingently issuable shares will be placed in escrow pending resolution of the contingency or contingencies.

The SEC has taken the position that contingencies from general warranties pursuant to a pooling cannot extend past the issuance of the first audited financial statements of the pooled company or one year after consummation, whichever comes first. The SEC has further taken a position that possible future share adjustments of over 10% of the shares issued in the business combination would raise questions as to the risk-sharing aspects of pooling.

The SEC's view on the acceptable longevity of general warranties appears to establish a separate standard on this point for public and nonpublic companies. It would appear such general management and balance sheet waranties may remain in force until resolved as long as they are not related to future events where nonpublic companies are pooled.

Employment contracts may be granted to former officer/stockholders of a combined company without giving rise to cash consideration in the exchange, provided the compensation agreed to is reasonable in relation to the services to be performed.

Absence of Planned Transactions

1. *No Reacquisitions of Stock Issued in Combination (paragraph 48a).*

   The combined corporation does not agree directly or indirectly to retire or reacquire all or part of the common stock issued to effect the combination.

An agreement to reacquire the issued shares for cash, referred to as a "bailout," changes the character of the transaction from a pooling to a cash transaction, and therefore a purchase. An immediate sale to purchasers other than the combined companies of shares received in a pooling based on the unrestricted right of the common sharcholders to sell their shares does not disqualify the pooling. There must, however, be no prior arrangements that require the sale of the shares.

The SEC in Accounting Series Releases (ASR) No. 130 and 135 imposed some restrictions on the disposal of shares issued pursuant to a pooling based on its view that continuity of ownership is required for some period after a pooling. In general, these state that any affiliate (as defined in Regulation S-X) receiving shares of common stock in a pooling may not dispose of any of such shares prior to the publication of combined sales and net income for a period of at least 30 days after the business combination. Although this requirement does not apply to poolings of nonpublic companies, a problem could exist with the SEC recognizing the pooling of interests in a filing pursuant to a later public offering if the SEC's restrictions on this matter were not complied with. These rulings are not intended to prevent the above-mentioned rights of common stockholders of a pooling company from selling their shares to third parties immediately after the pooling.

2. No Financial Arrangements (paragraph 48b).

The combined corporation does not enter into other financial arrangements for the former stockholders of a combining company, such as a guaranty of loans secured by stock issued in the combination, which in effect negates the exchange of equity securities.

This requirement parallels the preceding one in that, among other things, it provides that the combined corporation may not agree to use its financial strength to "bailout" former stockholders of a combined company.

3. No Plans to Dispose of Significant Assets (paragraph 48c).

The combined corporation does not intend or plan to dispose of a significant part of the assets of the combining companies within two years after the combination other than disposals in the ordinary course of business of the formerly separate companies and to eliminate duplicate facilities or excess capacity.

This condition establishes that significant disposals of assets would be contrary to the intent of the pooling requirements, in that the previous stockholders' interests would be changed significantly.

APPLYING POOLING OF INTERESTS ACCOUNTING

Principles of Pooling of Interests

At the date of consummation of a pooling of interests, the assets and liabilities of the combining companies are carried forward into the financial statements of the new combined entity at their book values. Accounting methods of the individual companies may be changed to provide consistent practices in the new combined entity, provided the changes are appropriate for the individual companies making the changes. Any such changes should be accounted for by retroactive restatement.

Stockholders' equity accounts, including retained earnings, retain their character and are similarly carried forward and combined. Certain reclassifications may be required in the financial statements of the new combined entity, depending on the relationship of the combined capital structures of the new entity. This may occur where the stated or par value of the outstanding stock of the issuing corporation after the combination exceeds the related amounts of the separate companies prior to the combination. The proper treatment of this situation is to reclassify an appropriate amount from additional paid-in capital to the capital stock account. If paid-in capital is exhausted, then an additional reclassification is made from retained earnings.

This principle is illustrated in the following example. Assume that the separate capital structures of Company A and Company B are shown below. Company A acquires all the outstanding shares of Company B in a pooling of interests in exchange for 20,000 newly issued shares of Company A stock, thereby increasing Company A's outstanding shares from 50,000 to 70,000.

	Before Combination		After Combination	
	Company A	Company B	Reclassification	Combined
Common Stock:				
50,000 shares, $10 par	$ 500,000			
100,000 shares, $1 par		$100,000		
	500,000	100,000	$100,000	$ 700,000
Additional paid-in capital	1,000,000	400,000	(100,000)	1,300,000
Retained Earnings	1,000,000	300,000		1,300,000
	$2,500,000	$800,000		$3,300,000

If elements of stockholders' equity of a combining company were adjusted to eliminate a deficit before or as part of the combination, the components of stockholders' equity before the adjustment should be used in accounting for the pooling.

Treasury Stock and Intercorporate Investments. If any of the shares issued to effect a pooling were held as treasury shares, these shares should be accounted for as if they were first retired, and new shares issued.

If the issuing company holds shares in the other combining company, those shares will be exchanged for shares issued in the pooling, resulting in the effective elimination of the investment. Any such shares should be accounted for as if retired as part of the combination.

Shares of the issuing company held by another combining company are in effect returned to the issuing company in the combination, and should be accounted for as treasury stock in the combined entity.

Expenses of a Pooling.   Expenses of effecting a business combination, such as registration fees, costs of furnishing information to stockholders, professional fees, and costs of combining operations should be charged to expense in the income statement of the combined entity in the period of consummation of the combination.

Expenses of the combination incurred by the separate companies prior to the combination may be deferred until the combination is consummated and then expensed in the income statement of the combined entity upon consummation. If at the end of a reporting period, amounts have been deferred pending a possible pooling, and it appears unlikely that the combination will be consummated, the amounts previously deferred should be charged to expense in the income statement of the separate company for that period.

If expenses of a pooling which are actually obligations of the combining companies or combined company are paid directly by stockholders, a capital contribution and an expense should be recorded. The SEC has taken the position that in poolings involving public companies, all expenses of the combination paid by stockholders should be charged to expense and added to capital, regardless of whether such expenses are legal liabilities of the companies.

Foreign Currency Translation in a Pooling.   Where a combination with a foreign operation is accounted for as a pooling of interests, it is treated as if the companies had always been combined. Therefore, the historical values of assets and liabilities and profit-and-loss items are translated from the acquiree's functional currency into the currency of the acquirer in accordance with FASB Statement No. 52 for all periods presented in the current and restated financial statements.

Financial Reporting of a Pooling

Financial Statement Presentation.   The new combined entity created by a pooling of interests is recognized as of the date the pooling is consummated. From that date forward, the combined financial position and results of operations are reported. All prior periods are restated including, in the fiscal year in which the pooling is consummated, the period from the beginning of the year to the date of consummation, so that all financial statements will be as if the previously separate entities had always been combined. In restating, all intercompany transactions involving long-term assets and liabilities need not be eliminated. They should be disclosed, however, together with the effects on earnings per share.

In the year in which a pooling is consummated, the financial statements should disclose that a pooling has taken place. The basis of combined presentation and restatement of prior periods should be disclosed either in the financial statements by captions or in notes to the financial statements. Paragraph 64 of APB Opinion No. 16 specifically requires that the notes to the financial statements include:

A. Name and brief description of the companies combined, except a corporation whose name is carried forward to the combining corporation.

B. Method of accounting for the combination—that is, by the pooling of interests method.

C. Description and number of shares of stock issued in the business combination.

D. Details of the results of operations of the previously separate companies for the period before the combination is consummated that are included in the current combined net income. The details should include revenue, extraordinary items, net income, other changes in stockholders' equity, and amount of and manner of accounting for intercompany transactions.

E. Descriptions of the nature of adjustments of net assets of the combining companies to adopt the same accounting practices and of the effects of the changes on net income reported previously by the separate companies and now presented in comparative financial statements.

F. Details of an increase or decrease in retained earnings from changing the fiscal year of a combining company. The details should include at least revenue, expenses, extraordinary items, net income, and other changes in stockholders' equity for the period excluded from the reported results of operations.

G. Reconciliations of amounts of revenue and earnings previously reported by the corporation that issues the stock to effect the combination with the combined amounts currently presented in financial statements and summaries. A new corporation formed to effect a combination may instead disclose the earnings of the separate companies which comprise combined earnings for prior periods.

The above information should be furnished on a pro forma basis in information that is given to stockholders regarding a proposed business combination expected to be accounted for as a pooling.

The following is an example of footnotes meeting the requirements for disclosure of a pooling of interests:

NOTE 2.   BUSINESS COMBINATION

On August 10, 19X3, Company A issued 625,000 shares of its common stock in exchange for substantially all the common stock of Company B. The combination was accounted for as a pooling of interests, and the consolidated financial statements have been restated to include the accounts of Company B since January 1, 19X2. Sales and net income of Company B were $17,850,000 and $1,670,000 in 19X2, and $14,800,000 and $2,830,000 in 19X3 from the beginning of the year to the date of the combination, respectively. Prior to the business combination, Company B reported on the basis of a fiscal year ending on June 30. The restated consolidated statement of income for 19X2 includes the results of Company A for the 12 months ended December 31, 19X2 combined with the results of Company B for the 12 months ended June 30, 19X3. The consolidated statement of income for 19X3 includes the results of both companies for the 12 months ended December 31, 19X3. Retained earnings have been adjusted for the net income of Company B for the six months ended June 30, 19X3 to $1,650,000 which, in the restated consolidated statement of income, has been duplicated. See Note 8 for the effects of the business combination on stockholders' equity.

NOTE 8.   CHANGES IN STOCKHOLDERS' EQUITY

The table on page 82 sets forth the changes in stockholders' equity for the years ended December 31, 19X2 and 19X3.

Reporting "In-Progress" Poolings.   Special reporting considerations apply when a pooling:

1. Is consummated after the end of a fiscal period but before issuance of the financial statements, or

2. Has been initiated but not consummated as of the date of the financial statements, and where the company is reasonably assured that the combination will meet the conditions of a pooling.

	Common Stock	Additional Paid-in Capital	Retained Earnings	Total
Balance, January, 19X2 as previously re-ported	$2,200,000	$15,400,000	$28,700,000	$46,300,000
Adjustment from pooling of interests (Note 2)	625,000	1,500,000	8,600,000	10,725,000
Balance, January 1, 19X2 as restated	2,825,000	16,900,000	37,300,000	57,025,000
Net income for the year			7,200,000	7,200,000
Balance, December 31, 19X2	2,825,000	16,900,000	44,500,000	64,225,000
Net income for the year			9,100,000	9,100,000
Adjustment to conform pooled company's fiscal year (Note 2)			(1,650,000)	(1,650,000)
Balance, December 31, 19X3	$2,825,000	$16,900,000	$51,950,000	$71,675,000

Because a pooling is recognized in the financial statements at the date of consummation, where a pooling is consummated after the end of the fiscal period, but before the issuance of a combining company's related financial statements, those statements are not retroactively restated to give effect to the business combination. The retroactive effect is not given to the pooling until financial statements covering the period of consummation are issued. The separate financial statements of the combining company should be issued for the fiscal period preceding the consummation. However, the combining company should disclose as supplemental information in the financial statements or in footnotes, the substance of the combination and effects on financial position and results of operation. The disclosures regarding results of operations should include:

1. Revenue.
2. Net income.
3. Earnings per share.
4. The effects of anticipated retroactive changes in accounting methods to conform with those to be used by the combined entity.

For "in-progress" poolings, in registration statements of public companies filed with the SEC, supplemental pro forma statements giving retroactive effect to the pooling are required to be filed, in addition to the historical financial statements filed in the annual report to stockholders. Only historical financial statements with appropriate footnote disclosures will normally be required in annual reports to stockholders, although in certain cases pro forma financial statements may be preferable. Form 10-K filings require only the same presentation as in the annual report to stockholders, except that if a registration statement containing pro forma combined financial statements was previously filed with the SEC, reference should be made to those statements in Form 10-K. These are general rules for these situations, but the specific requirements for individual registration forms and the circumstances (including such considerations as whether the auditor's report is dated before or after the consummation) should be carefully reviewed where filings with the SEC are involved to determine if pro forma financial statements or only footnote disclosures will be required.

At the end of a fiscal period where a company is party to a business combination that has been initiated but not consummated, intercorporate investments acquired for cash or other consideration are stated at cost in the balance sheet of the separate company, and stock acquired in exchange for stock of the issuing company is recorded at the proportionate share of the underlying net assets of the investee at the date acquired. Until the pooling is consummated and the pooling method determined to be appropriate, the investor company should recognize its share of net income or losses of the investee company as if on the equity method. Disclosure should be made of the effects of

restatement of operations for all periods presented, which will occur if
the combination is later consummated and meets the conditions for
the poolings of interest method.

The reporting process for a pooling simplifies greatly once financial
statements for the period of consummation have been issued, because
only combined statements for the current period and restated combined statements for prior periods are issued. This applies to annual
and quarterly financial statements.

An example of footnote disclosure of consummation of a pooling of
interests consummated after the end of the fiscal period but prior to
the issuance of the financial statements follows:

NOTE 10.   SUBSEQUENT EVENT—BUSINESS COMBINATION

In January 19X8, Company A exchanged 1,400,000 shares of its common stock for all the outstanding common stock of Company B. The
transaction will be accounted for as a pooling of interests, and in the
first quarter of 19X8, all prior periods will be restated to give retroactive effect to the combination. The following pro forma information
reflects the effects of the combination on the financial position and
results of operations of Company A and Company B.

FINANCIAL POSITION AT DECEMBER 31, 19X6

	Company A	Company B	Combined
Working capital	$17,300,000	$ 7,200,000	$24,500,000
Property, plant and equip- ment, net	39,700,000	16,500,000	56,200,000
Long-term debt	24,800,000	3,000,000	27,800,000
Stockholders' equity	33,500,000	17,300,000	50,800,000

RESULTS OF OPERATIONS, YEARS ENDED DECEMBER 31,

	19X7	19X6
Net sales:		
Company A	$178,000,000	$167,000,000
Company B	64,000,000	51,000,000
Combined	$242,000,000	$218,000,000

Net income:		
Company A	$ 18,625,000	$ 17,600,000
Company B	2,900,000	2,600,000
Combined	$ 11,525,000	$ 10,200,000
Net income per share:		
Company A	$6.21	$5.87
Company B (based on number of Company A shares issued in business combination)	2.07	1.86
Combined	$8.28	$7.73

Certain changes are expected to be made to conform the accounting practices of the companies. The effects of the changes are not expected to be significant.

See Appendix 5-1 for a listing of significant authoritative accounting pronouncements affecting both poolings and purchase method acquisitions.

APPENDIX 4-1: CHECKLIST FOR QUALIFYING FOR USE OF THE POOLING OF INTERESTS METHOD

The checklist below sets forth the major requirements of the pooling of interests method. Appropriate technical pronouncements should be referred to for proper application of these requirements and exceptions to the requirements.

AUTONOMY

1. Each of the combining companies must be autonomous and not have been a subsidiary or division of another corporation within two years before the plan of combination is initiated.

2. Each of the combining companies must be independent of the other combining companies. (Restrictions exist as to intercorporate investments permitted.)

MANNER OF COMBINING INTERESTS

1. The combination must be effected in a single transaction or completed in accordance with a specific plan within one year after the plan is initiated.
2. A corporation must offer and issue only common stock with rights identical to those of the majority of its outstanding voting common stock in exchange for substantially all (at least 90%) the voting common stock interest of another company at the date the plan of combination is consummated.
3. None of the combining companies may change the equity interest of voting common stock in contemplation of effecting the combination either within two years before the plan of combination is initiated or between the dates the combination is initiated and consummated.
4. Each of the combining companies may have reacquired shares of voting common stock only for purposes other than business combinations, and no company may have acquired more than a normal number of shares between the dates the plan of combination is initiated and consummated.
5. The ratio interest of individual stockholders to other common stockholders in a combining company must remain the same as a result of the exchange of stock to effect the combination.
6. The voting rights to which the common stockholders in the combined company are entitled are exercisable by the stockholders.
7. The combination is resolved at the date the combination is consummated and no provisions of the plan relating to the issue of securities or other considerations are pending.

ABSENCE OF PLANNED TRANSACTIONS

1. The combined corporation may not agree directly or indirectly to retire all or part of the common stock issued to effect the combination (no bailout arrangements).
2. The combined corporation may not enter into any other financial arrangements for the former stockholders of a combining company.
3. The combined corporation may not intend or plan to dispose of a significant part of the assets of the combining companies within two years after the combination other than disposals in the ordinary course of business of the formerly separate companies and to eliminate duplicate facilities or excess capacity.

APPENDIX 4-2: CHECKLIST OF DISCLOSURE REQUIREMENTS—POOLING OF INTERESTS COMBINATIONS

1. Nature and description of companies pooled during last period, number of shares issued, and basis of presentation and restatements (including reconciliation).
2. Revenues, extraordinary items, and net income of separate companies from beginning of period to date of consummation (or to end of most recent interim period prior to pooling).
3. Nature of adjustments to conform accounting practices and their effect on previously reported income of separate companies.
4. Details of changes in retained earnings from changing fiscal years.
5. Substance and effects, individually, of pooling consummated or reasonably assured of consummation after year-end but before statements are issued.
6. Nature of any precombination nonrecurring intercompany transactions involving long-term assets and liabilities that are not eliminated in preparing the pooled statements.

7. Separately, as an extraordinary item, any material amount of profit or loss (net of tax) resulting from disposal of a significant part of the assets or a separate segment of the previously separate companies within two years after the pooling was consummated.

8. Revenues, extraordinary items, and net earnings of the constituent companies for the preceding year on a combined basis if only single-year statements are presented for the year the pooling occurred.

5

ACCOUNTING FOR BUSINESS COMBINATIONS—THE PURCHASE METHOD

PRINCIPLES OF PURCHASE ACCOUNTING

General Principles

The purchase method of accounting is used for any business combination in which a controlling interest of another entity is acquired, which does not meet all the conditions for use of the pooling of interests method. The purchase method is also applicable where some or all of the stock of a minority interest is acquired, and also used in accounting for acquisition of investments accounted for by the equity method.

The principles of the purchase method are similar to the general accounting principles for acquisition of assets and issuance of stock. An overview of the methodology of the purchase method follows:

1. The total cost of the acquisition is determined.
2. The cost is allocated to identifiable assets acquired in proportion to their respective fair values.
3. If the total cost exceeds the fair value of the identifiable assets, the excess is allocated to goodwill; any excess of total fair value

of the identifiable assets over total cost is applied as a pro rata reduction of long-term assets.

4. Goodwill is amortized over a period not exceeding 40 years.
5. Prior periods are not restated; however, certain supplemental disclosures may be required.

Determining the Cost of an Acquisition

The general guidance in APB Opinion No. 16, paragraph 67, is that the cost of assets acquired in a purchase acquisition should be determined in accordance with the general principles for accounting for the acquisition of assets.

A. An asset acquired by exchanging cash or other assets is recorded at cost—that is, at the amount of cash disbursed or the fair value of other assets distributed.
B. An asset acquired by incurring liabilities is recorded at cost—that is, at the present value of the amounts to be paid.
C. An asset acquired by issuing shares of stock of the acquiring corporation is recorded at the fair value of the asset—that is, shares of stock issued are recorded at the fair value of the consideration received for stock.

The application of the above general principles of acquisition accounting sometimes involves a number of complex accounting considerations.

Many acquisitions are made by exchanging cash and/or incurring liabilities for the net assets or stock of another company. Alternatively, equity securities of the acquiring company may be issued in exchange for the assets or stock of the acquired company. Where market prices for the shares issued are known, the cost of the acquisition is normally measured by the market price of the stock exchanged at the date of acquisition. However, market prices for a reasonable period of time before and after the terms of the acquisition are agreed to and announced should be considered in establishing the value to be placed on the securities to avoid volatility of stock prices unduly affecting the recorded cost of the acquisition. Where restricted securities are issued in an acquisition, an appraisal of the value of such securities by qualified professionals, such as investment bankers, may be necessary to establish value.

When fair value of securities issued in an acquisition is not readily determinable, all factors present in the transition, such as an estimate of the value of the assets received, including a direct estimate of goodwill, should be considered in establishing the cost to be recorded.

Although cash paid, liabilities incurred, and securities issued will comprise the major portion of the cost of most acquisitions, numerous other items must be considered for inclusion in the cost of an acquisition. Following are some of the more common additional factors to be considered in determining the cost of an acquisition and establishing the carrying values of certain assets and liabilities.

1. *Direct Expenses of Acquisitions.* Acquisition costs should include direct expenses of the acquisition, such as finders' and directly related professional (for example, legal, accounting, and appraisal) fees and incremental in-house costs that were directly caused by and related to the acquisition. The normal costs of an internal acquisitions department, or officers or employees specifically concerned with acquisitions are not includable in the cost of acquisitions, because they are not incremental.

2. *Premium or Discount.* Purchase accounting requires recognition of present value concepts. Premium or discount on a debt security issued or assumed should be imputed to adjust the liability to present value based on current market interest or yield rates, if the stated interest or yield rate varies significantly from current market rates.

The procedure for assigning fair value to individual assets and liabilities (generally receivables or payables) requires discounting to present value or assigning a premium allocation.

After acquisition, interest expense or income should be recorded through amortization of the premium or discount, using the interest method.

3. *Assets Exchanged.* Assets conveyed to the seller as consideration in the acquisition should be included in the acquisition cost at fair value. Any deferred tax balances related to the assets given up should be removed from the balance sheet and applied as a reduction of the fair value of the acquired assets.

4. *Contingent Consideration.* Consideration contingent on future earnings of the acquired operation should be added to acquisition

cost when amounts of consideration to be payable are determinable beyond a reasonable doubt. Acquisition cost should be increased at that time, and the additional cost allocated to assets acquired in accordance with the purchase method, usually resulting in an adjustment to long-term assets or goodwill. The additional cost should be depreciated or amortized prospectively over the remaining useful lives of the related assets. Where stock has been given in consideration together with a contingency requiring the issuance of additional shares or payments of cash dependent on fluctuation in future security prices, issuance of additional shares does not result in a future adjustment of acquisition cost. The recorded value of shares previously issued is reduced by an amount equal to the fair value of the consideration (cash, stock, or other) paid upon resolution of the contingency.

Interest and dividends paid to an escrow agent on contingently issuable debt or securities should not be recorded as interest or dividends. Upon resolution of the contingency, if payment by the agent to the sellers is required, the amounts should be recorded as additional acquisition cost if the contingency was based on earnings. If the contingency was based on security prices, the treatment is the same as for contingently issuable securities in that the value of securities previously issued is reduced to result in no change to total recorded acquisition cost.

5. *Preacquisition Contingencies.* A negotiated adjustment to the purchase price related to the assumption of a contingency by the acquirer is properly includable in the cost of acquisition. Certain resolutions of contingencies after the acquisition can result in adjustments to acquisition costs.

6. *Valuation Adjustments for Tax Effects.* Where the book and tax basis of an acquired asset or assumed liability differ, the resulting differences to be reported in future book and taxable income and the resulting tax effects are considered an adjustment of fair market value, and require recognition as adjustments of the carrying values of the individual assets and liabilities.

Recording Assets Acquired and Liabilities Assumed

Recording a purchase acquisition requires the allocation of total acquisition cost to assets acquired and liabilities assumed on the basis of their respective fair values. If the total acquisition cost exceeds the fair values of identifiable net assets, the excess is allocated to good-will. If the fair value of identifiable assets and liabilities exceeds ac-quisition cost (sometimes referred to as negative goodwill), the defi-ciency is applied as a pro rata reduction of the assigned values of long-term assets, except for long-term investments in marketable se-curities. If long-term assets are eliminated by this procedure, any remaining negative goodwill is recorded as a deferred credit and am-ortized over a period not to exceed 40 years.

Where the acquisition was for less than 100% of the acquired com-pany, adjustments to carrying value of identifiable assets and liabili-ties are made only to the extent of the proportionate share acquired by the acquirer, and the portion of the acquired company to the remain-ing minority interest continues to be accounted for on a historical basis.

Appraisals. Although information such as the results of subsequent dispositions of assets are sometimes used as indications of fair value, independent appraisals are often the primary means of determining the estimated fair values to be used in assigning costs. In the absence of evidence that other amounts are better estimates, the appraised values are often used as the fair values.

In a formal appraisal, an amount may be assigned to goodwill to reflect the estimated value of the acquired operation's going concern value. The substance of the goodwill may be the existence of an exist-ing customer base or market share, an assembled and trained work force, or other intangibles of value. The appraiser may estimate the fair value of appraised goodwill based on guidelines, including per-centages of goodwill to total acquisition cost evidenced in recent com-parable acquisitions.

The appraiser may be aware of the total acquisition cost and may use this information in developing appraisals of individual items and the proportions of tangible and intangible assets. If the total appraised values of identifiable assets vary by an unusual amount from the total acquisition cost, ordinarily there should be an identifiable reason. For example, the acquisition cost of an unusually highly profitable busi-ness may include a higher than normal amount of goodwill. Con-versely, the acquisition cost of an operation that has been experienc-ing losses, or where the seller must sell under distress conditions for some reason, may be less than the fair values of the individual assets, resulting in negative goodwill.

In some cases the appraised values of individual assets must be adjusted to reflect certain accounting valuation adjustments required for purchase method acquisitions, including:

1. Adjustment of appraised fair value for the tax effects of differences between book and tax basis (illustrated later in this chapter).

2. Allocation of negative goodwill (illustrated later in this chapter).

3. Adjustment to a value indicated by additional information, which appears to be more indicative of fair value (such as a subsequent actual sale of one or more of the acquired assets at an amount differing from the appraised value).

The general guidelines included in APB Opinion No. 16, paragraph 87, for recording assets acquired and liabilities assumed are presented below together with a discussion of some of the more significant aspects of implementing the guidelines in practice. Unless otherwise stated, the quotations following are from subsections of APB Opinion No. 16, paragraph 87.

1. *Marketable Securities.*
   Marketable securities at current net realizable values.

2. *Receivables.*
   Receivables at present values of amounts to be received determined at appropriate current interest rates, less allowances for uncollectibility and collection costs, if necessary.

In practice, acquired trade accounts receivable expected to be collected in accordance with normal collection terms for most industries often will not be discounted to present value. However, where the receivable is expected to remain outstanding for a length of time that will result in a more significant discount factor, this should be reflected in the acquisition accounting.

Acquired notes receivable that bear an interest rate varying significantly from current market rates for a similar note should be adjusted for imputed discount or premium. The adjustment should result in additional interest income or expense from the date of acquisition to date of collection, reflecting a rate equal to current market rates on the adjusted receivable amount recorded at acquisition.

3. *Inventories.*
   (1) *Finished goods and merchandise at estimated selling prices less the sum of (a) costs of disposal and (b) a reasonable profit allowance for the selling effort of the acquiring corporation.*
   (2) *Work in progress at estimated selling prices of finished goods less the sum of (a) costs to complete, (b) costs of disposal, and (c) a reasonable profit allowance for the completing and selling effort of the acquiring corporation based on profit for similar finished goods.*
   (3) *Raw materials at current replacement costs.*

Purchase accounting for inventories is discussed in a separate section.

4. *Plant and Equipment.*
   Plant and equipment: (1) to be used, at current replacement costs for similar capacity unless the expected future use of the asset indicates a lower value to the acquirer, (2) to be sold or held for later sale rather than used, at current net realizable value, and (3) to be used temporarily, at current net realizable value recognizing future depreciation for the expected period of use.

If the total fair value of all identifiable assets acquired exceeds the total acquisition cost, the excess is applied as a proportionate reduction of the values assigned to long-term assets, including fixed assets. None of the excess is allocated to long-term marketable securities, nor would an allocation be appropriate to other long-term assets which have a cash equivalency with easy conversion. An illustration of this kind of allocation to fixed assets is at the top of page 96.

5. *Intangible Assets.*
   Intangible assets which can be identified and named, including contracts, patents, franchises, customer and supplier lists, and favorable leases, at appraised values.

Identifiable intangible assets should be valued before amounts are allocated to goodwill. Certain identifiable intangible assets may be amortized for tax purposes. In addition to the above, identifiable intangible assets may include customer lists, technology rights, patents and trademarks, computer programs and software.

	Fair Value (After Adjustment for Tax Effect of Differences in Book and Tax Basis)	Allocation of Excess of Fair Value Over Cost	Amount Assigned For Accounting Purposes
Current assets	$1,000,000		$1,000,000
Long-term assets:			
Fixed assets:			
Land	500,000	(111,200)	388,800
Building	2,000,000	(444,400)	155,600
Equipment	2,000,000	(444,400)	155,600
	4,500,000		3,500,000
Marketable securities	500,000		500,000
	$6,000,000	$(1,000,000)	$5,000,000

Total fair value, as above	$6,000,000
Total cost	5,000,000

Excess to be allocated	$1,000,000

Assets to be reduced:	$4,500,000

Percentage reduction	22.22%

Allocation		
Land	$ 500,000 × 22.22% = $ 111,200
Building	2,000,000 × 22.22% = 444,400
Equipment	2,000,000 × 22.22% = 444,400
	$1,000,000

FASB Interpretation No. 4 provides for the allocation of cost to indentifiable tangible and intangible assets, including:

1. *Any assets acquired in the combination that result from R&D activities of the acquired enterprise (such as patents, blueprints, formulas, and designs for new products).*

2. *Assets acquired to be used in R&D activities of the combined enterprise (such as materials, supplies, equipment, and specific research projects in process.*

Costs incurred related to research and development activities after an acquisition are accounted for in accordance with FASB Statement No. 2.

Additionally, if the agreement is structured to include a covenant that the seller will not compete with the acquirer for a specified period of time, this gives rise to an identifiable intangible that may be amortized for tax purposes.

6. **Other Assets.**

   Other assets, including land, natural resources, and nonmarketable securities, at appraised values.

7. **Accounts and Notes Payable.**

   Accounts and notes payable, long-term debt and other claims payable at present values of amounts to be paid determined at appropriate current interest rates.

The possible need to impute premium or discount to adjust stated interest rates to current market rates should be considered.

8. **Accrued Liabilities.**

   Liabilities and accruals—for example, accruals for pension cost warranties, vacation pay, deferred compensation—at present values of amounts to be paid determined at appropriate current interest rates.

Pension Costs. Purchase agreements will often provide for the continuation of pension plans maintained by the seller for the employees of the acquired company. The acquirer may agree to continue to provide retirement benefits for the employees of the acquired company at least equal to those under the plan maintained while the acquired company was owned by the seller. The pension plan and related fund assets may be transferred intact to provide continuation of the existing plan, or the employees may be integrated into a pension plan maintained by the acquirer. The agreement may require adjustments to the purchase price to be made for future benefits to be provided for previous service by the employees to the seller. For example, the seller may be required to make a payment to the acquirer or into the pension fund of an amount equal to any excess of vested benefits over fund assets related to pension plans as of the acquisition date.

Where the acquirer assumes the pension situation in its condition as of the acquisition date, the acquirer should include in the acquisition cost and in the acquired balance sheet an accrual for the present value of the excess of vested benefits over pension fund assets, if such exists.

Vacation Pay and Compensated Absences. Purchase agreements will frequently provide for a reduction in the purchase price in an amount equal to earned compensated absences, principally vacation pay, to be paid after the acquisition date. The liability should be included in computing the total acquisition cost, and a reflected as a liability in the acquired balance sheet.

FASB Statement No. 43, entitled "Accounting for Compensated Absences," sets forth the accounting standards for accruals for compensated absences. Under this pronouncement, vacation pay and other compensated absences must be recorded as balance sheet liabilities if the employees have earned vested right to such payments.

    9.   *Other Liabilities.*

       Other liabilities and commitments, including unfavorable leases, contracts, and commitments and plant closing expense incident to the acquisition, at present values of amount to be paid determined at appropriate current interest rates.

Purchase Accounting in Special Areas

Inventories. The guidelines for recording acquired inventories are similar to the guidelines for other assets in that they are intended to result in assigning the value the acquirer would theoretically have had to pay to acquire the inventory items individually in their current state. In the case of inventory, this includes compensating a manufacturer for the normal profit factor allocable to manufacturing work performed on work-in-process and finished goods inventories. Such amounts can be expected to be greater than the book value of the inventory in the balance sheet of the seller, as a result of both higher replacement costs for raw materials and the profit factor for manufacturing performed by the seller on inventory items prior to the acquisition.

The result of application of this valuation basis may cause a reduction of reported profits as a percentage of sales in the income statement of the acquirer for the period after the acquisition, as inventories sold in that period would bear a higher-than-normal cost. This lower profit reflects that the earning process performed by the acquirer with respect to the acquired finished goods (and work-in-process to a lesser extent) related only to the selling effort, and not to the manufacturing effort.

This is illustrated in the following example. Assume an acquired manufacturing operation normally sells at a 40% markup, 15% of which is considered to relate to manufacturing, and 25% to selling activities. The estimated sales amount to be realized from the sale of inventory is $2,000,000, 75% of which related to finished goods and 25% to work-in-process. The cost to complete the work in process is estimated at $50,000, and the work-in-process is 50% completed with respect to manufacturing operations. Costs of disposal are immaterial, and are ignored.

The table below indicates the manufacturing and selling profits which would normally occur on the acquired inventories.

	Finished Goods	Work-in-Process
Cost	$1,071,429	$357,143
Profit factors:		
Manufacturing (15%)	160,713	53,571
Selling (25%)	267,858	89,286
Selling price	$1,500,000	$500,000

Following is a computation of the amounts to be assigned to the acquired inventories.

Finished goods:

Estimated selling price	$1,500,000
Less, normal selling profit	(267,858)
Amount to be assigned	$1,232,142

Work-in-Process:

Estimated selling price	$ 500,000
Less:	
Normal selling profit	(89,286)
Manufacturing profit on 50% of work-in-process ($53,571 × 50%)	(26,786)
Cost to complete work-in-process	(50,000)
Amount to be assigned	$ 333,982

The following computes what would be reported in the income statement of the acquirer for the period after acquisition regarding the sale of the acquired inventories, assuming all items were sold.

	Total	Finished Goods	Work-in-Process
Sales	$2,000,000	$1,500,000	$500,000
Cost of sales:			
Inventory amounts recorded at acquisition	1,566,070	1,232,142	333,928
Additional costs incurred to complete	50,000	—	50,000
Total	1,616,070	1,232,142	383,928
Reported gross profit	$ 383,930	$ 267,858	$116,072
Reported gross profit as a percentage of sales	19.2%		

Assuming the same facts in a subsequent period where the inventories sold were manufactured by the acquirer, the following items would be expected to appear in the income statement.

Sales	$2,000,000
Cost of sales $2,000,000 ÷ 1.40	1,428,571
Profit	$ 571,429
Profit as a percentage of sales	28.6%

Occasionally, a purchase agreement may be structured so that the seller's inventory is acquired in exchange for a separate and distinct payment, which may be an amount equal to the book value of the inventories in the financial statements of the seller, or some other

negotiated amount that may vary from the amount which would be allocable based on the above method. The substantive terms of the purchase agreements should be carefully considered to determine if it is justifiable to treat the inventory acquisition separately from the acquisition of the other assets, and to assign lower amounts to the acquired inventories, resulting in higher reported gross profits in the period after the acquisition.

Special LIFO Inventory Considerations.   Where a business combination is taxable either for book or accounting purposes, and not taxable for the other, differences in the value assigned to LIFO inventories for book and tax purposes can result. In a purchase method acquisition, the acquirer is required to revalue the inventories to fair value at acquisition date, and the entire inventory is treated as a single LIFO layer acquired in the year of acquisition. For tax purposes, if the transaction has been a tax-free exchange, the previous LIFO inventory layers and values may be carried forward. This situation would ordinarily cause the book LIFO inventory balance to be greater than the tax LIFO inventory. If a taxable transaction is accounted for as a pooling of interests, the reverse would ordinarily occur—that is, that tax LIFO inventory amount would be greater than the book LIFO inventory amount.

The resulting differences between book and tax LIFO values and layers are carried forward from the date of acquisition. If inventory levels increase thereafter, book and tax cost of sales will generally be the same because the current year purchases or production will flow to cost of sales for both tax and accounting purposes. However, different values that may be allocated to fixed assets for tax and accounting purposes could create significant differences in depreciation charges allocated to production costs, which would be included in unit costs for cost of sales and incremental LIFO inventory layers. Where these differences are significant enough to require recognition for accounting purposes, differences in addition to those created in the acquisition accounting can arise. The additional differences, however, may exist where FIFO inventories, as well as LIFO inventories, are present.

If it appears that acquired LIFO inventory layers will not be liquidated in the foreseeable future, recognizing the tax effects of the differences in book and tax basis may not be necessary. Even if the layers were to be liquidated at some point in the future, the discounting of the future tax effects to present values to derive the amount that would represent the adjustment to fair value may result in the amount being immaterial.

Leases. Consistent with the basic principle that the values assigned to individual liabilities assumed should be based on fair value, when a lease assumed in a purchase bears a rental rate that is higher or lower than the current market rental rate for a similar lease, an intangible asset has been acquired, or an intangible liability has been assumed. Accordingly, the difference between rentals required under the assumed lease and current market rental rates, discounted to present value, should be included as an asset acquired or liability assumed in the acquisition and included in the acquired balance sheet.

The following illustrates the computation of the amount of an unfavorable lease commitment to be accrued in an acquisition. Assume an acquisition agreement provides that the acquirer assumes a lease on a 10,000 square foot factory building that bears an annual rental rate of $15 per square foot. Due to a decline in real estate values in the area, current leases on similar properties in the area provide for rentals averaging $10 per square foot. The remaining term of the lease is five years and rents are payable at the beginning of the year. The first annual rental payment is due the day after the acquisition. An appropriate discount rate is estimated at 12%.

	Effective Rental Rate	Market Rental Rate	Difference	
			Total	Present Value
1	$150,000	$100,000	$50,000	$ 50,000
2	150,000	100,000	50,000	44,643
3	150,000	100,000	50,000	39,860
4	150,000	100,000	50,000	35,589
5	150,000	100,000	50,000	31,776

Present value of unfavorable portion of assumed lease   201,868

Tax effect at 46%   (92,859)

Net liability included in acquisition
cost $109,009

The unfavorable lease liability would be included in the acquired balance sheet net of income tax effect, because the liability ordinarily would not be recognized for tax purposes until paid, resulting in different book and tax basis for the liability at the acquisition date.

Where the acquirer is required in an acquisition to assume a lease for an asset or facility that is of no use to the acquirer, the present value of the entire lease may be recorded as a cost of the acquisition. Similarly, where an asset or facility has only partial utility to an acquirer, the portion of future rental obligations pertaining to the portion not having utility may be recorded as a cost of the acquisition.

The mechanics of the above computation would apply to a "favorable lease," where the rental rate under the lease is less than the current market rate. The present value of the favorable portion of the lease would be recorded as an asset acquired in the acquisition, and amortized to expense over the term of the lease.

A lease assumed by the acquirer, which was classified by the seller in accordance with FASB Statement No. 13, retains its classification in the financial statements of the acquirer after the acquisition if no changes are made to the terms of the lease. If the provisions of the lease are modified, the revised lease is to be considered a new lease under FASB Statement No. 13, and the new lease should be classified and accounted for in accordance with the criteria set forth in that statement. A reclassification of the lease would not preclude recording the effects of an unfavorable or favorable operating lease as described above, which would still be required if applicable.

The above comprises the more frequent considerations related to leases assumed in an acquisition. A number of additional situations exist in areas such as the assumption of a leveraged lease as lessor, as to which appropriate accounting pronouncements should be referred to.

Preacquisition Contingencies.   Preacquisition contingencies of an acquired company can include the potential tax benefit of a tax loss carry-forward of an acquired operation, pending litigation at the acquisition date or a lawsuit filed shortly after the acquisition date, which related to events occurring before the acquisition, other contingent liabilities, contingent impairments of assets or, conversely, contingent assets.

Acquired Loss Carry-Forwards.   Special accounting procedures apply to an acquired loss carry-forward. At the date of acquisition, the tax benefits are recognized and reflected as a receivable in the acquired balance sheet only if realization is assured beyond a reasonable doubt. These cases will be rare in practice.

In the more normal case, the loss carry-forward is not recognized at the acquisition date. If the tax benefits are subsequently realized, the amount realized is retroactively recorded as a receivable with a corresponding reduction to the value assigned to other acquired assets. Reductions would first be applied to goodwill, and if goodwill is exhausted, or if no goodwill was recorded as a result of the acquisition, the values assigned to long-term assets (other than marketable securities) are reduced on a proportionate basis.

The actual restatement of prior balance sheets, and the resulting restatements to depreciation and amortization may in practice be done only where the effects are significant. Otherwise, recognition on a prospective basis for lesser amounts is a more practical approach.

An example of application of accounting for the tax benefit of an acquired loss carry-forward follows. Assume Company A acquires Company B stock for $12 million cash and that Company B has an unused loss carry-forward of $3 million. The following sets forth Company B's balance sheet at acquisition date after all purchase accounting adjustments, and the restated balance sheet after giving recognition to full realization of the tax benefit of the loss carry-forward at 46% rate for a tax recovery of $1,380,000.

COMPANY B
BALANCE SHEET AT ACQUISITION DATE

	As Originally Recorded	As Restated
Current assets	$ 3,000,000	$ 3,000,000
Tax recovery receivable	—	1,380,000
Fixed assets	10,000,000	10,000,000
Goodwill	2,000,000	620,000
	$15,000,000	$15,000,000
Current liabilities	$ 2,000,000	$ 2,000,000
Long-term debt	1,000,000	1,000,000
Equity	12,000,000	12,000,000
	$15,000,000	$15,000,000

The income statement for the year after acquisition would also be restated as follows, assuming that goodwill was being amortized over 20 years on a straight line basis.

Amortization charged in first year based on originally recorded goodwill	
$2,000,000 ÷ 20 =	$100,000
Amortization based on restated goodwill at acquisition date ($620,000 ÷ 20)	31,000
Restatement to reduce net income for first year (no tax reduction because goodwill is not tax deductible)	$ 69,000

Acquired Unused Investment Tax Credits.   The treatment given to unused investment tax credits of an acquired entity at acquisition date which are subsequently realized is different from the treatment given to loss carry-forwards. Any amounts of tax reductions achieved through realization of such tax credits after the acquisition are recorded as a reduction of the goodwill balance at the time of realization, and goodwill amortization is adjusted prospectively. If goodwill is fully eliminated, any additional amounts are recorded as reductions of other noncurrent assets, and then as deferred credits to be amortized over 40 years. These principles are included in FASB Interpretation No. 25, "Accounting for an Unused Investment Tax Credit."

Contingencies.   Preacquisition contingencies other than acquired loss carry-forwards are included in the purchase allocation in an amount equal to fair value. A period referred to as the *allocation period* ends when the acquirer is no longer waiting for information that it has arranged to obtain and that is known to be available or obtainable. Until this allocation period ends, the amounts assigned to specific assets and liabilities should be adjusted for the effects of current information regarding the contingency. The allocation period usually should not exceed one year from the date of consummation of the purchase acquisition. After the allocation period, any adjustments of the estimated fair values of contingencies previously recorded are included in the determination of net income for the period in which the adjustment is determined.

Fair value for inclusion in the purchase allocation can be determined by resolution of the contingency during the allocation period, or alternatively, fair value can be determined if the parties in negotiation agreed to an adjustment of the total purchase price by a specific amount as a result of the contingency.

If the fair value of a contingency cannot be determined during the allocation period, the contingency shall be included in the purchase allocation in an amount determined in accordance with the following criteria, contained in FASB statement No. 38:

(1) Information available prior to the end of the "allocation period" indicates that it is probable that an asset existed, a liability had been incurred, or an asset had been impaired at the consummation of the business combination. It is implicit in this condition that it must be probable that one or more future events will occur confirming the existence or the asset, liability, or impairment.

(2) The amount of the asset or liability can be reasonably estimated.

The above should be applied using the guidance in FASB Statement No. 5, "Accounting for Contingencies," and the related Interpretation No. 14, "Reasonable Estimation of the Amount of a Loss."

Adjustment of Fair Values for Tax Effects.   The valuation principles in APB Opinion No. 16 include an assumption that the utilization of an asset, whether through immediate expensing or future depreciation or amortization, should result in the acquirer receiving a normal tax benefit. Where the tax basis of an acquired asset is different than the fair value of that asset, the fair value must be adjusted to reflect that the normal tax benefit will not be received through the expensing of that asset. Similar reductions are made to liabilities that are included in the acquired balance sheet but are not recognized as liabilities for tax purposes. The payment of the related item may be treated as a deduction on the tax return, but for book purposes, the payment is not recognized as an expense, but the retirement of a liability.

Different basis in a purchase acquisition for book and tax purposes will result primarily from:

1.   Treatment of the acquisition for tax purposes as a tax-free exchange carrying over the tax basis of the seller, while revaluing the acquired assets for book purposes.

2.   The effects of different methods of allocating purchase price for book and tax purposes.

3.   Exclusion from acquisition cost for tax purposes of items for which immediate tax deductions can be obtained, while includ-

ing the items in acquisition cost for book purposes, and vice versa.

The net of tax procedure for valuing assets and liabilities with different book and tax basis is similar to providing deferred taxes. The tax effects recorded in an acquisition are not deferred taxes, however, but an element of fair value, and should, therefore, be shown in the balance sheet as an adjustment of the carrying value of the related asset or liability. In addition to differences caused by valuation adjustments recorded in purchase accounting, deferred taxes recorded by the seller should not be recorded in the balance sheet by the acquirer.

Although APB Opinion No. 16 prescribes the above net-of-tax classification, in practice some companies have established separate deferred tax balances for the tax effects of differences between book and tax basis. Although this may simplify record keeping, under present rules, the net-of-tax method is required.

The tax effect should be computed by multiplying the difference between the book and tax basis by the tax rate applicable to the item. That is, an asset or liability which normally impacts income taxed at ordinary rates should be tax-effected at ordinary rates, and assets expected to impact taxes at capital gains rates should be tax-effected at capital gains rates. The tax effect so computed should then be discounted to present value to reflect the impact of the timing of the tax effect. Unlike discounts applied to assumed liabilities payable in the future, discounts on tax effects are not amortized as interest expense in periods after the acquisition.

In practice, the discounting of the tax effect may not occur where the asset or liability is expected to be liquidated relatively soon after the acquisition. Discounting will generally be most relevant to property, plant, and equipment which will be depreciated over a relatively long period.

In periods after the acquisition, the realization of the tax effects are recognized as the related assets are depreciated or amortized, or the related liabilities are liquidated. This can cause an other-than-normal effective tax rate.

Foreign Currency Translation in a Purchase.   In a purchase acquisition of a foreign operation, the assets acquired and liabilities assumed are adjusted to fair values at the date of acquisition and translated at the exchange rate in effect at the date of acquisition. Any difference between the total cost of the acquisition in dollars and the translated net assets is accounted for as goodwill or negative goodwill. Future balance sheets are translated by converting the fair values at acquisition date into dollars at the exchange rate at the balance sheet date. Any difference caused by fluctuations in exchange rates are accounted for in accordance with FASB Statement No. 52.

Purchase Accounting and Minority Interests.   Where a minority interest remains outstanding after an acquisition, the adjustment of the recorded basis of assets and liabilities to current fair value resulting from purchase accounting are made only to the extent of the acquirer's proportionate share of the acquired company. The assets and liabilities prior to the acquisition remain the same to the extent of the percentage of minority interest remaining outstanding.

The following example illustrates the computation of acquisition adjustments where a minority interest remains outstanding. Assume that 75% of the stock of Company B is purchased by Company A for $7,500,000 cash.

	Company B Records	Fair Value (A)	Excess of Fair Value Over Historical Book Value	Consolidation Entries	Amounts Reported in Acquirer's Financial Statements
Current assets	$ 3,000,000	$3,500,000	$ 500,000	$ 375,000(B)	$ 3,375,000
Fixed assets	7,000,000	9,000,000	2,000,000	1,500,000(B)	8,500,000
Goodwill	—			1,500,000(C)	1,500,000
	$10,000,000			$3,375,000	$13,375,000
Current liabilities	$ 2,000,000	2,000,000			$ 2,000,000
Long-term debt	2,500,000	2,500,000			2,500,000
Equity	5,500,000			$2,000,000	7,500,000
Minority interest				1,375,000(D)	1,375,000
	$10,000,000			$3,375,000	$13,375,000

NOTES ON CONSOLIDATION ENTRIES:

(A)   After adjustment for tax effects in differences between book and tax basis. The write-up of inventories is to eliminate the "manufacturer's profit" in work-in-process and finished goods.

(B) Acquirer's share of excess of fair value over net book value of assets of Company B
       Current assets:

$$\$ \ 500{,}000 \times 75\% = \$ \ 375{,}000$$

       Fixed assets:

$$\$2{,}000{,}000 \times 75\% = \$1{,}500{,}000$$

(C) Goodwill:

Amount paid for stock		$7,500,000
Fair values of assets and liabilities:		
Current assets	$3,500,000	
Fixed assets	9,000,000	
Current liabilities	(2,000,000)	
Long-term debt	(2,500,000)	
	8,000,000	
Equity interest acquired	× 75%	6,000,000
Goodwill		$1,500,000

(D) Equity:

Company A investment in Company B	$7,500,000
Company B equity on historical basis	5,500,000
	$2,000,000
Minority Interest:	
Company B equity on historical basis	$5,500,000
Minority Interest percentage	× 25%
Minority Interest	$1,375,000

Where an acquirer purchases additional shares of ownership after its initial application of the purchase accounting method (sometimes referred to as a "step or incremental" acquisition), a separate determination of fair values of identifiable assets and liabilities is made at the time of each separate purchase, and the amount of goodwill computed accordingly.

RECORD KEEPING FOR PURCHASE ACCOUNTING ACQUISITIONS

Where the stock of a company has been acquired, two basic approaches for the record-keeping aspects of the revaluations required by purchase accounting are:

1. The accounting records of the acquired company are left the same as prior to the acquisition, and the revaluations and related effects on future income and expenses are recorded as consolidation adjustments.
2. The revaluations are recorded directly in the accounts of the acquired company, creating a new basis of accounting. This is referred to as the *push-down* method.

Either method is generally considered appropriate where 100% of an acquired company's stock has been purchased.

Where a continuing minority interest is substantial, the recording of the revaluation adjustments to assets and liabilities using the push-down method may not be appropriate, because this would disturb the historical accounting basis of the assets and liabilities underlying the minority interest.

Some accountants believe that the push-down method should not be used where any minority interest is present. Others believe it should be used only where a remaining minority interest is not significant. No authoritative pronouncements exist as to what would constitute a significant minority interest for this purpose. In any event, the use of the push-down method where a minority interest remains would require maintaining a separate accountability based on historical costs underlying the minority interest.

FINANCIAL REPORTING OF A PURCHASE ACQUISITION

The acquirer reports the results of operations of an acquired company after the date of acquisition. Notes to the financial statements of the acquirer should include the following disclosures (specified in APB Opinion No. 16, paragraph 95) for the period in which an acquisition accounted for as a purchase is completed.

A. Name and a brief description of the acquired company.

B. Method of accounting for the combination—that is, by the purchase method.

C. Period for which results of operations of the acquired company are included in the income statement of the acquiring corporation.

D. Cost of the acquired company and, if applicable, the number of shares of stock issued or issuable and the amount assigned to the issued and issuable shares.

E. Description of the plan for amortization of acquired goodwill, the amortization method, and period.

F. Contingent payments, options or commitments specified in the acquisition agreement and their proposed accounting treatment.

APB Opinion No. 16, paragraph 96, as amended by FASB Statement No. 79, requires that, where the acquirer is a public held company, notes to the financial statements for the period in which a purchase acquisition takes place include as supplemental information the following on a pro forma basis:

A. Results of operations for the current period as though the companies had combined at the beginning of the period, unless the acquisition was at or near the beginning of the period.

B. Results of operations for the immediately preceding period as though the companies had combined at the beginning of that period if comparable financial statements are presented.

The pro forma data need only be presented for the period of combination and the immediately preceding period. The minimum information to be disclosed in the pro forma information includes revenues, income before extraordinary items, net income, and earnings per share. In computing the pro forma results, the purchase accounting adjustments should be assumed to have taken place at the beginning of the period prior to the acquisition. The adjustments to actual data necessary to present the data on a pro forma basis will include any required changes to income taxes, preferred stock dividends, depreciation, and amortization.

The following is an example of disclosure of a purchase acquisition appropriate for inclusion in the notes to a publicly held acquirer's financial statements:

NOTE 5.   ACQUISITIONS

On June 1, 19X7, the Company acquired all the stock of Company B, a manufacturer of automotive accessories, for $12,000,000 in cash. The acquisition has been accounted for as a purchase, and net assets and results of operations of Company B have been included in the Company A consolidated financial statements since the acquisiton date. The excess of cost over net assets acquired amounted to $670,000, and is being amortized over a 40-year period. The following sets forth unaudited pro forma consolidated results of operations assuming the acquisition had occurred on January 1, 19X6. The unaudited pro forma data includes the effects of all significant adjustments related to the acquisition, including interest expense from January 1, 19X6 on $5,000,000 in 12% subordinated debentures issued by Company A on May 1, 19X7 deemed to have provided funds for the acquisition.

	19X7	19X6
Net Sales	$84,500,000	$77,600,000
Net Income	6,750,000	6,200,000
Net Income per common share	$1.93	$1.77

ILLUSTRATION OF PURCHASE ACCOUNTING

The following example illustrates the application of purchase accounting, including adjustments of fair values for differences in book and tax basis. Assume that Company A acquires all the stock of Com-

COMPANY B
BALANCE SHEET BEFORE ACQUISITION

	Tax	Book
Current assets	$2,500,000	$2,500,000
Fixed assets, net	2,500,000	5,000,000
Other assets	300,000	600,000
	$5,300,000	$8,100,000
Current liabilities	$1,200,000	$1,200,000
Deferred taxes		1,400,000
Long-term debt	2,000,000	2,000,000
Equity	2,100,000	3,500,000
	$5,300,000	$8,100,000

pany B for $12 million cash in a tax-free transaction. For tax purposes, the basis of assets and liabilities of Company B are carried over, but for accounting purposes the assets must be revalued in accordance with the purchase accounting method. The balance sheets for book and tax purposes of Company B prior to the acquisition are shown below. Independent appraisals indicated fair values of identifiable assets as follows: fixed assets, $10 million; other assets (including trademarks and patents), $1 million. Inventories are valued at $3 million in accordance with principles of purchase accounting. Assume ordinary tax rates of 46% and capital gains rates of 30%. A discount rate of 14% is considered appropriate for present value computations.

COMPANY B
ACQUISITION ACCOUNTING SUMMARY

	Tax Basis	Fair Value Before Tax Effects	Tax Effects	Amounts Assigned for Books
Current assets	$2,500,000	$ 3,000,000	$ (230,000) (1)	$ 2,770,000
Fixed assets, net	2,500,000	10,000,000	(824,000) (2)	9,176,000
Other assets	300,000	1,000,000	(168,000) (3)	832,000
Goodwill		(400,000)	1,130,000 (5)	730,000
	$5,300,000	$13,600,000	$ (92,000)	$13,508,000
Current liabilities	1,200,000	$ 1,200,000		$ 1,200,000
Unfavorable lease		200,000	$ (92,000) (4)	108,000
Long-term debt	2,000,000	2,000,000		2,000,000
Equity	2,100,000	12,000,000		12,000,000
	$5,300,000	$13,600,000	$ (92,000)	$13,508,000

NOTE 1. INVENTORIES

Book value before tax effects	$3,000,000
Tax basis	2,500,000
Difference	500,000
Tax Rate	46%
Tax effect	$ 230,000

The above tax effect is not discounted to present value because the inventory is expected to turn over completely in the next year, resulting in discount having an insignificant effect.

NOTE 2. FIXED ASSETS

	Land	Building	Equipment	Total
Book basis	$1,000,000	$3,000,000	$6,000,000	$10,000,000
Tax basis	300,000	800,000	1,400,000	2,500,000
Difference	700,000	2,200,000	4,600,000	$ 7,500,000
Tax rate	30%	46%	46%	
Tax effect	$ 210,000	$1,012,000	$2,116,000	$ 3,338,000
Present value	$ –0– [a]	$ 130,000[b]	$ 694,000[c]	$ 824,000
Adjusted book basis	$1,000,000	$2,870,000	$5,306,000	$ 9,176,000

[a] Because the land is expected to be held for an indefinite period, the effect of discounting would be to make the discounted present value immaterial. For example, the present value of $210,000 paid at the end of 39 years would be as follows: $210,000 × .02 = $4,200. Therefore for all practical purposes, the present value is considered to be insignificant.

[b] Buildings: Book life, 30 years; tax life remaining, 10 years. On straight line basis for first 10 years, depreciation is $100,000 per year for books and $80,000 for taxes for difference of $20,000. Tax effect at 46% is $9200 per year. For years 11 through 30, depreciation is $100,000 for books and zero for taxes for a difference of $100,000. Tax effect at 46% is $46,000 per year. Discounted present value at 14% of a flow of $9200 per year for 10 years, followed by a flow of $46,000 per year for 20 years is $130,244, rounded to $130,000.

[c] Equipment: Book life, 15 years; tax life remaining, 7 years. On straight line basis for first 7 years depreciation is $400,000 per year for books and $200,000 for taxes, for a difference of $200,000. Tax effect at 46% is $92,000 per year. For years 8 through 15, depreciation is $400,000 per year for books and zero for taxes, for a difference of $400,000. Tax effect at 46% is $184,000 per year. Discounted present value at 14% of a flow of $92,000 for 7 years, followed by a flow of $184,000 per year for 8 years is $694,101, rounded to $694,000.

NOTE 3. OTHER ASSETS

	Trademarks	Other	Total
Book basis	$400,000	$600,000	$1,000,000
Tax basis	–0–	300,000	3,000,000
Difference	400,000	300,000	$ 700,000
Tax rate	46%	46%	
Tax effect	$184,000[a]	$138,000[b]	$ 322,000

[a] Trademarks: 10-year life for books; straight line over 10 years for tax effect of $18,400 per year, discounted at 14% equals $95,974, rounded to $96,000.
[b] Other: Computation not shown. Total present value of tax effects is $168,000.

NOTE 4.   UNFAVORABLE LEASE

(4)   Unfavorable portion of assumed lease is already stated at present value. Therefore, pretax effect amount multiplied by 46% tax rate equals present value of tax effect of $92,000.

NOTE 5.   GOODWILL

(5)   In this type of computation, goodwill becomes the balancing amount and is computed by difference.

In future years, the above differences would be expected to result in a higher than normal income tax rate. For example, assume no other permanent differences or tax credits exist, and pretax income for Company B is $200,000

The following demonstrates the effect on the tax provision for the Year after the acquisition.

Pretax income				$2,000,000
Taxes at statutory 46% rate				$ 920,000 (46.0%)
Tax effects of permanent differences:				
Inventory				230,000
Depreciation and amortization				

	Books	Taxes	Difference
Buildings	$ 95,667	$ 80,000	15,667
Equipment	353,733	200,000	153,733
Other assets	83,200	30,000	53,200
Goodwill	18,250	–0–	18,250

240,850 × 46% =   110,791

Provision for income taxes	$1,260,791 (63%)
Net income	$ 739,209

The above example represents the impact of Company B in the consolidated balance sheet and results of operations of Company A, after all adjustments to apply the purchase method.

Appendix 5-1: Significant Authoritative Accounting Pronouncements on Business Combinations

The following list is intended to provide guidance in referring to the significant accounting pronouncements on mergers and acquisitions, but it is not necessarily an all-inclusive index of professional requirements that may have a bearing on the subject.

APB OPINIONS

No.	Date	Title (and description)
15	5/69	Earnings Per Share (effects on earnings per share of mergers and acquisitions
16	8/70	Business Combinations (the comprehensive professional standard on accounting for business combinations)
17	8/70	Intangible Assets (accounting for goodwill and other purchased intangibles)
19	3/71	Reporting Changes in Financial Position (reporting acquisitions in the Statement of Changes in Financial Position)
20	7/71	Accounting Changes (changes in the reporting entity)
21	871	Interest on Receivables and Payables (discounting to present value)

APICPA ACCOUNTING INTERPRETATIONS

No.	Date	Title (and description)
N/A	See description	Unofficial Accounting Interpretations of APB Opinion No. 16 (39 separate brief interpretations issued on various dates between 12/70 and 3/73 dealing with specific technical questions on business combination accounting).
N/A	3/73	Unofficial Accounting Interpretations of APB Opinion No. 17 (deals with goodwill in a step acquisition).

FASB STATEMENTS

No.	Date	Title (and description)
10	2/75	Extension of "Grandfather" Provisions for Business Combinations (extended indefinitely certain exceptions in requirements for pooling of interests accounting for cases where intercorporate investments existed prior to October 31, 1970).
12	12/75	Accounting for Certain Marketable Securities (establishes accounting for allowance accounts in consolidated and separate company financial statements and for allowance accounts of equity method investees).
16	6/77	Prior Period Adjustments (accounting principles for realization of income tax benefits of preacquisition operating loss carry-forwards).
38	9/80	Accounting for Preacquisition Contingencies of Purchased Enterprises (guidelines for allocating cost of an acquisition to preacquisition contingencies).
79	2/84	Elimination of Certain Disclosures for Business Combinations by Nonpublic Enterprises (amends APB Opinion No. 16 by eliminating certain pro forma disclosures where a nonpublic enterprise engages in a purchase method acquisition).

FASB INTERPRETATIONS

No.	Date	Title (and description)
4	2/75	Applicability of FASB Statement No. 2 to Business Combinations Accounted for by the Purchase Method (establishes principles for assigning cost to assets resulting from research and development which have been acquired in a business combination accounted for by the purchase method).
9	2/76	Applying APB Opinions No. 16 and 17 when a Savings and Loan Association or a Similar Institution is Acquired in a Business Combination Accounted for by the Purchase Method (interpretation provides that purchase accounting principles as stated in APB No. 16 and 17 apply to acquisitions of savings and loan associations).
21	4/78	Accounting for Leases in a Business Combination (describes accounting principles for leases assumed in a business combination).
25	9/78	Accounting for an Unused Investment Tax Credit (provides for adjustment of goodwill or other assets at date of realization of unused investment credits of an acquired company at acquisition date in purchase method acquisitions).

APPENDIX 5-2: CHECKLIST OF DISCLOSURE REQUIREMENTS—PURCHASE METHOD ACQUISITIONS

1. Name and brief description of purchases during latest period; cost and, if applicable, number of shares issued or issuable, and amount assigned thereto; and period for which results of operations are included in income statement.

2. Contingent payments, options, or commitments and their proposed accounting treatment.

3. For unresolved preacquisition contingencies assumed in business combinations initiated prior to December 16, 1980, for which the specific provisions of FASB Statement No. 38 are not applied, the amount and nature of such contingency adjustments determined after December 15, 1980, which are reported other than as specified in FASB Statement No. 38. Include a description of how those adjustments are reported and the effect of the adjustments on current or expected future cash flows of the enterprises.

4. Plan for amortization (including method and period) of any acquired goodwill or any excess of acquired net assets over cost (negative goodwill).

5. For publicly held companies, supplemental pro forma information on results of operations for the:

   a. Current period as though the companies had combined at the beginning of the period, unless the acquisition took place at or near that date.

   b. Immediately preceding period as though the companies had combined at the beginning of that period if comparative financial statements are presented.

NOTE

Information relating to several relatively minor acquisitions may be combined.

6

FEDERAL INCOME TAX CONSIDERATIONS

This chapter will discuss the more relevant U.S. federal income tax considerations relating to corporate mergers, acquisitions, and divestitures based on the Internal Revenue Code of 1954 (hereinafter referred to as the IRC or the Code), updated through changes made by the Tax Reform Act of 1984 (the 1984 Act). The Tax Equity and Fiscal Responsibility Act of 1982 (TEFRA) and the 1984 Act are the last major tax-related legislations which affected this area. Tax-related legislation enacted in 1983 was concerned primarily with technical corrections which are reflected, as appropriate, in the materials contained in this chapter. To the extent that the material discusses transactions from the seller's viewpoint, the areas discussed cover the tax aspects of divestitures.

A few definitions are in order at this point. For purposes of this chapter, the term "corporate acquisition" will be used to refer to transactions in which one corporation obtains control over another corporation. "Control" usually occurs for business purposes when the buyer corporation obtains more than 50% of the voting stock of the acquired corporation. However, the term "control" for tax purposes, as defined in IRC Section 368(c)(1), refers to the acquisition of 80% or more of the voting and nonvoting stock of the acquired corporation. Control, in compliance with this tax definition (that is, the acquisition of 80% of both voting and nonvoting stock), is a prerequisite to utilization of most forms of reorganization commonly associated with tax planning for mergers and acquisitions.

The term "corporate merger" is used to refer to the acquisition of one corporation by another followed by the legal termination of existence of the acquired corporation with the buyer corporation surviving and succeeding to the assets, rights, and obligations of the acquired corporation. Corporate mergers are discussed in greater detail later in this chapter in the sections concerning reorganizations.

Finally, the term "corporate divestiture" is used to refer to the disposition or other transfer by one corporation of one or more of its businesses to another entity.

Tax considerations often influence how transactions are structured, but often tax considerations are secondary to overriding business, legal, and other concerns. The structure of a transaction may and sometimes should disregard tax considerations because of such overriding concerns, but it is important to understand and quantify the associated tax benefits or costs of any given structure.

Major questions with respect to the tax aspects of an acquisition include the following:

1. Is it taxable or nontaxable?
2. What is the character (ordinary versus capital) of any gain or loss that may be recognized now or in the future?
3. Is there any recapture of tax credits or depreciation?
4. If capital assets are received, what is the holding period for each asset?

Any transaction will be either taxable, tax-free, or partially taxable. The fundamental tax principle is that all transactions are fully taxable—unless the transaction or parts of it fit within one of the specifically defined tax-free exceptions within the Code. This general rule has its roots in IRC Section 61, which provides that " . . . gross income means all income from whatever source derived . . . " The Courts and the Internal Revenue Service (IRS) use this general rule as the starting point in analyzing the taxability of any transaction. It is broadly interpreted, and exceptions to it (i.e., situations qualifying for tax-free treatment) are narrowly defined.

In a tax-free transaction involving corporations, the seller (the acquired corporation or target corporation or their shareholders, if relevant) generally recognizes no gain or loss. The buyer (the acquiring corporation or acquirer) carries over the seller's tax basis, holding period, and other tax attributes. The seller avoids recapture of tax credits, depreciation, and other adverse tax consequences. This tax deferral can be a significant benefit in a tax-free transaction in the form of the cash savings that otherwise would be expended to satisfy tax liabilities arising from the transaction. Additionally, tax attributes such as earnings and profits and net operating losses may also be received or carried over by the buyer. Strict requirements as to structure exist, however, and restrictions often apply to the utilization of tax benefits that have been carried over in a tax-free transaction.

A large portion of the tax-free merger and acquisition area is covered by reorganizations under IRC Section 368 and related sections. Certain defined and qualified reorganizations are permitted by the tax laws to occur tax-free of any tax liabilities in order to encourage and permit businesses to organize and structure themselves in an economic and efficient manner. Each type of reorganization has its own requirements. These requirements and the underlying policies are discussed in detail later in this chapter.

If a reorganization qualifies under IRC Section 368 and related sections as a tax-free transaction, two or more corporations will exchange stock for stock, or assets for stock, without incurring any tax liability. Taxation is deferred by the substitution or carrying over of tax attributes. If a purported reorganization fails to qualify under IRC Section 368, then the transaction generally will be taxable to the seller but not to the buyer. The seller recognizes gain to the extent that the fair market value of the property received (stock or other property of the buyer) exceeds the tax basis in the property transferred (stock or assets of the target corporation). The buyer generally recognizes no gain or loss under IRC Section 1032 on the exchange of its stock for the stock or assets of the seller, even in an unsuccessful reorganization attempt.

The structure of a merger or acquisition will determine the tax ramifications to both parties to the transaction. However, the IRS and the Courts have the capability of denying taxpayers anticipated tax benefits, even in carefully structured transactions, by using their broad powers to reallocate income, deductions, and credits among the parties. Judicial concepts such as "no business purpose," "sham transaction," and "substance over form" have long been successfully utilized by the Courts and the IRS in unexpectedly reshaping a transaction for tax purposes—much to the disappointment and to the financial loss of the taxpayers.

Additionally, there are certain statutes that give the IRS enormous capability to restructure any transaction. For example, under IRC Section 482 the IRS is given the authority and power to restructure any transaction between commonly controlled entities or organizations to prevent evasion of taxes or to reflect income. IRC Section 269 provides that the IRS may disallow any deductions, tax credits, or other allowances resulting from mergers or acquisitions made to evade or to avoid income tax.

All of the preceding judicial and statutory danger zones must be carefully considered as potential tax structures and consequences from mergers and acquisitions are analyzed and planned.

Generally, the buyer and seller will be in conflict over tax considerations, because what is good for one is usually bad for the other. Often the IRS will permit the parties great latitude in structuring transactions, provided that the structure and tax treatment are consistent with the economic substance and the arm's length reality of that negotiated transaction.

There are occasions when the tax goals and interest of the buyer and seller provide the tax planner with an opportunity to obtain above-normal tax benefits for both parties. These transactions may be subject to close IRS scrutiny and extra care must be exercised by the tax planner.

This chapter will address these areas in some depth, but it must be stressed that these areas can involve especially complex tax considerations, many of which are not apparent to other than the highly qualified tax specialist who should be consulted regarding the tax aspects of any merger or acquisition.

CHANGES MADE BY TEFRA AND THE 1984 ACT

Some of the significant changes made by TEFRA and the 1984 Act include the following:

TEFRA

Faster depreciation write-offs under former IRC Section 168(b)(1)(B) and (C)—175% and 200% declining balance depreciation, respectively—have been eliminated, which affects cash flow planning for some mergers and acquisitions.

IRC Section 334(b)(2) has been replaced by new IRC Section 338 dealing with step-up in asset basis in qualified stock purchases. If the requirements of IRC Section 338 are satisfied, a purchase of stock can be treated by the purchaser as a direct purchase of assets, resulting in a step-up in the tax basis of the assets in the hands of the purchaser, but with possible recapture income to the seller.

New IRC Section 269A was added, which provides the IRS with broad powers to reallocate income among personal service corporations and their employee-owners.

TEFRA repealed the partial liquidation provisions under IRC Section 346. IRC Section 311 now controls the tax consequences of a partial liquidation and will generally result in dividend treatment to corporate shareholders.

The 1984 Act

Tax deductions are generally allowed only after complying with the new "economic performance" test under IRC Section 461(h) as well as the traditional "all events" test.

Real property placed in service after March 15, 1984 is depreciated over 18 years instead of 15 years. Depreciation rates for such real property simulate the 175% declining balance depreciation method. A mid-month averaging convention is also required.

"Golden parachute" payments triggered by a change in ownership in equity or assets may result in a denial of part or all of the tax deductions for such payments under new IRC Section 280G. A 20% excise tax may also apply under new IRC Section 4999 to part or all of such payments.

1976 revisions to net operating loss carry-forward rules under IRC Section 382 were again postponed.

Rules under IRC Section 341 were tightened, including raising the percentage of realized income from one-third to two-thirds in order to avoid classification as a collapsible corporation.

TAXABLE MERGERS AND ACQUISITIONS

General Concepts and Requirements

As a general rule, all transactions are taxable unless they fall within one of the specific tax-free provisions of the Internal Revenue Code (Treasury Regulation Section 1.1002-1(a)). In a taxable acquisition, generally only the seller recognizes gain or loss. If the buyer gives up not only cash but also property, however, the buyer may also recognize gain or loss on the exchange.

Taxable Mergers and Acquisitions—The Buyer's Viewpoint

For tax purposes, the purchase of the assets of a business is treated as a purchase of each separate tangible and intangible asset in that business. Even though the buyer may view the transaction as the purchase of a going business concern, each asset must be separately identified and valued for computation of the seller's gain or loss and for establishing the buyer's tax basis in the acquired assets.

The buyer of assets will desire to allocate most of the purchase price to depreciable assets to maximize future tax depreciation deductions. Conversely, the seller will desire to minimize allocation to the same assets in order to reduce depreciation recapture. Instead, the seller will desire to allocate much of the purchase price to nondepreciable assets such as goodwill and know-how in order to obtain favorable long-term capital gain treatment. Therefore, the allocation of the purchase price among the various assets becomes an important issue to both the buyer and the seller.

If the buyer purchases stock and the transaction qualifies under IRC Section 338, the buyer may elect under IRC Section 338 to step-up the tax basis in the assets of the acquired corporation. This election may trigger recapture income on the acquired assets, resulting in higher federal income taxes to the seller. The tax consequences of an election under IRC Section 338 to step-up the basis in the assets in the acquired corporation will have to be carefully analyzed and understood by both the buyer and the seller. It is an issue for negotiations because it will directly impact the net after-tax cost of the acquisition to the buyer as well as the federal income taxes payable by the seller. The cash flow of the buyer and the seller will also be affected by an election under IRC Section 338.

Taxable Mergers and Acquisitions—The Seller's Viewpoint

There are three major areas to be addressed in determining the tax consequences to the seller in a taxable merger or acquisition. The specifics of all three areas must be carefully considered by the tax planner in determining the tax consequences of a taxable merger or acquisition.

The first major area involves the calculation of the amount of gain or loss that will be recognized by the seller. This calculation is made by determining the amount received by the seller and subtracting from it the tax basis in the assets given up by the seller. The last two major areas concern the character (capital versus ordinary) of the gain or loss recognized by the seller and the timing for recognizing such gain or loss.

Computing Gain or Loss. IRC Section 1001(b) provides that "the amount received from the sale or other disposition of property shall be the sum of any money received plus the fair market value of the property other than money received." Also included in the amount received by the seller are any liabilities of the seller or liabilities associated with the transferred property that are assumed by the buyer.

A taxable merger or acquisition can involve the purchase of stock, assets, or both. If the buyer pays only cash, the amount received by the seller is simply equal to the amount of the U.S. dollars paid by the buyer. If the purchase involves the receipt by the seller of cash as well as property of the buyer, then two sales have actually taken place— one by the seller and one by the buyer to the extent of property transferred by the buyer to the seller. Again, the fair market value of all assets must be ascertained in order to determine the amounts received by the seller and buyer.

The tax basis under IRC Section 1011 and related sections is calculated by determining the seller's original purchase price (cost) and subtracting allowable depreciation benefits. The resulting amount is the seller's adjusted tax basis. Gain or loss is determined by subtracting the adjusted tax basis from the amount received. Incidentally, TEFRA added an adjustment to the tax depreciation basis by providing in IRC Section 168(g) that for purposes of depreciation, the basis is reduced by one-half of the amount of investment tax credits associated with the property, unless the taxpayer claims a reduced investment tax credit. For purposes of calculating gain or loss, however, no such adjustment in the basis for investment tax credits should be made.

Ordinary Versus Capital Gain or Loss. Gain or loss will be characterized as either capital gain or loss or ordinary gain (income) or loss to the seller. Corporate as well as noncorporate sellers generally prefer to have all income characterized as captial gains (taxed at rates of 28 and 20%, respectively) and all losses taxed as ordinary losses (highest effective tax benefits of 46 and 50%, respectively).

Many factors are involved in determining the character of any gain or loss. One of the most important factors is the nature and use of the asset sold. Generally, if the asset sold is a capital asset (as defined in IRC Section 1221), the seller will receive long-term capital gain tax treatment if the asset has been held for longer than six months. If the asset is not a capital asset and not inventory held for sale, then IRC Section 1231 may qualify the asset for capital gain treatment if the asset is depreciable property, was held for more than six months, and was used in the trade or business of the seller.

If the asset was subject to an allowance for depreciation, recapture of depreciation provisions under IRC Section 1245 and 1250 will override all other sections, including IRC Sections 1231 and 453, and characterize all such gain as ordinary income to the extent of prior tax depreciation deductions taken by the seller. Disposition of assets that have been held for less than five years may also result in recapture of investment tax credits under IRC Section 47.

The effect of tax depreciation and investment tax credit provisions can best be understood by use of an illustration. Assume that X Company purchases a new machine at a total cost of $1000. Assuming that this machine has a useful life for tax purposes of five years, X Company is entitled to a $100 ($1000 × 10%) investment tax credit. The tax basis of the machine is reduced by 50% of the investment tax credit, giving X Company a tax basis in the machine equal to $950 ($1000 − 0.5 ($100)).

Assume after three years, X Company has taken $550 in tax depreciation deductions on the machine. Further assume that X Company then sells the machine for $800 to NEWCO. The amount of taxable gain to X Company on the sale is calculated as follows:

Amount received	$800
Less adjusted tax basis ($1000 − 550)	(450)
Taxable gain	$350

Ordinarily, if the machine qualified under IRC Section 1231, the $350 of gain may be taxed at a 28% corporate capital gain tax rate. X Company would owe $98 in federal income taxes. However, depreciation recapture provisions under IRC Section 1245 will require that to the extent of depreciation deductions taken on the machine, the gain on the sale of the machine must be characterized as ordinary income. Therefore, the $350 of gain to X Company will generate $161 in federal income taxes, assuming a 46% corporate tax rate. In addition, because X Company owned the machine for less than five years, there will be investment tax credit recapture upon the sale of the machine. IRC Section 47 provides that 15-, 10-, or 5-year property that is held for three full years is subject to a 40% recapture of investment tax credit. Therefore X Company will have investment tax credit recapture of $40. Consequently, the total income tax liability to X Company on the sale of the machine will be $201 ($161 + $40).

Other factors are also important in determining the character of any gain or loss. If assets were used in a trade or business, if the assets are depreciable assets or if they are assets held for the sale to customers in the ordinary course of business (e.g., inventory), then different tax consequences may result.

Special provisions also apply whenever parties are related. For example, under IRC Section 1239, gain from transactions involving depreciable property between related (80% or more owned) corporations is always characterized as ordinary gain. Under IRC Section 267(b), losses from transactions between a wide range of related parties are disallowed.

Timing of Recognition of Taxable Gain or Loss.   As a rule, gain or loss is recognized by the seller in the same year in which the merger or acquisition occurs. However, if the seller receives at least one payment after the close of the taxable year in which the merger or acquisition occurred, then the sale may qualify for installment sales method tax treatment under IRC Section 453. The provisions in this section provide for recognizing gain only when cash or other property is received by the seller. Additionally, if a sale qualifies under IRC Section 453, then the gain from such sale is automatically deferred under IRC Section 453 unless the seller elects to currently recognize all gain (i.e., elects out of IRC Section 453). However, the 1984 Act added new IRC Section 453(i) which requires all depreciation recapture income to be recognized in the year of disposition.

To illustrate, assume X Company purchases a machine for $1000, takes $550 in tax depreciation deductions and $100 in investment tax credits, and sells the machine at the end of three years for $1,200 to NEWCO. The purchase price is to be paid in equal installments over a four-year period. Each $300 payment received by X Company will contain $50 of gain calculated as follows:

$$\frac{\text{Total gain on sale}}{\text{Total purchase price}} \times \text{amount of payment} = \begin{array}{l}\text{taxable gain}\\ \text{portion of payment}\\ \text{received by seller}\\ \text{(X Company)}\end{array}$$

$$\frac{\$200}{\$1,200} \times \$300 = \underline{\underline{\$50.00}}$$

In the year of disposition, X Company will recognize taxable income of $600 ($550 in depreciation recapture plus $50 in gain) as well as $40 in investment tax credit recapture income. X Company will recognize taxable income of $50 in years 2, 3 and 4.

Allocation of Purchase Price in an Asset Purchase

When assets are transferred in a taxable transaction, the purchase price must be allocated among the various assets. This is true even though the purchase price is based on the acquisition of an ongoing business enterprise. When stock is purchased, each share of stock receives its own allocated portion of the purchase price, which becomes its tax basis. Special allocation rules apply when more than one class of stock is purchased.

The allocation that is set forth in the sales contract is usually binding on both the buyer and seller for purposes of tax basis allocation.

What is a good allocation to one party is generally not the best allocation to the other party. This adversary relationship between buyers
and sellers provides the rationale for IRS general acquiescence to the
allocation established by the parties. To the extent that the IRS believes the allocations are not indicative of an arm's length transaction,
however, the IRS may attempt to reallocate the purchase price among
the assets according to its own valuation.

The purchase price must be allocated for tax purposes according to
the fair market value of all tangible and intangible assets. In theory,
this is best achieved through independent appraisals that establish the
fair market value of each asset. In practice, independent appraisals are
often expensive and time-consuming. Therefore, the parties will often
look for other ways of establishing the fair market value of each asset.

One of the more common methods used for establishing the fair
market value of each asset is the use of the net book value method. If
the purchase price is greater or less than the net book value of the
purchased assets, then an equation is used to allocate the purchase
price. The numerator of the equation consists of the net book value of
the individual assets to which the purchase price is being partially
allocated, and the denominator of the equation consists of the total net
book value of all assets. This equation is multiplied by the purchase
price, resulting in the amount of the purchase price which is allocated
to that individual asset.

For example, assume that the total purchase price in a merger or
acquisition was $10,000 for all assets. These assets have a total net
book value of $6000. If an asset has a net book value of $1200, then the
amount of the purchase price allocated to the asset will be equal to the
following:

$$\frac{\$1200}{\$6000} \times \$10,000 = \$2000$$

If asset X is depreciable tangible property, then the buyer will be
able to deduct $2000 in depreciation over the tax life of asset X. Inci-
dentally, if asset X originally cost $3000 and has an adjusted tax basis
of $500 to the seller, then the $1500 gain ($2000 − $500) to the seller
will be characterized as ordinary income under the depreciation recapture provisions in IRC Section 1245.

Two other methods are sometimes used in allocating the purchase
price among assets. One is the original acquisition cost method for

which the same mechanical process as shown in the above example is used, except that the numerator in the equation is the original acquisition cost of each individual asset, and the denominator of the equation is the total original cost of all the assets. This fraction is then multiplied by the total purchase price. The other method involves using replacement values in the same type of computation.

Regardless of what method is used to allocate the purchase price among the various assets, the method must be supportable and result in each asset receiving an allocated amount of the purchase price, which is representative of the fair market value of that asset.

Care must be exercised when establishing the fair market value of used and intangible assets. Acquired facilities often have assets that have been fully depreciated for book purposes, but are still in use in that facility and of value. Additionally, any method of valuation that allocates very little or nothing to intangible assets such as goodwill, going concern, and know-how, if relevant, will invite IRS scrutiny and possible reallocation. For tax purposes, no deductions are allowed for these types of assets.

As discussed above, tax rules require that the purchase price must be allocated to all assets, tangible and intangible, in proportion to their fair market values. This approach differs greatly from the residual approach of allocation used in purchase accounting for book purposes, where whatever acquisition cost remains in excess of the fair market values of tangible assets is allocated to intangible assets. The following is an illustration of the application of tax allocation on the basis of relative fair market values of all assets acquired, including goodwill.

Assume Company A acquires assets from Company B for $11 million in cash. For tax purposes, the purchase price will be allocated as follows:

| | Appraised Value | | Allocation of Cost for Tax Purposes |
	Amount	Percentage	
Receivables	$ 1,000,000	8.70%	$ 957,000
Inventories	3,000,000	26.09%	2,869,900
Fixed Assets	6,500,000	56.51%	6,216,100
Goodwill	1,000,000	8.70%	957,000
	$11,500,000	100.00%	$11,000,000

Contrast the above approach used for tax purposes with the following residual cost approach used in financial accounting:

	Appraised Values	Allocation of Cost for Financial Reporting Purposes
Receivables	$ 1,000,000	$ 1,000,000
Inventories	3,000,000	3,000,000
Fixed Assets	6,500,000	6,500,000
Goodwill	1,000,000	500,000
	$11,500,000	$11,000,000

Using the residual approach, the amount assigned to goodwill ($500,000) is the amount needed to balance to total cost ($11 million) after costs equal to fair values have been assigned to tangible assets. The residual approach has had limited acceptance for tax purposes, making the allocation in accordance with relative fair values generally the acceptable method of allocating cost for tax purposes.

It should be noted that in the above example, an additional adjustment to the values to be established for financial reporting purposes would be required for the tax effects of the differences between the book and tax basis of assets acquired. This area is discussed in Chapter 5.

If cash or cash equivalents are among the acquired assets, an allocation of purchase price (cost) equal to the dollar amount of the cash or cash equivalent is appropriate for tax as well as for book purposes. The remaining purchase price would be allocated to the remaining acquired assets in accordance with their relative fair market values.

An important tax benefit can be obtained by the buyer by allocating a portion of the purchase price to the cost of a covenant not to compete by the seller. To enable this tax treatment, the purchase agreement should specifically state that a portion of the consideration paid for the acquired operation relates to the covenant not to compete. The amount assigned to this asset is normally amortizable for tax purposes over the life of the agreement.

Allocating Basis in a Stock Purchase

When a buyer purchases stock, the basis in that stock is equal to the purchase price. As a general rule, the tax basis of the assets in the underlying corporation is not stepped-up to reflect the purchase price. This is disadvantageous to the buyer who has expended funds for a nondepreciable asset (stock) that is not eligible for investment tax credits.

There is an exception to this rule under IRC Section 338. This section provides that a buyer who acquires stock may elect to treat the transaction as the purchase of assets, thereby achieving a step-up in the depreciable basis of such assets. This section was enacted under TEFRA and replaced similar provisions in IRC Section 334(b)(2).

The statutory theme of IRC Section 338 is to achieve conformity or parity in the tax treatment between a purchase of assets and a purchase of stock. The target corporation (seller) under IRC Section 338 is "deemed" for tax purposes to have sold all of its assets on the acquisition date under the provisions of IRC Section 337. The next day a "new" corporation is deemed to have purchased the same assets for an amount equal to the total purchase price.

In general, there are three requirements under IRC Section 338 that must be satisfied in order for the buyer to achieve a step-up in the basis of the assets equal to the purchase price. First, the buyer must be a corporation (IRC Section 338(a) and (d)(1)). Second, the buyer must obtain control (as defined in IRC Section 338(d)(3)) equal to 80% or more of the voting stock and nonvoting stock of the target (selling) corporation. Stock that is limited and preferred as to dividends is not included when testing for the 80% or more control. Control must be acquired within a 12-month acquisition period (IRC Section 338(d)(3)). Third, the buyer must make an election by the fifteenth day of the ninth month beginning after the month of acquisition of the target corporation (IRC Section 338(g)(1)).

If these and other statutory requirements are satisfied, then the buyer can achieve a step-up in the tax basis of the assets in the target corporation equal to the purchase price of the stock. Recapture income (e.g., depreciation) remains in the target corporation (seller) and is an economic item to be negotiated. The tax history of the corporation, including any losses, disappear and may constitute a major disadvantage of electing under IRC Section 338 to step-up the basis in the assets of the acquired corporation.

Care must be exercised in this area, because IRC Section 338 is a new provision and contains many complex rules such as the "all-or-nothing" rules under IRC Section 338(f) and provisions governing redemptions under IRC Section 338(e)(2).

TAX-FREE MERGERS AND ACQUISITIONS

General Concepts and Requirements

Section 368(a)(1) defines and describes seven basic forms of corporate reorganizations. Each form of corporate reorganization has its own requirements, although several requirements and concepts are common to most forms of reorganizations. Some of these reorganizations have well-known variances such as forward and reverse triangular mergers under IRC Section 368(a)(2)(D) and (E).

Reorganizations that involve the transfer of assets generally require that "substantially all" of the assets of the seller be transferred to the buyer. By transferring specified minimum percentages of assets, transactions can fall within defined safe harbors for qualifying as substantially all of the assets. However, the type of assets transferred (for example, operating assets versus investment assets) is also important in determining whether or not substantially all of the assets of the seller have been transferred to the buyer.

Reorganizations involving stock require that the buyer obtain in exchange for stock "control" over the seller. Control is generally defined as acquiring 80% or more of the voting and nonvoting stock (IRC Section 368(c)(1)).

Another concept that is common to most forms of reorganizations is the doctrine of continuity of interest. In order to satisfy the doctrine of continuity of interest, the sellers must maintain specified minimum proprietary interests in the business after the reorganization is completed. In theory, a tax-free reorganization involves only a structural change in a business without changing ownership. The doctrine of continuity of interest is a test for determining whether the transaction is only a structural change, or whether the purported reorganization is in reality a winding up of the business affairs of the entity—which may be treated as a taxable liquidation.

Statutory provisions under IRC Sections 269 and 482 also provide broad powers to the IRS to restructure a purported tax-free transaction into a taxable event that conforms to the underlying economic reality of such a transaction.

In any transaction that qualifies as a reorganization, the tax attributes of the seller (earnings and profits, net operating losses, tax basis of assets, etc.) are generally carried over and acquired by the buyer as provided in IRC Section 381, although this section does not apply to all reorganizations. This subject is discussed later in this chapter.

Finally, in some reorganizations, a buyer and seller are permitted to exchange, in addition to stock, limited amounts of other property which, although taxable to the extent of such other property, will not cause the transaction to fail as a reorganization. This property, which is partially taxable in an otherwise tax-free exchange, is called boot.

The Courts and the IRS can utilize a variety of judicial doctrines and statutory provisions which enable them to restructure an attempted tax-free transaction into a taxable event if they believe such is appropriate. For example, "form over substance," "sham transaction," and "no business purpose" are three separate although related doctrines that look to the underlying economic reality of a transaction in determining tax consequences. Additionally, the step transaction doctrine is the integration of all related steps into a single transaction in determining the true nature of the transaction. Under the step transaction doctrine, a series of legally separate transactions that are pursuant to a common plan or goal can be collapsed into one single transaction and taxed accordingly by the IRS.

These judicial doctrines, statutes, and also technical requirements must all be considered by the tax planner in structuring any transaction.

Specific Types of Reorganizations

Type A Reorganization—Statutory Mergers.   A Type A reorganization is defined in IRC Section 368(a)(1)(A) as "(A) a statutory merger or consolidation. . . ."

There are two basic requirements for a Type A reorganization—a merger or consolidation, usually under state law, of two or more corporations, and the maintenance of the requisite level of continuity of interest.

A Type A reorganization involves the acquisition of the assets of the seller in exchange for the stock of the buyer. Only the buyer corporation is in existence after the transaction. This necessarily requires that all of the assets are obtained by the buyer. This should be contrasted with some reorganizations under IRC Section 368(a)(1) which only require that substantially all the assets be obtained by the buyer (see, for example, IRC Section 368(a)(1)(C) and IRC Section 368(a)(2)(B)).

In an A reorganization, if 100% of the consideration paid is in stock and/or securities of the buyer corporation, then no gain or loss is recognized to any party to the reorganization. Up to 50% of the consideration paid can be boot and the IRS will still view this transaction as a valid A reorganization (Rev. Proc. 77-37 CB-2 568). Anything less than 50% is subject to possible challenge by the IRS. Determining the mix of good to bad (boot) consideration is a form of testing for continuity of interest.

Figure 1 illustrates a Type A reorganization involving a statutory merger. Steps (1) and (2) involve the transfer to X Company of all the assets and liabilities of Y Company in exchange for the transfer of X Company stock to the shareholder(s) of Y Company. The merger is completed by the legal termination of the existence of Y Company. It is also common for two or more existing corporations (e.g., X Company and Y Company) to be merged and disappear into a newly created company (e.g., NEWCO). This latter form constitutes a statutory consolidation under IRC Section 368(a)(1)(A).

Type A reorganizations (mergers and consolidations) must satisfy all appropriate requirements under state law. Shareholder B as well as the creditors of Y Company will automatically become shareholders and creditors of X Company by operation of law.

Whenever the consideration paid by the buyer consists of stock,

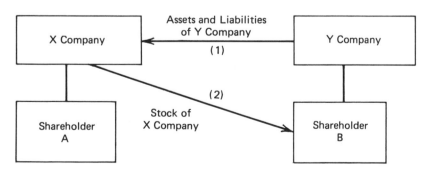

Figure 1. Type A.

warrants, convertible debentures, and so on, other aspects of the doctrine of continuity of interest come into play. Each variation of consideration must be separately analyzed and weighed by the tax planner to determine if the requirements under the doctrine of continuity of interest are satisfied, thereby permitting the transaction to fall within the protection of the tax-free provisions of IRC Section 368(a)(1).

Type B Reorganization—Stock Acquisitions. A Type B reorganization is defined in IRC Section 368(a)(1)(B) as:

> (B) the acquisition by one corporation, in exchange solely for all or a part of its voting stock (or in exchange solely for all or a part of the voting stock of a corporation which is in control of the acquiring corporation), of stock of another corporation if, immediately after the acquisition, the acquiring corporation has control of such other corporation (whether or not such acquiring corporation had control immediately before the acquisition) . . .

Reorganizations under IRC Section 368(a)(1)(B) involve the acquisition of control of the seller by the buyer by obtaining the requisite stock of the seller in exchange for stock of the buyer corporation. At least 80% or more of the stock of the seller must be received by the buyer (IRC Section 368(c)). Only the voting stock of the buyer can be exchanged. Anything else will be boot and taxable under IRC Section 356. For ruling purposes, there cannot be any boot paid directly or indirectly for the stock of the seller corporation in a B reorganization.

Figure 2 illustrates a Type B reorganization and the exchange of stock. Steps (1) and (2) involve the transfer of voting stock of X Com-

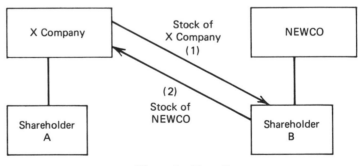

Figure 2. Type B.

pany to Shareholder B in exchange for stock of NEWCO. The X Company must acquire at least 80% of the voting and nonvoting stock of NEWCO unless such stock is limited and preferred as to dividends. After the exchange, NEWCO is a subsidiary of X Company and Shareholder B possesses only voting stock of X Company.

There cannot be a creeping B reorganization, which involves the exchange of stock, 80% or more of which is acquired over a period of time pursuant to a common plan of reorganization. Such a creeping reorganization is permitted under IRC Section 368(a)(1)(C) and will be discussed in greater detail later in this chapter.

Type C Reorganization—Asset Acquisitions.   A Type C reorganization is defined in IRC Section 368(a)(1)(C) as:

> (C) the acquisition by one corporation, in exchange solely for all or a part of its voting stock (or in exchange solely for all or a part of the voting stock of a corporation which is in control of the acquiring corporation), of substantially all of the properties of another corporation, but in determining whether the exchange is solely for stock, the assumption by the acquiring corporation of a liability of the other, or the fact that property acquired is subject to a liability, shall be disregarded . . .

This type of reorganization involves the acquisition of the assets of the seller. It is similar to an A reorganization in this respect. Unlike an A reorganization, however, only "substantially all" of the assets of the seller need to be exchanged for stock of the buyer. Up to 20% of the fair market value of the assets of the seller corporation can be acquired by payment of boot (IRC Section 368(a)(2)(B)).

Figure 3 illustrates a Type C reorganization. Steps (1) and (2) involve the transfer of substantially all the assets of NEWCO to X Company in exchange for the voting stock of X Company. This stock may be given directly to the shareholders of NEWCO or may be given directly to NEWCO, which then liquidates and distributes the stock of X Company to the shareholders of NEWCO.

The 1984 Act requires that after a C reorganization, in order to preserve tax free status, the seller must distribute all remaining assets, including stock obtained in the reorganization. Exceptions require IRS consent.

For ruling purposes, substantially all the assets in a reorganization means at least 90% of the net value of the assets *and* 70% of the gross

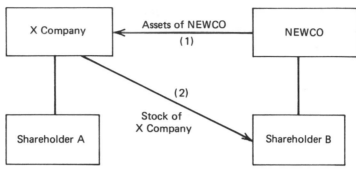

Figure 3. Type C.

value of the assets (Rev. Proc. 77-37, supra). If the transferred assets consist of all the operating assets, however, then the Courts have allowed tax-free treatment where as little as 51% of the total assets of the seller are transferred in a valid reorganization.

A valid C reorganization can occur over a period of time (a creeping reorganization) if pursuant to a common plan of reorganization.

There are two final comments. The doctrine of continuity of interest requires minimum participation by the former equity holders. Again, stock warrants, convertible debentures, and so on, must be considered by the tax advisor dealing with this requirement. Care must also be exercised in trying to separate wanted from unwanted assets. Attempts to spin-off or to otherwise transfer only selected assets to the buyer may invalidate the purported reorganization because of the failure to satisfy the requirement that "substantially all" of the assets must be transferred in a Type C reorganization.

Type D Reorganization—Corporate Divisions. A Type D reorganization is defined in IRC Section 368(a)(1)(D) as:

> (D) a transfer by a corporation of all or part of its assets to another corporation if immediately after the transfer the transferor, or one or more of its shareholders (including persons who were shareholders immediately before the transfer), or any combination thereof, is in control of the corporation to which the assets are transferred; but only if, in pursuance of the plan, stock or securities of the corporation to which the assets are transferred are distributed in a transaction which qualifies under section 354, 355, or 356. . . .

Based on changes in the 1984 Act, "control" in certain D reorganizations is achieved under IRC Section 368(c)(2) with 50% or more voting stock or 50% or more of the total value of the stock of the acquiring corporation. Reasons why D reorganizations are executed include desire or need to sell part of a corporation, preparation for liquidation, or to break a shareholder deadlock.

There are two basic types of transactions that will qualify as a D reorganization. These are (1) transfers to a controlled corporation followed by a liquidation of the transferor corporation, and (2) corporate divisions effected by spin-offs, split-offs, and split-ups.

Transfers to a Controlled Corporation. To illustrate this type of Type D reorganization, assume Company X transfers part or all of its assets to a controlled corporation followed by a complete liquidation of Company X.

The assets referred to in step (1) of Figure 4 can be all, substantially all, or only part of the assets of Company X. Where less than all the assets have been conveyed to NEWCO, remaining assets of Company X will be distributed to Shareholders A and B upon the liquidation of Company X.

Spin-offs, Split-offs, and Split-ups. There are three methods of accomplishing a corporate division. These are a spin-off, split-off, and a split-up. In a spin-off, the parent corporation transfers assets to a

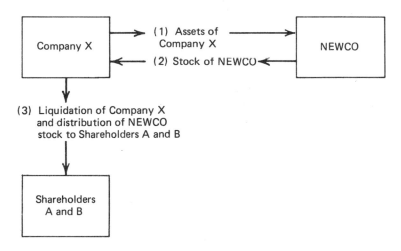

Figure 4. Type D.

subsidiary corporation in return for stock. The parent then distributes the stock to its shareholders. In a split-off, the parent corporation again transfers assets to a subsidiary corporation, but the shareholders of the parent exchange part of their stock in the parent corporation in return for the stock of the subsidiary corporation. Finally, in a split-up, the parent distributes all its assets to two or more subsidiaries in exchange for stock. The parent is then liquidated and the stock distributed to the shareholders of the liquidated parent.

Figure 5 illustrates the carrying out of a corporate division by spin-off. In a split-off, the transaction would be the same, except that in exchange for stock of the Subsidiary Company in step 3, Shareholders A and B would convey to Company X part of their stock in Company X.

Figure 6 illustrates the carrying out of a split-up. Whichever method is used, all D reorganizations have to meet several requirements, some of which are unique to D reorganization. As with all reorganizations, the doctrines of business purpose, sham transaction, step transaction, and so on, apply. In addition, IRC Section 368(a)(1)(D) also requires the transfer of all or part of the assets of the parent as well as the distribution of the stock or securities received by the parent to the shareholders of the parent as provided in IRC Section 354, 355, or 356. This last requirement, satisfying IRC Section

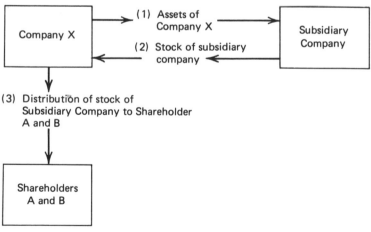

Figure 5.

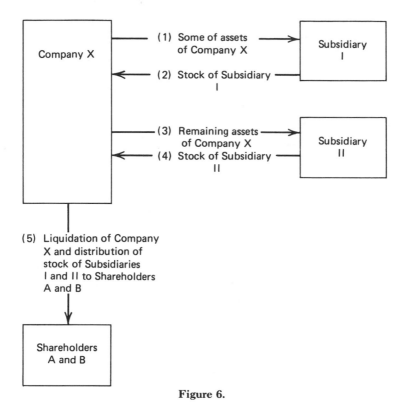

Figure 6.

354, 355, or 356, is where the tax planner will encounter the greatest complexity in qualifying any transaction as a valid D reorganization. As will be seen below, each of these sections has its own special requirements and potential pitfalls.

IRC Section 354 provides that no gain or loss shall be recognized in a reorganization if stock or securities in a corporation are exchanged solely for stock or securities in such corporation or in another corporation that is a party to the reorganization. Some exceptions are made regarding securities. These exceptions are intended to protect the Treasury against a bail-out of earnings and profits at capital gain rates. Additionally, IRC Section 354(b)(1) states that substantially all of the assets of the transferor must be transferred in order to qualify under IRC Section 354, as well as requiring that the transferee must distribute all stock, securities, and other property to its shareholders. Again, these provisions are intended as safeguards against a bail-out of earnings and profits at capital gain rates.

IRC Section 355 deals with the distribution of stock and securities. Stock is not required to be exchanged or otherwise redeemed from the shareholders. This section permits the transfer of less than substantially all of a corporation's assets in an exchange for stock and/or securities of the transferee. Distribution of stock does not have to be pro rata to the shareholders. However, IRC Section 355 contains several requirements that again are designed to prevent a bail-out of earnings and profits at capital gain rates. For example, the most obvious safeguard is the requirement under IRC Section 355 that distributions cannot be a "device" for the distribution of earnings and profits (IRC Section 355(a)(1)(B)). Also required is an active trade or business as provided in IRC Section 355(b). This means that the transferor and/or its controlled corporation must be engaged in an active trade or business for the previous five years. These and other requirements must be considered by the tax planner in qualifying any transaction under IRC Section 368(a)(1)(D).

IRC Section 356 provides a degree of flexibility regarding the receipt of boot in a D reorganization. As a general rule, if boot is received in an exchange to which IRC Section 354 or 355 would apply, then gain will be reorganized to the extent of the boot received (IRC Section 356(a)(1)). However, the transaction will continue to qualify as a tax-free reorganization. Again, boot includes cash and other property. IRC Section 356(a)(2) determines the character (capital versus ordinary) of such gain. This section provides a test that tries to determine whether the exchange has the effect of a dividend. Special rules apply when using this dividend test as well as when more than one class of stock or securities are received in the exchange.

Hybrid Reorganizations—Forward and Reverse Triangular Mergers

Forward Triangular Mergers. The forward triangular or subsidiary merger method has the advantage of effecting a tax-free merger, while keeping the acquired business operation as a separate legal entity. This will provide some insulation to the parent from unforeseen liabilities that may arise from prereorganization activities of the acquired corporation. Such hidden liabilities include tax liabilities, product liability, antitrust suits, and so on.

A forward triangular merger occurs when the actual buyer is a subsidiary corporation. The transaction consists of two steps instead of the usual one step that involves only the exchange of stock of the buyer for the stock or assets of the seller. In a forward triangular merger the parent corporation of the buyer first contributes its stock to a new or preexisting buyer corporation (a subsidiary) in an exchange that is tax-free under IRC Section 351. In return, the parent receives stock in the subsidiary, although receipt of such stock is not required if the subsidiary is already existing. The second step involves the usual reorganization exchange with the buyer (subsidiary corporation) receiving the assets of the seller in exchange for the stock of the parent.

Figure 7 illustrates the carrying out of a forward triangular merger. Stock of Company X is contributed in step (1) to the Subsidiary Company. If the Subsidiary Company is already in existence, step (2) can be eliminated. Stock of Company X is retransferred to the Target Company in exchange for substantially all of the assets of the Target Company, which is then merged and disappears into the Subsidiary Company.

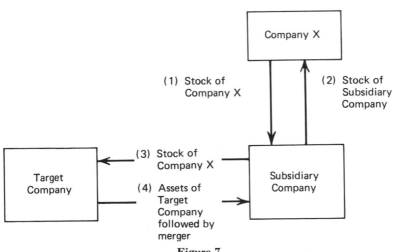

Figure 7.

There are four requirements for a tax-free forward triangular merger under IRC Section 368(a)(2)(D). First, the buyer must obtain substantially all the assets of the seller. Second, the seller must be merged into the subsidiary and not merely consolidated. Third, the merger must constitute a valid 368(a)(1)(A) reorganization if it had hypothetically involved only the parent and the buyer. This valid A reorganization requirement is tested under tax laws and not state laws (Rev. Rul. 74-297, 1974-1 CB 84). Finally, no subsidiary stock can be used, although some flexibility exists for the use of other forms of consideration. If any subsidiary stock is used, it will invalidate the attempted IRC Section 368(a)(2)(D) reorganization.

The subsidiary corporation may assume liabilities of the seller, but any assumption of liabilities by other than the subsidiary corporation or a joint assumption by the parent and its subsidiary could potentially invalidate the reverse triangular merger (Treasury Regulation Section 1.368-2(b)(2) and Rev. Rul. 73-257, 1973-1 CB 189).

Care must be exercised by the tax planner in following these requirements. Variations from these requirements in form or in substance can invalidate the purported forward triangular merger.

Reverse Triangular Mergers.   Another form of triangular merger is the reverse triangular merger or subsidiary merger. The reverse triangular merger offers insulation of the parent corporation from hidden tax and legal liabilities as discussed under IRC Section 368(a)(2)(D). Additionally, this form of tax-free merger has application where assets of the target company cannot be freely transferred, such as in regulated industries.

The reverse triangular merger is similar to the forward triangular merger under IRC Section 368(a)(2)(D). First, the parent corporation exchanges its stock in an IRC Section 351 transaction with the stock of a new or existing buyer (subsidiary corporation). Second, the seller corporation and the buyer merge, with the shareholders of the seller receiving stock of the parent of the buyer. In the reverse triangular merger, however, it is the seller corporation that survives the merger and the buyer disappears, with the stock of the seller now being held directly by the parent of the former subsidiary corporation.

In a reverse triangular merger, substantially all of the assets of both the seller and the buyer must end up in the surviving seller corporation. Additionally, the shareholders of the seller corporation must exchange 80% or more control of the seller corporation for the voting stock of the parent. There is no creeping reorganization permitted under IRC Section 368(a)(2)(E). The parent must obtain at least 80% control in a single transaction between its subsidiary and the seller corporation. Any consideration in excess of the 80% stock requirement can be boot and still satisfy the requirements of IRC Section 368(a)(2)(E).

Figure 8 illustrates the carrying out of a reverse triangular merger. Stock of Company X is contributed in step (1) to the Subsidiary Company. If the Subsidiary Company is already in existence, step (2) can be eliminated. Stock of Company X is retransferred to the Shareholders of the Target Company, step (3), in exchange for the voting stock of the Target Company, step (4). Step (5) is the merger (and disappearance) of the Subsidiary Company into the Target Company.

As usual, the doctrine of continuity of interest applies. The buyer is also permitted to pay cash in lieu of fractional shares, to pay cash for

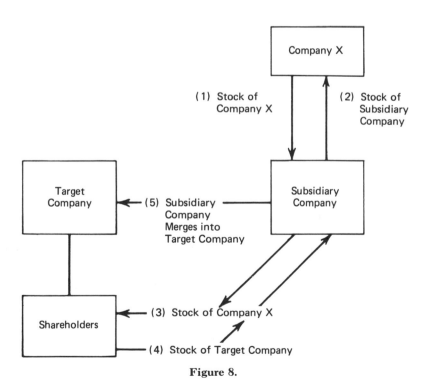

Figure 8.

reorganization expenses, and to buy out dissenters with cash and still have a valid reorganization (Rev. Rul. 77-307, 1977-2 CB 117).

Type E Reorganization—Recapitalizations. A Type E reorganization is defined in IRC Section 368(a)(1) as "(E) a recapitalization".

This reorganization under IRC Section 368(a)(1)(E) involves the readjustment or reshuffling of the financial structure of a single corporation. Examples of recapitalizations can be found in Treasury Regulation Section 1.368-2(e) and include exchange of bonds for preferred stock (Treasury Regulation Section 1.368-2(e)(1)), preferred stock for common stock (Treasury Regulation Section 1.368-2(e)(2) and (3)), common stock for common stock or preferred stock for preferred stock (Rev. Rul. 54-482, 1954-2 CB 148 and Rev. Rul. 56-586, 1956-2 CB 214), and a variety of other exchanges.

The doctrine of continuity of interest is not applicable to recapitalizations (Rev. Rul. 77-415, 1977-2 CB 311). Similarly, IRC Section 381 is not applicable. Care must be exercised whenever a corporate creditor exchanges debt. For example, if a creditor exchanges debt for stock and the stock has a fair market value that is less than the principal amount of the old debt, the corporate-debtor has no cancellation of indebtedness income on such an exchange (Rev. Rul. 59-222, 1959-1 CB 80). However, if the creditor exchanges debt for new debt and the new debt has a principal amount that is less than the old principal amount, the corporate-debtor may have cancellation of indebtedness income (Rev. Rul. 77-437, 1977-2 CB 28).

Care must also be exercised even if all the formal requirements of IRC Section 368(a)(1)(E) are satisfied. For example, in one transaction, common stock was exchanged for common stock, and bonds were distributed to shareholders on a pro rata basis. Even though the transaction satisfied the formal requirements of IRC Section 368(a)(1)(E), the court held that this was a taxable event and there was no valid reorganization. The court found that the distributing corporation had large earnings and profits and there was no valid business reason or purpose for the transaction. The court held that the shareholders who received the bonds had dividend income to the extent of the fair market value of the bonds received in the distribution.

Type F Reorganization—Changes in Identity, Form, or Place. A Type F reorganization is defined in IRC Section 368(a)(1) as "(F) A mere change in identity, form, or place of organization of one corporation, however effected."

Reorganizations under IRC Section 368(a)(1)(F) involve the change in the identity, form, or place of organization of a single corporation. For example, a corporation that is reincorporated in another state is a valid F reorganization (Rev. Rul. 57-276, 1957-1 CB 126). A transaction that involves only a change in the name of the corporation and the issuance of new stock still constitutes a valid F reorganization (Rev. Rul. 72-206, 1972-1 CB 104). In fact, if any A, C, or D reorganization also qualifies as an F reorganization, then the transaction will be treated as an F reorganization for purposes of IRC Section 381(b) (Rev. Rul. 57-276, supra). However, shift in ownership or other proprietary interests in a corporation is not an F reorganization.

Tax Attributes In Reorganizations

Generally, the tax attributes of the seller will be carried over and taken by the buyer in a tax-free reorganization. For example, the buyer will carry over the seller's tax basis in the stock or assets received from the seller (IRC Section 362(b)). The buyer corporation has nonrecognition of gain or loss on the exchange of its stock per IRC Section 1032. Tax-free treatment also applies to a subsidiary that uses the stock of its parent (Rev. Rul. 57-278 1957-1 CB 124). The buyer corporation also receives "tacking" under IRC Section 1223(2) for the time that the acquired assets or stock were held by the seller. "Tacking" permits qualified buyers to increase their holding period for acquired assets, including stock, by the period for which such property was held by the seller. Other tax attributes that normally carry over in a tax-free acquisition include earnings and profits, capital loss carry-overs, net operating loss carry-overs, tax credit carry-overs, and other items. The treatment of many of these tax attributes is governed by IRC Sections 381(b) and (c).

Section 381 sets forth rules that govern the treatment of tax attributes other than basis and holding period. However, IRC Section 381 applies only to two groups of transactions. First, IRC Section 381 governs the tax attributes in a transaction that involves the liquidation of a subsidiary corporation and to which IRC Section 332 applies. The second group of transactions to which IRC Section 381 applies is to reorganizations under IRC Section 368(a)(1)(A), (C), (D), (F), or (G). The tax planner who is involved with a reorganization that is not within IRC Section 381 will probably be forced to interpret and to rely on a series of cases in order to determine the carry-over, if any, of various tax attributes of the seller to the buyer corporation. This area is discussed in greater detail in this chapter in the materials that discuss the utilization of losses and tax credits by corporations which are parties to a reorganization.

The seller in a tax-free acquisition generally takes a substituted basis in the stock received in the reorganization under IRC Section 358(a). Special rules apply where more than one class of stock is exchanged. The tax basis of the seller is increased by any gain recognized by the seller and any liabilities assumed by the seller (IRC Section 358(a)). Basis is decreased by any loss recognized in the exchange as well as by boot received and liabilities of the seller that are assumed by the buyer (IRC Section 358(a)(B)). Special care must be exercised in dealing with liabilities because complex rules apply to reorganizations that involve liabilities.

Sellers that qualify under IRC Section 1223(a) also receive tacking onto the holding period of the stock received by the seller from the buyer corporation for the time which the property transferred to the buyer was held by the seller.

TAX LOSSES AND TAX CREDIT CARRY-OVERS OF ACQUIRED CORPORATIONS

At one time, a frequent motive for many corporate acquisitions or mergers was the availability of tax loss and/or tax credit carry-overs in the acquired corporation which could be used to offset taxable income of the acquiring corporation. Such "loss corporations" were often advertised for sale in business magazines and newspapers. The price for a loss corporation often was based on a discounted value of such tax loss or tax credit carry-forwards. However, a series of tax reforms enacted by Congress, including IRC Sections 269, 381, 382, and 383, have greatly restricted the ability to offset the buyer's taxable income by the tax loss and/or tax credit carry-overs of the acquired corporation.

As a general rule, unused net operating losses may be carried back by the corporation that sustained such losses "to each of the three taxable years preceding the taxable year of such loss" (IRC Section 172(b)(1)(A)). Thereafter, any excess net operating losses may be carried forward "to each of the 15 taxable years following the taxable year of such loss" (IRC Section 172(b)(1)(B)). Unused investment tax credits are also carried back for three years and carried forward for 15 years (IRC Section 46(b)).

In a taxable acquisition of assets, the tax loss and tax credit carry-overs of the acquired corporation cannot be transferred to the buyer. If an acquired corporation is subsequently liquidated, any tax loss and/or tax credit carry-forwards may disappear and be lost forever. If a major concern in a corporate acquisition or merger is the preservation of tax loss and/or tax credit carry-forwards of the acquired corporation, then the tax planner must understand the maze of complex statutory provisions and cases that control this area.

IRC Sections 381, 382, and 383 are the statutory provisions that apply to and govern the carry-over and realization of tax benefits related to the carry-over of tax losses as well as tax credits in many mergers and acquisitions. As a general rule, IRC Section 381 and the regulations thereunder permit the carry-forward of tax losses and tax credits to a corporation that acquires the assets of another corporation in certain liquidations and reorganizations. If the merger or acquisition is outside IRC Section 381, guidelines become fuzzy or disappear altogether. If IRC Section 381 does not apply, one must look to cases to provide guidelines in order to determine the availability to the buyer corporation of tax loss and/or tax credit carry-forwards from the acquired corporation. Additionally, the IRS may challenge any attempted carry-over and utilization of tax loss and/or tax credit carry-forwards under IRC Section 269. This provision gives the IRS broad powers to disallow any tax deduction or tax credit if such tax benefit was acquired pursuant to an acquisition made to evade or avoid taxes (a "bad intent" test).

IRC Sections 382 and 383 are the major policing provisions utilized by the courts and the IRS to reduce or eliminate net operating loss (IRC Section 382) and tax credit (IRC Section 383) carry-forwards. The availability of such tax losses and credits generally depends on how well the tax planner can avoid these provisions as well as IRC Section 269.

The operating rules and requirements of IRC Section 382 also apply to IRC Section 383. Through these provisions enacted in 1954, Congress attempted to establish mechanical rules that could be easily applied by the courts, IRS and taxpayers. Such rules were perceived to be needed to reinforce IRC Section 269 which has a "bad motive or intent" test which the IRS felt was too difficult to prove in order to be an effective weapon against tax loss and tax credit trafficking.

IRC Sections 382 and 383 were extensively revised by the Tax Reform Act of 1976, but the effective dates for these revisions has been postponed to 1/1/86. Unless otherwise noted, reference to IRC Sections 382 or 383 will be to the pre-1976 provisions that remain in effect until 1/1/86.

IRC Section 382, and therefore IRC Section 383, is structured to apply to two types of transactions. IRC Section 382(a) applies to the purchase of a corporation which is accompanied by a change in its trade or business. IRC Section 382(b) applies to changes in ownership resulting from a reorganization specified in IRC Section 381(a)(2) (i.e., type A, C, F, G, and certain D reorganizations). There is no "change in a trade or business" requirement under IRC Section 382(b). Reorganizations not covered by IRC Section 381 are governed by case law.

IRC Section 382(a) provides that if 50% or more of a corporation's stock is purchased within a two-year period, and if such corporation has not continued to carry on a trade or business substantially as that conducted before any change in ownership, then any net operating losses of that corporation are lost forever. Tax credits will also be lost under IRC Section 383.

It is important to note that after a stock purchase, the net operating loss carry-forward of the acquired corporation may only be utilized against future taxable income of that acquired corporation, even if the acquired corporation is included in a consolidated tax return with other corporations reporting taxable income. Tax planning for utilization of acquired net operating losses sometimes includes the contribution to the acquired corporation of profitable divisions or operations, which has the effect of increasing future profits of the acquired corporation. However, all such actions must have a valid purpose other than tax reduction, and must not violate the "continuity of business" requirement of IRC Section 382(a).

IRC Section 382(b) applies whenever the shareholders of the loss corporation receive, in a reorganization listed in IRC Section

381(a)(2), less than 20% of the fair market value of the stock of the acquiring corporation. Net operating loss carry-forwards are reduced by 5% for each percentage point below 20% received by shareholders of the loss corporation. Tax credits will also be reduced by IRC Section 383. Net operating loss carry-forwards may be utilized to offset post-acquisition taxable income of only the acquired corporation (Treasury Regulation Section 1.1502-21). As with stock purchases, tax planning involving tax-free reorganization sometimes includes the contribution to the acquired corporation of profitable divisions or problems.

Under the changes scheduled to take place on 1/1/86, the "continuity of business" requirement is eliminated, but continuity of ownership requirements are greatly increased. If these changes become effective, in general the ability to utilize acquired tax loss and credit carry-forwards will be greatly reduced.

This entire area is very complex, and a tax specialist should be consulted.

Consolidated Regulations

The consolidated regulations apply to a group of two or more affiliated and includable corporations that have filed a proper election under IRC Section 1501. In general, affiliated corporations means one or more chains of corporations "connected through stock ownership with a common parent corporation" (IRC Section 1504(a)). Such stock ownership must consist of 80% or more of all voting stock and 80% or more of the total stock value except nonvoting stock that is limited and preferred as to dividends (IRC Section 1504(a)). Includable corporations are defined to include any corporation except foreign corporations, Domestic International Sales Corporations (DISC), certain insurance companies, and corporations exempt from taxation under IRC Section 501 (IRC Section 1504(b)). Subchapter S corporations cannot be a member of a consolidated group by definition under IRC Section 1361(b)(2)(A).

An affiliated group of corporations that has filed the proper IRC Section 1501 election will file only a single tax return. This group of corporations will pay only a single tax based on its combined taxable income (CTI). However, separate taxable incomes (STI) must be calculated for each corporation in the consolidated group in order to determine CTI. These computations involve a variety of adjustments and eliminations, an explanation of which is beyond the scope of this chapter.

One of the major advantages of electing a consolidated return is the ability to offset the income of one corporation by the losses and/or tax credits occurring in another member corporation. The utilization of losses may be limited if such losses occurred in a separate return limitation year as defined in Treasury Regulation Section 1.1502-21. However, a variety of other limitations and special rules also apply to losses, tax credits, and to other tax provisions and computations when applied to a consolidated group of corporations. (For example, see Treasury Regulation Section 1.1502-3 dealing with tax credits and Treasury Regulation Section 1.1502-23 dealing with Section 1231 net gain or loss computations.)

The theme of the consolidated code provisions and the regulations thereunder is to treat a consolidated group of corporations as a single taxpayer for purposes of computing federal income taxes. IRC Section 1502 delegates to the Secretary broad powers to formulate and implement regulations to govern the taxation of consolidated groups of corporations. For example, the consolidated regulations provide that on the sale or exchange of property from one member corporation to another member corporation, where both corporations are members of the same consolidated group, gain or losses may not be recognized until such property is transferred outside the consolidated group (Treasury Regulation Section 1.1502-13(c)). If the deferred intercompany sale or exchange involves depreciable property, the buying member will receive a basis equal to the purchase price (Treasury Regulation Section 1.1502-31(a)). The selling member will have gain that is deferred until the property is either transferred outside the consolidated group or depreciation deductions are taken by the buying member (Treasury Regulation Section 1.1502-13(c)).

PRIVATE LETTER RULINGS

Sometimes the need for certainty as to tax consequences or the involvement of large dollars will dictate that the parties to a merger or acquisition seek a private letter ruling from the IRS. Private letter rulings are the official IRS sanction that confirm that certain stated tax consequences will or will not occur as a result of a proposed merger or acquisition.

Private letter rulings can be obtained for completed transactions. As a practical matter, however, private letter rulings are not generally requested for completed transactions. Once a transaction is completed, the taxpayer cannot retroactively adjust either the form or the substance of the merger or acquisition and an adverse ruling by the IRS will result in a high audit probability of the merger or acquisition.

The procedure for obtaining a private letter ruling generally involves providing detailed information to the IRS concerning the nature and type of merger or acquisition as well as information about the parties. As a general rule, no printed forms are required for most ruling requests. One exception is for rulings that request a change of accounting methods or accounting periods.

Although the taxpayer is given a great deal of flexibility in the form in which materials are submitted, a variety of regulations and revenue procedures set forth various materials that are required to be submitted prior to the IRS ruling on the tax consequences of a merger or acquisition. Treasury Regulation Section 601 and Revenue Procedure 81-1, IRB 1983-1, 16, are two major source documents that are often referred to by taxpayers in preparing requests for private letter rulings. All requests for private letter rulings should also include a description of the transaction, including all underlying documents, as well as a supporting brief that explains the taxpayer's position and sets forth all relevant authorities. This process can be time-consuming (often 6 to 24 months or longer), expensive ($5,000 to $10,000 or more for accounting, legal, and similar fees), and may result in a negative IRS ruling that is forwarded to the local IRS district director of the taxpayer.

Finally, Revenue Procedures should be reviewed for those areas in which the IRS has stated no rulings will be issued to taxpayers.

MISCELLANEOUS

This chapter has highlighted many of the major tax issues involved in corporate mergers and acquisitions. There are numerous other tax issues that also must be considered by the tax planner.

For example, most corporations have pension and/or profit sharing plans. These plans and related funds can involve substantial sums of money as well as potential liability. To transfer or carry over these plans from one corporation to another can be complex and often involves obtaining prior IRS approval through the issuance of a determination letter.

The transfer of employees from one corporation to another, even within a consolidated group, may trigger additional employer FICA payments for these employees, as well as additional FUTA payments.

State and local income, sales and use taxes also must be analyzed. Such state and local taxes are triggered by the sale of tangible property as well as intangible property. For example, the sale of all the assets in a manufacturing facility would be within the scope of most state sales and use taxes. However, many states offer a variety of exemptions for the sale of assets used in manufacturing. Statutory tax exemption provisions in each state must be separately analyzed in order to determine their potential application to any proposed merger or acquisition. Consequently, the acquisition of a corporation that has assets located in several states may provide the taxpayer with the opportunity to save thousands of dollars by properly timing the purchase of such stock or assets in states that have favorable income, sales, use, and/or property tax exemptions.

APPENDIX 6-1: TAX CHECKLIST FOR CORPORATE MERGERS AND ACQUISITIONS

IS THE MERGER OR ACQUISITION TAXABLE OR NONTAXABLE?

General rule is that all sales, exchanges, or other dispositions are taxable unless clearly within a specific statutory exception within the Internal Revenue Code.

IF TAXABLE

Seller

First: Determine the dollar amount received by the seller which includes:

Cash,

Fair market value of other property received, plus

Liabilities of the seller assumed by the buyer.

Second: Determine the adjusted basis in the stock and/or assets transferred to the buyer.

Original cost plus improvements less allowable depreciation.

Third: Determine the amount of gain or loss to the seller.

Subtract adjusted basis from the amount received.

Fourth: Determine character of the gain or loss to the seller.

Capital gain or loss if capital assets under IRC Section 1221.

Gain or loss may be characterized as capital or ordinary depending on computations if qualified IRC Section 1231 trade or business assets.

Ordinary income generally includes everything that does not fall within capital asset (IRC Section 1221) or trade or business assets (IRC Section 1231) designation.

Fifth: Determine the timing for recognizing gain or loss to the seller.

General rule is that all gain or loss is recognized at the time of the sale, exchange, or other disposition. Exceptions to this rule includes IRC Section 453 installment sales.

Sixth: Determine the amount, if any, of recapture of depreciation and tax credits associated with the transferred assets.

Buyer

First: Determine the purchase price paid by the buyer which includes:

Cash,

Fair market value of any property transferred to the seller, (which may itself be a taxable event to the buyer), plus

Liabilities assumed by the buyer or purchase money liabilities.

Second: Determine the basis in assets purchased.

Equal to the purchase price which is allocated among the assets based on their fair market value.

Third: Determine the holding period of any capital assets.

IF NONTAXABLE

Reorganization Requirements

Type A—Merger or Consolidation of Two or More Corporations under State Law

Buyer corporation survives and seller corporation disappears.

Buyer absorbs all assets and liabilities of seller.

Continuity of interest required.

Flexibility and consideration paid—up to 50% can be boot and still be valid reorganization for ruling purposes.

Watch out for existence of stock warrants, convertible debentures, and other similar property, as well as assumption of liabilities.

Type B—Stock for Stock Exchange

Very strict requirements with little flexibility.

Exchange must be "solely" for voting stock of buyer.
    No de minimis rule.

Control (80% or more) must be obtained by the buyer in a single transaction.
    No creeping B reorganizations permitted.

Continuity of interest required.

No boot permitted as part of purchase price.

Type C—Stock of Buyer Exchanged for "Substantially all" the Assets of the Seller

Buyer must acquire "substantially all" the assets of the seller.
    As little as 51% of total assets may be okay if representing 100% of operating assets of seller.

70% of gross assets and 90% of net assets test for ruling purposes.

Seller must distribute all assets, including stock obtained in the reorganization.

Continuity of interest required.

Type D—Spin-off, Split-off, and Split-up of Corporate Assets

Vehicle to provide equity ownership to key employees, break shareholder deadlocks, etc.

No "substantially all" requirement

Transferred assets can represent few, many, or all of the assets of transferor corporation.

Continuity of interest required.

Stock and/or securities received by transferor corporation must be distributed to shareholders per IRC Section 354, 355, or 356.

Cannot be device for bail-out of earnings and profits.

Forward Triangular Mergers—Target Company Merges and Disappears into Subsidiary Company

Parent company drops down stock into subsidiary that retransfers and exchanges parent stock for assets of Target Company.

Must be voting stock of parent.

Target Company must transfer substantially all assets.

Target Company must merge into subsidiary.

Target Company disappears.

Hypothetically a valid Type A reorganization.

Target Company cannot receive stock of subsidiary company.

Continuity of interest required.

Reverse Triangular Mergers—Subsidiary Company Merges and Disappears into Target Company

Parent company drops down stock into subsidiary company, which retransfers and exchanges parent stock for stock of Target Company.

Must be voting stock of parent.

Subsidiary company must merge and disappear into Target Company.

Continuity of interest required.

Target Company cannot receive stock of subsidiary company.

"Substantially all" of the assets must be held by surviving corporation.

Limited amount of boot is permitted to be part of the purchase price.

Type E—Readjustment or Reshuffling of Financial Structure of a Single Corporation

No continuity of interest required.

Broad range of exchanges permitted.

Possible cancellation of indebtedness income on debt exchanges.

Type F—Change in Identity, Form, or Place of a Single Corporation

Continuity of interest required.

Any Type A, C, or D reorganization that also qualifies as a Type F will be treated as a Type F reorganization.

Tax Attributes—Seller

First: Determine the tax basis of the seller in the stock received from the buyer.

The seller takes a substituted tax basis in the stock received from the buyer (i.e., the tax basis in the stock received by the seller is the same as that of the property transferred to the buyer).

Possible adjustments to the tax basis of the seller under IRC Section 358 for any gain recognized, other property received, liabilities of the seller assumed by the buyer, etc.

Special allocation rules may apply if more than one class of stock is received by the seller.

Second: Determine the holding period of the seller in the newly acquired stock of the buyer.

Seller usually receives tacking (i.e., seller includes the period for which the seller held the property exchanged).

Tax Attributes—Buyer

First: Determine the tax basis of the seller in the stock and/or assets received from the seller.

> Buyer takes a carry-over tax basis under IRC Section 362 (i.e., the tax basis in the stock and/or assets received by the buyer is the same as the tax basis of that property when held by the seller).
>
> Possible adjustments under IRC Section 362 for any gain recognized by the buyer.
>
> No special allocations necessary due to carry-over of tax basis of seller.

Second: Determine the holding period of the buyer in the assets received from the seller.

> IRC Section 1223(2) provides the buyer with tacking (i.e., buyer includes the period for which the seller held the property received by the buyer).

7

DIVESTITURES

AN OVERVIEW OF THE PROCESS

In the last few years, the aggressive acquisition trends of many large companies have been reversed to a trimming down of operations. Many of those companies, previously committed to growth and diversification by acquisition, discovered that they had spread themselves too thin and are now returning to concentrate on the lines of business and products they know best.

In tough economic times, when profits and cash flow decline, companies tend to reexamine their business plans, many times leading to decisions to change business direction, redeploy capital, or flee troublesome, unprofitable businesses. Furthermore, in economic downturns companies may look to divestiture as a way to raise needed cash.

Many companies are discovering that businesses which were acquired because of a good historical profit or return on investment do not fit with their main line of business, and that they cannot manage a new, unfamiliar business well, leading to a decision to divest. Occasionally, divestitures are made as a result of government or regulatory decrees.

Many smaller, privately owned companies are sold as a result of the owner's desire to retire or move on to other business interests.

Once the decision to divest has been made, whether the decision is based on one of the above motivations, or some other reason, an orderly program for carrying out the divestiture should be developed, including:

1. Deciding on the method of divestiture
2. Preparing for the divestiture by:
    a. Organizing the divestiture team
    b. Preparing a written presentation
    c. Taking actions to "dress up" the entity being sold to be an attractive acquisition target for buyers
3. Determining the asking price
4. Finding a buyer
5. Structuring and negotiating the sale
6. Consummating the sale
7. Assisting the buyer in transition
8. Handling continuing details after the divestiture has been completed

Methods of Divestiture

Three major ways of making a divestiture are: sale, spin-off, and liquidation.

Sale. The simplest way to divest and the method preferred by most selling companies is the sale of stock of a corporate subsidiary rather than the sale of assets. This avoids many of the difficulties that can arise in the disposition of liabilities and also the valuation of assets, because these matters will become issues only if the sale agreement includes warranty clauses on these points.

An alternative is to sell the assets without selling the corporate shell. Because the seller often retains the liabilities in this type of transaction, he or she can normally negotiate a better selling price since the acquirer is not concerned with the assumption of any "hidden" liabilities.

Leveraged Buy Outs. Two types of sales of businesses that have received recent publicity are the leveraged buy out and the sale to employees. The leveraged buy out is the sale of a business, many times to the existing management team, using the debt capacity of the business to borrow funds (sometimes by the seller holding notes) to finance the purchase. The seller may also receive common or preferred stock from the new corporation. In essence, the sale is structured so that the purchase price is paid by the future earnings of the divested unit, earned under the management of the purchaser.

Because the leveraged buy out often results in a highly leveraged entity, with heavy future debt service burden, where the seller is holding notes, he or she should be confident that the business and new management both have the potential to produce the cash flow needed to cover internal operating needs plus the debt service.

Special considerations may apply to accounting for a divestiture effected through a leveraged buy out; these are discussed in the following section on accounting for divestitures.

Spin-off. In a spin-off, the business to be disposed of is set up as a separate corporation and the stock is distributed, usually on a pro rata basis, to the existing shareholders of the parent company. Advantages of this type of divestiture to the parent company are that any debt of the subsidiary is removed from the parent company's balance sheet, and that it has withdrawn from exposure to the future capital needs of the spun-off unit. This arrangement, however, can work only where the management team of the divested company is in place and it can operate without further management and administrative support from the parent company. A potential advantage to shareholders of a public company is that a public market is established which may value the separate companies greater than the previous value of the parent alone. Spin-offs are often structured as tax-free exchanges and the parent company will often request an Internal Revenue Service Ruling on the tax-free nature of the transaction.

An alternative to the distribution of stock is to distribute assets in kind to the shareholders. This type of distribution may either be pro rata to the shareholders or may be non-pro rata to a select group of shareholders in exchange for an amount of stock equal to the fair market value of the assets distributed; this will usually work best when dealing with a small group of shareholders.

Liquidation. Another form of divestiture is the liquidation or abandonment of the real property, fixed assets, and intangibles of the unwanted business unit.

In some cases, where a seller is trying to dispose of an unprofitable business, potential buyers may not be willing to pay a price for the ongoing business which equals the amount that could be obtained by selling the assets individually. If this becomes apparent, the seller should consider liquidating the business and selling the assets individually in an orderly fashion. In fact, in some cases, a seller may be better advised to liquidate the individual assets for cash, where the sale of an unprofitable ongoing business may require the seller to hold notes.

Preparing for a Divestiture

Certain fundamental steps should be taken when preparing to dispose of a business, whether the seller is a corporation selling a subsidiary or division, or whether the sellers are individuals selling a privately owned company. Some of these are:

1. Form the divestiture team, including arranging for competent professional help in the legal and accounting area to negotiate, structure, and administer the sale, and consider the use of a business broker to locate qualified and interested buyers.

2. Prepare a professionally written presentation on the entity, which describes the industry, the organization, history, and potential. The presentation should include financial data, including balance sheets, operating statements, and major assets and liabilities. The operating statements should indicate effects of nonrecurring and unusual items. Projected financial results may be included, but must not imply guarantee of attaining projected results.

3. Arrange the business so that it stands on its own and does not give the impression that continuation of present ownership, support from the parent organization, or management by present owners are essential to continuation of the business.

4. To the extent possible, simplify the structure of the entity being sold from an organizational, legal, and financing standpoint.

The period prior to placing the entity on the market should be devoted to preparing the entity for sale. Such factors as a few key capital expenditures and repair and maintenance projects can enhance the attractiveness of the entity. A smoothly running data processing and financial control system will also be a plus to buyers interested in acquiring a well-run operation.

Determining the Asking Price

Various traditional methods of estimating the value of a business were discussed in Chapter 1. When a divestiture is planned, the seller may use these techniques in developing an estimated asking price. Significant objectivity is needed, however, particularly where the company being sold is a privately owned company whose owners may be dealing with significant personal assets. The value of a company in the marketplace may be noticeably different than the hypothetical value computed using a statistical or comparative method. The realities are that the seller has to find a buyer who will actually pay the settlement price for the company.

In a larger company, determining the asking price may be a project that requires the involvement of many departments. For example, financial personnel would ensure that all assets are listed and take steps to establish estimated fair market value, tax personnel would evaluate the tax basis and tax liability or benefit that will result from various prices and transaction structures, and operating and general businesspeople who are familiar with the industry would be able to offer much insight to pricing the entity being sold.

The most realistic way to select an asking price is to analyze prices recently paid to purchase similar companies. Similar companies for this purpose might be described as those in the same industry, with comparable assets, sales, earnings, and growth trends.

It can take a seller a long time to locate a qualified buyer who will actually make a meaningful offer. Consequently, it makes much sense to ask a reasonable price at the outset if the desire is to sell within a relatively short period. Furthermore, where an initial asking price may be unreasonably high, resulting in no offers, dropping the asking price to a more realistic level at a later date can give an impression of desperation on the part of the seller, or an indication that something may be wrong with the entity being sold.

Finding the Buyer

Several ways to find a buyer are:

1. Rely completely on a business broker.

2. Rely on other types of intermediaries, such as investment bankers.

3. Spread the word through banks, lawyers, accountants, and any other professional who may have clients that may be interested in acquiring the entity being sold.

4. Advertise in trade publications and make the availability of the entity being sold known to members of industry associations.

5. Advertise in the classified advertising sections of newspapers.

A business broker will normally charge a fee based on a percentage of the gross selling price. Brokers normally operate with a sliding fee scale under which smaller percentages of the sale price are paid for larger transactions. Although other arrangements exist with respect to brokers' fees, the percentage of gross selling price basis is the most common.

After a potential buyer has been located, a careful assessment of the potential buyer's ability to finance the transaction should be performed. This should include an examination of the buyer's financial position and source of funding for consummating the acquisition. If the buyer is strong financially and in a position to pay cash for the entity, and sincerely wants to consummate the acquisition, the seller's position is relatively comfortable. Where the seller must hold promissory notes for part of the sale price, a key factor to evaluate is the buyer's ability to operate the business successfully to generate cash to pay the note held by the seller. All too often in the sale of small companies in particular, the buyer is not able to operate the business as successfully as the seller, resulting in a default on the notes held by the seller. The seller is usually faced with taking the damaged business back to repair and continue operating, or to sell again.

Where notes are involved, sometimes arrangements can be made for the seller to continue participating in the management of the company until the notes are fully or partially paid.

Structuring and Negotiating the Sale

This subject was discussed in Chapter 1 from the perspective of an acquirer. Many of the same considerations apply to a divestiture, although the viewpoint will be somewhat different. The seller in a divestiture will want to structure the deal so that as much cash as possible is received up front, thereby reducing future risk with respect to the transaction.

Also, the seller will normally prefer to sell stock of a corporation to conclude the transaction as cleanly as possible. This can be done by selling stock of an existing corporation, or by transferring assets and liabilities of an ongoing business into a new corporation prior to the sale.

The tax structure of the transaction may be important to the seller, but if the seller is under pressure to divest, this type of consideration may be considered of lesser importance.

Consummating the Sale

This area was discussed in Chapter 1 from the perspective of an acquirer. Generally, the same considerations would apply to a seller.

Assisting the Buyer in Transition

The buyer may need significant assistance in the transition of the acquired company. The areas involved may include administrative, financial, systems, or any other area of a company's activities, including general management or operations. See Chapter 3 for a discussion of these areas from the acquirer's viewpoint.

Sometimes specialists from both the seller and acquirer organizations will work together on task forces to effect orderly transitions in each area.

After the Divestiture

The aftermath of the divestiture of an ongoing business often results in many lingering details that remain long after the divestiture is complete.

The transfer of responsibility that occurs from a definite cutoff at the date of sale has a way of causing many problem transactions to surface, particularly in the receivables and payables area. These problems can arise whether the divestiture was a sale of stock, or the sale of assets, in that even if the sale was one of stock, the purchase price may have been contingent on the realizability of specific balance sheet accounts, such as receivables and payables.

For example, receivables may include balances from longtime customers who purchase substantial amounts on a continuing basis. A sizable receivable balance, which turns over continuously, may exist at all times, and depending on the company's system the balance may not show up as overdue. In the context of applying the first payments made after the divestiture, it may be discovered that the customer has a disputed item or items. A three-way dispute can result in this kind of situation between the seller, the acquirer, and the customer.

If the disposal was of a sizable, high-volume business, there will very likely be a continuing trickle of customer claims and unpaid bills, many of which may be small, but all of which demand attention. Where the seller retains responsibility for these, someone in the seller organization should be given responsibility for handling them. These kinds of transactions may surface for a year or more after a divestiture.

ACCOUNTING FOR DIVESTITURES

General

The major accounting principles for divestitures are set forth in Accounting Principles Board (APB) Opinion No. 30, "Reporting the Results of Operations," which emphasizes special disclosures as well as the fundamental principles of accounting recognition. The first step in accounting for a divestiture is to determine if the divestiture qualifies as a disposal of a segment of a business under the criteria set forth in APB Opinion No. 30. The Opinion provides that where a significant divestiture qualifies as a disposal of a segment of a business, separate presentation of operating results is required and the Opinion recommends consideration of separate balance sheet presentation of net assets and liabilities of the divested entity. This presentation gives the reader a clear indication of the separate continuing and discontinued portions of the entity.

The recognition criteria in accounting for divestitures are the same whether the divestiture qualifies as a disposal of a segment of a business or not, and require immediate recognition of losses expected to be incurred as a result of the divestiture on the date on which management having the authority to approve the action commits itself to a formal plan (the "measurement" date). The plan would normally be expected to be carried out within one year after the measurement date. Estimated gains are recognized when realized (normally on the "disposal" date). Losses recognized at the measurement date should include any operating profits or losses expected for the period between the measurement date and disposal date, except that future operating profits may be given recognition at the measurement date only to the extent of the estimated loss on disposal. Where an estimated gain on disposal exists at the measurement date, estimated future operating profits should be recognized when realized.

Changes in estimates in periods following the recording of amounts pursuant to a disposal are reported in the period of the change in estimate.

Principles of Accounting for Divestitures

The fundamental definition of a disposal of a segment of a business is set forth in APB Opinion No. 30, paragraph 13, and is as follows:

> For purposes of this Opinion the term "segment of a business" refers to a component of an entity whose activities represent a separate major line of business or class of customer. A segment may be in the form of a subsidiary, a division, or a department, and in some cases a joint venture or other nonsubsidiary investee, provided that its assets, results of operations, and activities can be clearly distinguished, physically and operationally and for financial reporting operations, and activities of the entity. Financial statements of current and prior periods that include results of operations prior to the measurement date (as defined in paragraph 14) should disclose the results of operations of the disposed segment, less applicable income taxes, as a separate component of income before extraordinary items. . . . The fact that the results of operations of the segment being sold or abandoned cannot be separately identified strongly suggests that the transaction should not be classified as the disposal of a segment of the business. The disposal of a segment of a business should be distinguished from other disposals of assets incident to the evolution of the entity's business, such as the disposal of part of a line of business, the shifting of production or marketing activities for a particular line of business from one location to another, the phasing out of a product line or class of service, and other changes occasioned by technological improvements. The disposal of two or more unrelated assets that individually do not constitute a segment of a business should

not be combined and accounted for as a disposal of a segment of business.

AICPA Accounting Interpretations of APB Opinion No. 30 contains the following guidelines for distinguishing between transactions that are disposals of a segment of a business and those that are not:

The following are illustrative of disposals that should be classified as disposals of a segment of a business:

(1) A sale by a diversified enterprise of a major division that represents the enterprise's only activities in the electronics industry. The assets and results of operations of the division are clearly segregated for internal financial reporting purposes from the other assets and results of operations of the company.

(2) A sale of a meat packing enterprise of a 25 percent interest in a professional football team that has been accounted for under the equity method. All other activities of the enterprise are in the meat packing business.

(3) A sale by a communications enterprise of all its radio stations that represent 30 percent of gross revenues. The enterprise's remaining activities are three television stations and a publishing enterprise. The assets and results of operations of the radio stations are clearly distinguishable physically, operationally and for financial reporting purposes.

(4) A food distributor disposes of one of its two divisions. One division sells food wholesale primarily to supermarket chains and the other division sells food through its chain of fast food restaurants some of which are franchised and some of which are owned by the enterprise. Both divisions are in the business of distributing food. However, the nature of selling food through fast food outlets is vastly different from that of wholesaling food to supermarket chains. Thus, by having two major classes of customers, the enterprise has two segments of its business.

Certain disposals would not constitute disposals of a segment of a business because they do not meet the criteria in the Opinion. For example, the following disposals should not be classified as disposals of a segment of a business:

(5) The sale of a major foreign subsidiary engaged in silver mining by a mining enterprise that represents all of the enterprise's activities in that particular country. Even though the subsidiary being sold may account for a significant percentage of gross revenue of the consolidated group and all of its revenues in the particular country, the fact that the enterprise continues to engage in silver mining activi-

ties in other countries would indicate that there was a sale of a part of a line of business.

(6) The sale of a petrochemical enterprise of a 25-percent interest in a petrochemical plant that is accounted for as an investment in a corporate joint venture under the equity method. Since the remaining activities of the enterprise are in the same line of business as the 25 percent interest that has been sold, there has not been a sale of a major line of business but rather a sale of part of a line of business.

(7) A manufacturer of children's wear discontinues all of its operations in Italy that were composed of designing and selling children's wear for the Italian market. In the context of determining a segment of a business by class of customer, the nationality of customers or slight variations in product lines in order to appeal to particular groups are not determining factors.

(8) A diversified enterprise sells a subsidiary that manufactures furniture. The enterprise has retained its other furniture manufacturing subsidiary. The disposal of the subsidiary, therefore, is not a disposal of a segment of the business but rather a disposal of part of a line of business. Such disposals are incident to the evolution of the entity's business.

(9) The sale of all the assets (including the plant) related to the manufacture of men's woolen suits by an apparel manufacturer in order to concentrate activities in the manufacture of men's suits from synthetic products. This would represent a disposal of a product line as distinguished from the disposal of a major line of business.

Companies will often prefer that a divestiture qualify as a disposal of a segment of a business in that companies will often dispose of their less successful businesses, and the separate presentation on the income statement often presents a better image of continuing operations.

The "Measurement Date" and the "Disposal Date." These terms are defined in APB Opinion No. 30, paragraph 14, as follows:

Definition of Measurement and Disposal Dates. For purposes of applying the provisions of this Opinion, the "measurement date" of a disposal is the date on which the management having the authority to approve the action commits itself to a formal plan to dispose of a segment of the business, whether by sale or abandonment. The plan of disposal should include, as a minimum, identification of the major assets to be disposed of, the expected method of disposal, the period expected to be required for completion of the disposal, an active program to find a buyer if disposal is to be by sale, the estimated results of operations of the segment from the measurement date to the disposal date, and the estimated proceeds or salvage to be realized by disposal. For purposes of applying this Opinion, the "disposal date" is the date of closing the sale if the disposal is by sale or the date that operations cease if the disposal is by abandonment.

A plan of disposal of a segment of a business would be expected to be carried out within one year from the measurement date.

Determination of Gain or Loss on Divestitures. The principles for determining a gain or loss on a divestiture are the same whether or not the divestiture qualifies as a disposal of a segment of a business.

The basic computation is as follows:

The carrying value of the entity is deducted from the net proceeds (sale price, less direct transaction costs) realized or expected to be realized.

Other costs related to the disposal are deducted from the gain or loss.

Income or losses (to the extent predictable with reasonable accuracy) expected from projected operations of the entity from the measurement date to the disposal date are computed, and sometimes used in the computation of gain or loss at the measurement date.

The income tax effects of the gain or loss are measured and included in the computation of gain or loss.

The gain or loss on a divestiture should not include adjustments, costs, and expenses associated with normal business activities that should have been recognized on a going concern basis up to the measurement date.

The two basic components of the overall gain or loss will be (1) the gain or loss on disposal, and (2) the estimated profit or loss from operations of the entity disposed of from the measurement date to the disposal date. The following table outlines whether the gain or loss is reported in the measurement period.

If the estimated operations from measurement date to disposal date are a:	And, if the result of the disposal is a:	
	Gain	Loss
Loss	If a net gain— recognize when realized. If a net loss— recognize at measurement date.	Recognize at measurement date.
Gain	Recognize when realized	If a net gain— recognize when realized. If a net loss— recognize at measurement date.

Direct Transaction Costs. These include those costs that are directly associated with the transaction, such as accounting, legal and brokers' fees, sales and use taxes, and other costs of conveyance.

Other Costs Related to the Disposal. Types of costs in this category specifically mentioned in APB Opinion No. 30 include severance pay, additional pension costs, employee relocation expenses, and future rentals on long-term leases to the extent they are not offset by sublease rentals.

Although costs such as the above are clearly caused by the decisions to divest, there are many other costs that will be triggered by the divestiture. Furthermore, there will be cases where judgment will be required in distinguishing between costs that should be recognized partly as gain or loss on divestiture and partly as normal operating expenses of the divested entity for periods prior to the measurement date. Several examples follow:

1. Accounts Receivable—Additional accounts may become uncollectible because the parent is divesting the business unit. Furthermore, many smaller customer claims may surface after a divestiture where there is a question as to whether the seller or acquirer is responsible.

2. Inventories—Certain inventory related costs can be caused by a divestiture. Examples are purchase commitments not assumed by the buyer which obligate the seller to make future payments for which no benefits are received, excess parts or supplies inventories retained by the seller which will not be used and merchandise inventories not purchased by the acquirer which become obsolete because of the acquirer's decision not to carry the product line.

3. Prepaid Expense Writeoffs—These may include writeoff of insurance premiums, rents, rental deposits, or any other prepaid expense item that would have otherwise carried benefit to a future period.

4. Plant and Equipment—Some writeoffs of fixed assets are caused by a divestiture if the acquirer will not take the items, and the seller has no use for them without the divested business unit. These costs should include costs of dismantling and shipping for disposal, reduced by any amounts recovered by sale proceeds. Also, the costs of carrying unused facilities until their sale should be included as a cost of the divestiture.

5. Commitments—Expenditures made to satisfy contractual commitments for which future benefit would have been derived were it not for the divestiture are properly includable in gain or loss on divestiture. Examples include consulting and service agreements, advertising commitments, and purchase commitments.

Accounting for Income Taxes in a Divestiture. At the time of recognition of gain or loss on a divestiture on a pretax basis, the related income tax effects should be recognized. The precise amount of income tax effect can be affected by various interrelated factors:

1. Income or loss may be subject to ordinary tax rates or capital gains rates depending on the structure of the sale and the nature of the assets sold.

2. Even where the assets sold would appear to be an asset for which the sale would be taxed at capital gains rates, there may be recapture of depreciation, subjecting some or all of a gain to ordinary tax rates, or recapture of investment credits previously recognized as reductions of income tax expense.

3. Deferred tax balances related to the entity or assets sold are "reversed" as a result of the divestiture. The rates at which the taxes were provided may differ from effective tax rates realized on the divestiture, which may cause additional abnormalities in the effective tax rate.

The following examples illustrate some of the principles of providing income taxes on divestitures and their relationship to income taxes of preceding periods.

Assume that Company A acquired all the outstanding stock of Company B three years ago for a cash payment of $2055. As a result of the purchase acquisition accounting, goodwill of $1100 was created on a book basis of which $100 was amortized over the next three years. Equipment was revalued to $2064, its appraised fair market value, adjusted by the tax effect of the difference between book and tax basis of the equipment. Company A operated Company B for three years, including Company B in its consolidated financial statements and consolidated federal income tax return for the three-year holding period. We will illustrate the accounting for two types of divestitures at the end of the three-year holding period:

1. Where Company A sells 100% of its stock in Company B for $4 milllion in cash.

2. Where Company A sells 75% of the assets of Company B, together with the business related to 75% of Company B's product lines and operations.

Following are the book and tax balance sheets of Company B at the divestiture date, and data that sets forth book and tax activity of Company B during the holding period.

COMPANY B BALANCE SHEET AT DIVESTITURE DATE

	Book	Tax
Current assets	$1,000	$1,000
Equipment	2,064	1,500
Less, allowance for depreciation	<414>	<942>
	1,650	558
Goodwill	1,000	—
Total assets	$3,650	$1,558
Current liabilities	$1,000	$1,000
Deferred taxes	185	—
Stockholder's equity:		
Common stock	10	10
Additional paid-in-capital	2,045	355
Retained earnings	410	193
	2,465	558
Total liabilities and stockholder's equity	$3,650	$1,558
Equipment valuation at date of acquisition of Company B by Company A:		
Appraised fair market value	$2,800	$2,800
Tax basis:		
Cost	1,500	
Less, depreciation deducted on tax returns	<300>	
Tax basis	1,200	
Differences between fair market value and tax basis	1,600	
Tax effect of difference between fair market value and tax basis (46%)	$ 736	736
Amount for financial reporting at acquisition date		$2,064

Book depreciation after acquisition:
Annual depreciation ($2064 divided
    by 15 years) $ 138
Number of years   ×   3
                                              414

Tax depreciation after acquisition:
Annual depreciation ($1500 divided
    by seven years)   214
Number of years   ×   3
                                              642

Excess of tax over book depreciation
   expense $ 228

Attributable to:
Permanent differences from differences between book and tax basis
   ($58 × 3) $<174>
Timing differences from use of different depreciation methods and lives
   to extent book and tax basis were
   equal ($214 less 80 multiplied by
   three years) (See Note A)   402
Excess of tax over book depreciation
   expense $ 228

NOTE A

If the book basis had been equal to the tax basis ($1200) at the date of
acquisition, using straight line depreciation over 15 years, annual
book depreciation expense would have been $80. Because the re-
ported annual book depreciation expense of $138 was based on the
amount established for financial reporting at acquisition ($2064) de-
preciated on a straight line basis over 15 years, the difference of $58
($138 less 80) is the annual amount attributable to the permanent
difference that arose from the tax effect of the difference between the
book and tax basis of the assets at acquisition date.

Computation of pretax income of Company B during holding period:

	Book	Tax
Income before depreciation and amortization	$1,000	$1,000
Depreciation expense	<414>	<642>
Goodwill Amortization	<100>	—
Pretax income	$ 486	$ 358

Computation of taxable income of Company B during holding period:		
Pretax income	$ 486	$ 358
Depreciation permanent difference ($58 × 3)	174	—
Goodwill amortization	100	
Taxable income	$ 760	$ 358

Computation of income tax expense of Company B during holding period:		
Taxable income	$ 760	$ 358
Tax rate	46%	46%
Income tax expense	$ 350	$ 165

Computation of current and deferred income tax expense during holding period per books:	
Currently payable	$ 165
Deferred ($350 less $165)	185
Total income tax expense	$ 350

Computation of net income and retained earnings of Company B during holding period:		
Pretax income	$ 760	$ 358
Income tax expense	350	165
Net income and retained earnings	$ 410	$ 193

Divestiture Example No. 1   For income tax expense purposes, the divestiture of the stock of Company B is a capital transaction for Company A. The recording of the earnings of Company B increased the carrying value of Company B in the consolidated financial statements of Company A, and this entire carrying value must be removed from the balance sheet upon the disposition of Company B's stock. The taxes payable from the disposal produce an effective tax rate on the disposal of 35.5% (taxes of $545 divided by the pretax book gain of $1535).

Following are schedules setting forth the computation of the tax effect, the net gain, and the net cash realized from the disposal.

Computation of pretax book gain on disposal:	
Sale price for stock of Company B	$4,000
Less, carrying value of investment in Company B on equity method	2,465
Pretax gain on book basis	$1,535

Computation of tax gain on disposal:	
Sales price for stock of Company B	$4,000
Less, tax basis of stock	2,055
Tax gain	$1,945

Computation of income taxes on gain:	
Tax gain	$1,945
Capital gains tax rate	28%
Income taxes on gain on disposal	$ 545

Computation of net gain on disposal of Company B:	
Pretax gain on book basis	$1,535
Income taxes	545
Net gain on disposal	$ 990

Computation of net cash realized by Company A on disposal of Company B:	
Gross sales price	$4,000
Less, income taxes to be paid	545
Net cash realized	$3,455

Divestiture Example No. 2. In the second example to be illustrated, Company A sells 75% of the assets and business of Company B for $4000 in cash, with Company B retaining all its liabilities. The example illustrates the fundamentals of allocation of selling price to individual assets (assumed to have been done proportionately in relation to fair market values), the tax rate effects of depreciation and investment credit recapture, and removal of goodwill and deferred tax balances related to the assets sold from the balance sheet.

From the seller's standpoint, this transaction was effected in such a way that there was a disproportionate tax liability caused by allocation of $1000 of the selling price to goodwill, which from the standpoint of Company B (the seller in the transaction) had no tax basis. Although this transaction may have been structured better for the seller from a tax standpoint, it illustrates well the fundamentals of computing taxes on a disposal.

Following are schedules computing the income tax impact, net gain, and net cash realized in Divestiture Example No. 2.

Allocation of selling price and computation of taxes payable:

	Allocation of Selling Price	Tax Basis	Gain	Tax Rate	Tax
Current assets	$1,000	$ 750	$ 250	46%	115
Equipment	2,000	419	1,581	(A)	570
Goodwill	1,000	—	1,000	28%	280
	$4,000	$1,169	$2,831		$965

NOTE A

Computation of taxes on disposal of equipment:
   Original cost for tax purposes:
      $1500 × 75% = $1,125
   Depreciation deducted for tax pur-
      poses: $942 × 75% =   706
   Tax basis of equipment sold $ 419

Depreciation recapture taxed at ordinary rates ($706 × 46%)		$ 325
Balance of gain taxed at capital gains rates ($1,581 − 706 × 28%)		245
		$ 570

Computation of income taxes and net gain on disposal:

Total proceeds of sale		$4,000
Carrying values to be removed from the balance sheet:		
Current assets— $1,000 × 75% =		750
Equipment— $2,064 × 75% =	$1,548	
Less, accummulated Depreciation—$ 414 × 75% =	<311>	1,237
Goodwill— $1,000 × 75% =		750
		2,737
Pretax book gain on disposal		1,263
Income tax expense:		
Tax on gain on disposal	965	
Add: Investment tax credit recapture (assumed)	25	
Deduct: Deferred tax balances applicable to assets sold ($185 × 75%)	<138>	852
Net gain on disposal		$ 411
Computation of net cash realized by seller:		
Gross proceeds		$4,000
Less, income taxes currently payable		
Tax on gain on disposal	965	
Investment tax credit recapture	25	<990>
Net cash realized by seller		$3,010

Adjusting Prior Estimates. Paragraph 25 of APB Opinion No. 30 requires that an adjustment to a gain or loss on a divestiture that was reported in a prior period be reported as an element of current income or expense, unless it meets the criteria for a prior period adjustment.

An adjustment that does not meet the prior period adjustment criteria should be separately disclosed as to year of origin, nature, and amount and classified separately in the current period in the same manner as the gain or loss on disposal.

Footnote 6 to paragraph 15 of APB Opinion No. 30 also touches on this area by stating that when a divestiture is originally expected to be completed within one year, and this is subsequently revised to a longer period of time, any revision of the net realizable value of the segment, which would include estimated future operating income or losses, should be treated as a change in estimate.

Measurement Dates Occurring After the End of an Accounting Period. Footnote 5 to paragraph 15 of APB Opinion No. 30 addresses the situation where a measurement date occurs after the end of an accounting period, but prior to the issuance of the financial statements. Information at the measurement date which provides evidence of conditions that existed at the date of such statements and affects estimates made in preparing the financial statements should be reflected in the financial statements.

Gain or Loss on a Leveraged Buy Out. Where an especially high amount of leverage is present in a divestiture in the form of the seller holding notes, it may not be appropriate to recognize the divestiture for accounting purposes. This concept has particular applicability to public companies, in that Securities and Exchange Commission Staff Accounting Bulletin No. 30 specifically states that where the seller retains the usual risks and evidences of ownership, the divestiture should not be recognized for accounting purposes. Evidence of ownership would include continued participation in the operation at the board or managerial levels. Risks of continued ownership would be present when the buyer has made a small down payment and the funds to be provided for the rest of the purchase price must come from future operations of the acquired entity.

Where a leveraged sale of an operation does not qualify for accounting as a divestiture, the assets and liabilities of the operation should continue to be reported in the balance sheet in a segregated presentation, and operating losses of the entity should be recognized in the financial statements of the seller if there is a significant dependence by the seller on the operations of the entity to realize the balance of the selling price.

A gain in such a transaction should be recognized only when realization is assured beyond a reasonable doubt; an indicated loss should be recognized immediately.

Financial Reporting of Divestitures

Income Statement Presentation. The requirements for income statement presentation and disclosure are set forth in paragraphs 8 through 12 of APB Opinion No. 30, and require separate income statement disclosure for a divestiture that qualifies as a disposal of a segment of a business as defined in paragraph 13 of the same opinion.

Under these requirements, the results of continuing operations are reported separately from discontinued operations, and any gain or loss from disposal of a segment of a business is reported in conjunction with the related results of discontinued operations. Specifically, this is done by reporting operations of a segment that has been or will be discontinued separately as a component of income before extraordinary items and the cumulative effect of accounting changes (if applicable) in a manner similar to the following:

Income from continuing operations before Provision for income taxes	$xxxx
Provision for income taxes	xxxx
Income from continuing operations	xxxx
Discontinued operations (Note X):	
Income (loss) from operations of discontinued business (less applicable income taxes of $XX)	xxxx
Loss on disposal of discontinued business, including provision of $XX for operating losses during phase-out period (less applicable income taxes of $XX)	xxx
Loss from discontinued operations	xxxx
Net income	$xxxx

When necessary, the above captions should be modified when an entity reports an extraordinary item and/or the cumulative effect of a change in accounting principle. In such cases, the presentation of per share data will need similar modification.

Amounts of income taxes applicable to the results of discontinued operations and the gain or loss from disposal of the segment should be disclosed on the face of the income statement or in related notes. Revenues applicable to the discontinued operations should be separately disclosed in the related notes.

Paragraph 9 of APB Opinion No. 30 provides that earnings per share data for income from continuing operations and net income should be presented on the face of the income statement. Per share data for the results of discontinued operations and gain or loss from disposal of the business segment may be presented. If it is, such presentation may be on the face of the income statement or in a related note.

Balance Sheet Presentation. Footnote 7 to paragraph 18 of APB Opinion No. 30 suggests that consideration be given to segregating remaining assets and liabilities of a discontinued segment of a business in the balance sheet. The suggested presentation is that the net assets and liabilities be disclosed in captions for net current and noncurrent assets and liabilities. In making such a presentation, only liabilities that will be assumed by others should be designated as liabilities of the discontinued segment.

Other Disclosures. Paragraph 18 of APB Opinion No. 30 contains various footnote disclosure requirements, which are as follows:

1. The identity of the segment of business that has been or will be discontinued.
2. The expected disposal date, if known.
3. The expected manner of disposal.
4. A description of the remaining assets and liabilities of the segment at the balance sheet date, to the extent not adequately disclosed on the face of the balance sheet.
5. The income or loss from operations and any proceeds from disposal of the segment during the period from the measurement date to the date of the balance sheet.

For periods subsequent to the measurement date and including the period of disposal, notes to the financial statements should disclose the information listed in items 1 through 4 above and also the information listed in item 5 above compared with the prior estimates.

Footnote 7 to paragraph 18 of APB Opinion No. 30 also requires that a statement be made that a loss on disposal cannot be estimated within reasonable limits, if this is the case.

Divestitures That Are Not Disposals of a Segment of a Business. It was previously noted that for divestitures which do not fit under the definition of "disposal of a business segment" as included in APB Opinion No. 30, gain or loss on the transaction should be computed and recognized on the same basis as for a disposal of a segment of a business. However, the financial statement presentation is different. The pretax gain or loss on the disposal should be reported as a separate component of pretax income from continuing operations. No separate earnings per share presentation may be given on the face of the income statement. Revenues and expenses prior to the disposal should be reported as part of normal revenues and expenses from continuing operations.

APPENDIX 7-1: SIGNIFICANT AUTHORITATIVE ACCOUNTING PRONOUNCEMENTS ON DIVESTITURES

The following list is intended to provide guidance in referring to significant accounting pronouncements on divestitures, but it is not necessarily an all-inclusive index of professional pronouncements that may have a bearing on the subject.

APB OPINIONS

No.	Date	Title (and description)
30	6/73	Reporting the Results of Operations (specifies the accounting and reporting for disposal of a segment of a business).

AICPA ACCOUNTING INTERPRETATIONS

No.	Date	Title (and description)
N/A	11/73	Accounting Interpretations of APB Opinion No. 30 (clarifies determination of kinds of transactions that constitute disposal of a segment of a business, and reporting for those divestitures that do not qualify as disposal of a segment of a business).

FASB Statements

No.	Date	Title (and description)
52	12/81	Foreign Currency Translation (requires reversal and inclusion in computation of gain or loss the cumulative translation adjustment upon disposal of a foreign entity).

FASB Interpretations

No.	Date	Title (and description)
29	2/79	Reporting Tax Benefits Realized on Disposition of Investments in Certain Subsidiaries and Other Investees (provides guidance on classification of tax benefits realized on disposition of a subsidiary or investee which files a separate tax return).
37	7/83	Accounting for Translation Adjustments upon Sale of Part of an Investment in a Foreign Entity (provides clarification that a pro rata portion of any cumulative translation adjustment should be included in determining gain or loss).

APPENDIX 7-2: CHECKLIST OF DISCLOSURE REQUIREMENTS FOR DIVESTITURES

For divestitures qualifying as disposals of a segment of a business:

1. Report separately as a component of income after continuing operations and before extraordinary items and the cumulative effect of accounting changes (net of applicable income taxes, which should be disclosed either in the income statement or in the notes):
   a. Results of operations.
   b. Gain or loss from disposal. (If loss cannot be reasonably estimated, disclose that fact.)
2. All prior periods presented should be restated to disclose the results of operations of the discontinued business segment in a manner consistent with item 1.
3. Disclose revenues applicable to discontinued operations in a note.
4. Disclose the following in the notes for the period in which the measurement date falls:
   a. Identity of business segment that has been or will be discontinued, expected disposal date if known, and expected manner of disposal.
   b. Description of remaining assets and liabilities of the segment at the balance sheet date (may be segregated in balance sheet).
   c. Income or loss from operations and proceeds from disposal of segment during the period from measurement date to balance sheet date.
5. Disclose the following in notes for periods after the measurement date, including the period of disposal:
   a. Same information as described in 4a and 4b.
   b. Same information as described in 4c above compared with prior estimates.

6. An adjustment, in the current period, of a loss on disposal reported in a prior period should be disclosed, including the year of origin, nature, and amount. Gain or loss from the adjustment should be classified separately in the current period as gain or loss on disposal of a segment, unless the item is a correction of an error.

8

CORPORATE JOINT VENTURES

A GENERAL BUSINESS PERSPECTIVE

A corporate joint venture is an indirect form of business combination. Two or more separate entities become the stockholders of the joint venture corporation (JVC), which may be a previously existing corporation or a newly formed one. Sometimes joint ventures are formed as partnerships. However, the material in this chapter will be presented generally from the perspective of the joint venture, and the joint venturers, being corporations.

The term *joint venture* can be defined as the sharing of risk and commitment by two or more parties in the hope of making a profit. The term implies a more direct involvement in the investee than where just a passive investment is made by an investor. The equity method of accounting is normally used by investors in accounting for joint ventures, because the investors are usually in a position to influence the activities and policies of the JVC.

Corporate joint ventures are defined in APB Opinion No. 18, paragraph 3d, as follows:

"Corporate joint venture" refers to a corporation owned and operated by a small group of businesses (the "joint venturers") as a separate and specific business or project for the mutual benefit of the members of the group. A government may also be a member of the group. The purpose of a corporate joint venture frequently is to share risks and rewards in

developing a new market, product or technology; to combine complementary technological knowledge; or to pool resources in developing
production or other facilities. A corporate joint venture also usually
provides an arrangement under which each joint venturer may partici-
pate, directly or indirectly in the overall management of the joint venture. Joint venturers thus have an interest or relationship other than as
passive investors. An entity which is a subsidiary of one of the "joint
venturers" is not a corporate joint venture. The ownership of a corporate
joint venture seldom changes, and its stock is usually not traded publicly. A minority public ownership, however, does not preclude a corporation from being a corporate joint venture.

The forming of a JVC may involve the continuation of an existing
business or the creation of a new one, with the joint venturers contributing resources and financial support to assist the JVC in achieving its
goals. The JVC will typically have a board of directors comprised of
representatives of the investor entities, and the management team of
the JVC may include personnel who were previously employees of
the investor entities, in addition to personnel hired from the outside.

Why Corporate Joint Ventures Are Formed

Corporate joint ventures are formed for a variety of reasons, including:

1. The desire of the joint venturers to pursue a business endeavor
    that requires more capital or commitment of resources than
    either venturer is willing or able to commit individually.
2. A combination of complementary strengths of each of the joint
    venturers (e.g., combining of the strengths of a strong manufac-
    turing company with those of a strong marketing company).
3. A partial divestiture by one of the joint venturers where that
    party has decided for internal reasons not to continue the com-
    mitment of resources and management attention required for a
    wholly owned or majority owned subsidiary.

Structuring and Forming Corporate Joint Ventures

The formation of a corporate joint venture usually results in each of
the investor entities owning specified percentages of the voting shares
of the JVC. The simplest, most familiar structure is where two entities

each own 50% of the voting shares of the JVC. However, more than two entities can be involved in a joint venture.

In some cases, different classes of voting common stock may be issued to the joint venturers, or even voting preferred stock with specifically stated dividend and profit and loss sharing provisions.

The contributions that joint venturers make to a JVC can take many different forms, including contribution of cash, a promise to contribute cash at a future date or as needed by the JVC, stock of existing corporations, the assets and liabilities associated with an ongoing business, or particular skills and technology. Where the value of the contributions made by one joint venturer is greater than the value of the contributions of the other joint venturer, the transaction may involve some form of compensatory payment to the joint venturer contributing the greater value. These arrangements can be provided by a direct payment from one joint venturer to the other, or by measures taken in structuring the JVC, such as the issuance of debentures of the new JVC to one of the joint venturers.

Ordinarily, joint venturers will attempt to structure the formation of a JVC as a tax-free transaction to the extent possible.

Administration of Corporate Joint Ventures

The formation of a new JVC often involves the splitting off of a portion of one or more of the joint venturer's organizations. Although these business units may be complete operating divisions or corporations in their own right, there may have been significant dependence on the parent organizations for administrative and other functional support. Upon formation of a new JVC, it is important to ensure that these support functions will be adequately provided in the future. Particular functional areas of concern, where individual subsidiaries or divisions may not be self-sufficient from the standpoint of staff support, may include:

1. Legal
2. Tax
3. Personnel and employee benefits
4. Insurance
5. Data processing

In addition, the JVC may need support in other business areas, such as research and development, manufacturing (for example, safety considerations, ability to evaluate OSHA requirements, and development of manufacturing methods), marketing (for example, training of salespeople and advertising), and public relations, to name just a few.

It is important to ensure that the new organization will have adequate professional support in all these areas. This can be achieved by the new organization hiring its own qualified personnel, or by calling on specialists from the joint venturer organizations to provide staff support on a part-time basis. With respect to services performed by personnel from the joint venturer organizations for the JVC, consideration should be given to executing consulting or service agreements between the JVC and joint venturer to evidence the arms' length relationship that should exist between the separate corporations.

JOINT VENTURE ACCOUNTING

When a JVC is formed, one must be concerned with accounting from two perspectives: (1) the separate entity financial statements of the JVC, and (2) the accounting by the investor for its investment in the JVC.

Separate Entity Financial Statements of the Joint Venture Corporation

From the perspective of the JVC, the formation of the new corporation will ordinarily be viewed as a purchase accounting transaction. The JVC will have exchanged its shares of voting stock for the consideration received from the joint venturers. A new basis of accountability is established for the net assets received by the JVC based on fair market values.

Fair market value should be based on the most readily determinable and conclusive information available, which in the formation of a JVC may be difficult to determine. Because the stock issued will normally not be publicly traded, it will be difficult to estimate a value for the stock, often leading to the valuation of the net assets acquired in exchange for the stock being the determinant of fair value to be assigned to the transaction. In some cases, an independent appraisal of the assets may be required if their values are not apparent from other sources, such as the amounts of monetary assets contributed by one joint venturer where the agreement between the parties calls for equal or proportionate contributions.

In establishing the opening balance sheet of the JVC, the values assigned to assets for financial reporting purposes may differ from the tax basis of the assets, particularly where the assets are written up to amounts exceeding their net book values previously on the books of the joint venturer, coupled with a tax-free transfer where the previous tax basis is carried over. In such cases, the adjustments of fair value for the tax effects of differences in book and tax basis required by APB Opinion No. 16 are required in the separate entity financial statements of the JVC.

Where evidence of values determined in the exchange of shares indicates that intangible assets have been contributed to the JVC, assignment of value to intangible assets, including goodwill, may be appropriate. When this question arises, however, all facts and circumstances should be carefully evaluated to determine if intangible value is, in fact, present.

After establishing the opening balance sheet of the JVC, normal separate entity accounting in accordance with generally accepted accounting principles is applied to the future transactions of the JVC.

Accounting for Investments in Corporate Joint Ventures

Paragraph 16 of APB Opinion No. 18 specifically states that the equity method should be used in accounting for investments in corporate joint ventures. Even if this requirement were not specifically stated, the more general requirements of paragraph 17 of the same opinion provide that the equity method be used for investments in common stock where the investor is in a position to exercise significant influence over the operating and financial policies of the investee, which would apply to most corporate joint ventures. The Opinion provides that an investment of 20% or more of the voting stock of an investee leads to a presumption that an investor has the ability to exercise significant influence over an investee in the absence of evidence to the contrary.

The general principles of the equity method are that the initial investment in the JVC is recorded at cost as a one-line investment in the balance sheet of the investor; the investment is increased or decreased by the investor's proportionate share of the net income or loss of the JVC; and the investment is reduced by any dividends received.

Any difference between the carrying value of an equity method investment and the investor's proportionate share of the net assets reported in the separate financial statements of the JVC should be amortized in a similar manner to goodwill or negative goodwill.

Income taxes that will be payable at the time the JVC remits dividends to the investor should be accrued as an expense at the time the investor recognizes its share of the net income which will be remitted as future dividends. The "indefinite reversal criteria" exception to this rule provides that if the intent of the investor is to leave the earnings in the JVC as a permanent investment, then income taxes that would assume a dividend distribution or some other taxable event need not be accrued.

The specifics of conditions for use of the equity method and the fundamentals of applying the equity method are primarily set forth in APB Opinion No. 18, "Equity Method for Investments in Common Stock," and are dealt with in more detail in the following section.

Principles of the Equity Method.   The basic principles for applying the equity method of accounting are set forth in paragraph 19 of APB Opinion 18, and are as follows:

1. Intercompany profits and losses should be eliminated until realized by the investor or investee.
2. A difference between the cost of an investment and the amount of underlying equity in net assets for an investee should be considered goodwill and amortized over a period not to exceed 40 years, unless the difference can be related to specific accounts of the investee. In any event, this difference should be recognized systematically as part of the income and loss recognized by the investor.
3. Investments in common stock should be shown in the balance sheet of an investor as a single amount, and the investor's share of earnings or losses of investees should ordinarily be shown in the income statement as a single amount except that the investor's share of extraordinary items and its share of prior-period adjustments reported in the financial statements of an investee

should be classified in a similar manner unless they are immaterial in the income statement of the investor.

4. A transaction of an investee of a capital nature that affects the investor's share of stockholders' equity of the investee should be accounted for as if the investee were a consolidated subsidiary.

5. The investor ordinarily should discontinue applying the equity method when the investment (and net advances) has been reduced to zero and should not provide for additional losses unless the investor has guaranteed obligations of the investee or is otherwise committed to provide further financial support for the investee. If the investee subsequently reports net income, the investor should resume applying the equity method only after its share of that net income equals the share of net losses not recognized during the period the equity method was suspended. An investor should, however, provide for additional losses when the imminent return to profitable operations by an investee appears to be assured. For example, a material, nonrecurring loss of an isolated nature may reduce an investment below zero even though the underlying profitable operating pattern of an investee is unimpaired.

6. When an investee has outstanding cumulative preferred stock, an investor should compute its share of earnings (losses) after deducting the investee's preferred dividends, whether or not such dividends are declared.

7. When an investment in voting stock of an investee company falls below 20% of the investee's outstanding voting stock and the investor thereby loses the ability to influence policies of the investee, the investor should discontinue accruing its share of the earnings or losses of the investee, since the investment no longer qualifies for the equity method. The earnings or losses that relate to the stock retained by the investor and that were previously accrued should remain as a part of the carrying amount for the investment. However, dividends received by the investor in subsequent periods which exceed his share of earnings for such periods should be applied in reduction of the carrying amount of the investment.

8. When an investment in common stock of an investee that was

previously accounted for on other than the equity method becomes qualified for use of the equity method by an increase in the level of ownership, the investor should adopt the equity method of accounting. The investment, results of operations (current and prior periods presented), and retained earnings of the investor should be adjusted retroactively in a manner consistent with the accounting for a step-by-step acquisition of a subsidiary.

Capitalization of Interest Costs.   Joint venture corporations should capitalize interest in the separate financial statements of the JVC in accordance with FASB Statement No. 34, "Capitalization of Interest Cost."

FASB Statement No. 58 was issued to clarify the principles to be followed by investors in regard to capitalization of interest costs concerning equity method investments. For purposes of capitalization of interest costs, an investor's investment in an equity method investee is an asset qualifying for interest capitalization if the investee is in the process of undergoing activities necessary to commence its planned principal operations, and if the activities of the investee include the use of funds to acquire qualifying assets for its operations. The important distinction is that to the investor, the equity method investment is the qualifying asset—not the individual qualifying assets of the investee.

When the investee commences its planned operations, the investor shall cease treating the equity method investment as an asset qualifying for capitalization of interest.

Income Taxes on Undistributed Earnings.   APB Opinion No. 23, paragraph 17, provides that unless certain criteria are met, deferred income taxes should be provided on timing differences that arise from the inclusion of a proportionate share of earnings of a corporate joint venture in pretax accounting income of an investor where the earnings are not included in taxable income of the investor. Where such taxes are provided, this will normally be equal to the income taxes which would have been required if the earnings had been remitted as dividends in the current period.

The criteria which, if met, permit the investor not to provide such deferred taxes are referred to as the "indefinite reversal" criteria. This is defined in paragraph 12 of APB Opinion No. 23 as where there is sufficient evidence that the investor has invested or will invest the undistributed earnings indefinitely or that the earnings will be remitted in a tax-free liquidation.

With respect to changes in circumstances causing an investor to change its decision of whether or not to provide income taxes on unremitted earnings in prior years, the income tax expense of the current year should be adjusted for the cumulative amount of taxes required, or to be reversed.

Financial Statement Disclosures.   Paragraph 20 of APB Opinion 18 sets forth the primary disclosures required for equity method investments in the financial statements of the investor:

1. Parenthetically, in notes to financial statements, or in separate statements or schedules (A) the name of each investee and percentage of ownership of common stock, (B) the accounting policies of the investor with respect to investments in common stock, and (C) the differences, if any, between the amount at which an investment is carried and the amount of underlying equity in net assets and the accounting treatment of the difference.

2. The names of any significant investee corporations in which the investor holds 20% or more of the voting stock, for which the investment is not accounted for using the equity method, together with the reasons why the equity method is not considered appropriate, and the names of any significant investee corporations in which the investor holds less than 20% for which the investment is accounted for on the equity method, together with the reasons why the equity method is considered appropriate.

3. For those investments in common stock for which a quoted market price is available, the aggregate value of each identified investment based on the quoted market price. It should be noted that this disclosure is not required for investments in common stock of subsidiaries.

4. Summarized information as to assets, liabilities, and results of operations should be presented in the notes or separate statements should be presented for unconsolidated subsidiaries,

corporate joint ventures, or other equity method investments either individually or in groups, where they are, in the aggregate, material in relation to the investor's financial statements.

5. Material effects of possible conversions of outstanding convertible securities, exercises of outstanding options or warrants or contingent issuances of additional shares of an investee should be disclosed in notes to the financial statements of an investor.

Related Party Disclosures. FASB Statement No. 57, "Related Party Disclosures," established disclosure requirements for transactions between related parties, which includes transactions between investors and equity method investees. Accordingly, certain disclosures will be required in separate financial statements of equity method investees and investors where significant intercompany transactions exist, which could have resulted in different operating results or financial position if the entities were not related.

These disclosures include the following specific types of transactions that could occur between an investor and equity method investee:

1. Sales, purchases, and transfers of realty and personal property.
2. Services received or rendered, such as accounting, management, engineering, and legal services.
3. Leases.
4. Borrowings and lendings.
5. Guarantees.
6. Maintenance of bank accounts as compensating balances for the benefit of another.
7. Intercompany billings based on allocations of common costs.

In this area, the disclosure requirements are the important consideration, rather than accounting principles. A transaction between an investor and an equity method investee on other than an arms' length basis (such as the investor performing services for the investee without charge), creates only the need for a disclosure. There is no need for imputation of revenue or costs other than as reported.

With respect to any material related party transactions, the following should be disclosed:

1. The nature of the relation(s) involved.

2. A description of the transaction (for each of the periods for which income statements are presented).

3. The dollar amounts, if any, of the transactions (for each of the periods for which income statements are presented).

4. The effects of any change from the preceding period in the method of establishing the terms of transaction.

5. Amounts receivable from or payable to the related parties (as of the date of each balance sheet presented) and, if not otherwise apparent, the terms and manner of settlement.

6. Any other information deemed necessary to an understanding of the effects of the transactions on the financial statements. This might include, for example, the name of the related party.

Representation should not be made in the disclosures that transactions between related parties were on an arm's-length basis unless that representation can be substantiated.

Disclosure of Guarantees. FASB Interpretation No. 34, "Disclosure of Indirect Guarantees of Indebtedness of Others," contains disclosure requirements that will have applicability to some JVC situations. Sometimes the investors in a JVC will assist the JVC in obtaining credit by an investor's guarantee of the indebtedness of the JVC, or by the investor executing an agreement committing the investor to transfer funds to the JVC upon occurrence of specified events, such as falling below specific financial ratios. Interpretation No. 34 requires that any such indirect guarantees be disclosed.

Income Tax Disclosures. The financial statement disclosures required under APB Opinion No. 23, paragraph 14, related to undistributed earnings of corporate joint ventures on which taxes have not been provided are:

1. A declaration of an intention to reinvest undistributed earnings of a subsidiary to support the conclusion that remittance of those earnings has been indefinitely postponed, or a declaration that the undistributed earnings will be remitted in the form of a tax-free liquidation.

2. The cumulative amount of undistributed earnings on which the parent company has not recognized income taxes.

Other disclosure requirements in paragraphs 56 through 64 of APB Opinion No. 11 may also apply. Disclosure of other matters such as available tax credits and deductions may be desirable.

APPENDIX 8-1: SIGNIFICANT AUTHORITATIVE ACCOUNTING PRONOUNCEMENTS ON THE EQUITY METHOD OF ACCOUNTING

The following list is intended to provide guidance in referring to significant accounting pronouncements on the equity method of accounting, but it is not necessarily an all-inclusive index of professional pronouncements which may have a bearing on the subject.

APB OPINIONS

No.	Date	Title (and description)
18	3/71	The Equity Method of Accounting for Investments in Common Stock (establishes the fundamental provisions of the equity method).
20	7/71	Accounting Changes (requires restatement in investor financial statements where entities change to or from the equity method).
23	4/72	Accounting for Income Taxes—Special Areas (sets forth principles for providing income taxes on undistributed earnings of corporate joint ventures).
24	4/72	Accounting for Income Taxes (sets forth principles for providing income taxes on undistributed earnings of investments where holdings of common stock are accounted for by the equity method—other than subsidiaries and corporate joint ventures).

AICPA ACCOUNTING INTERPRETATIONS

No.	Date	Title (and description)
N/A	11/71 & 2/72	Accounting Interpretations of APB Opinion No. 18 (provides guidance on elimination of intercompany profits, unincorporated entities).

FASB STATEMENTS

No.	Date	Title (and description)
58	4/82	Capitalization of Interest Cost in Financial Statements that Include Investments Accounted for by the Equity Method (provides that investors should capitalize interest of amounts of equity method investments where the investee is undergoing activities necessary to commence its operations where the investee is using funds to obtain "qualifying" assets).

FASB INTERPRETATIONS

No.	Date	Title (and description)
29	2/79	Reporting Tax Benefits Realized on Disposition of Investments in Certain Subsidiaries and Other Investees (provides guidance on classification of tax benefits realized on disposition of a subsidiary or investee which files a separate tax return).
34	3/81	Disclosure of Indirect Guarantees of Indebtedness of Others (may require disclosure of investor's commitment to provide funds to JVC upon occurrence of specified events).

35	5/81	Criteria for Applying the Equity Method of Accounting for Investments in Common Stock (provides guidance for decision of whether investor has influence significant enough to require equity method and discusses certain limitations on using the equity method).

FASB TECHNICAL BULLETINS

No.	Date	Title (and description)
79–19	12/79	Investor's Accounting for Unrealized Losses on Marketable Securities Owned by an Equity Method Investee (provides that an investor shall reduce its equity section by its proportionate share of the reduction of the equity section of an investee accounted for by the equity method as a result of an adjustment to the carrying value of a long-term portfolio of marketable securities).

APPENDIX 8-2: CHECKLIST OF DISCLOSURE REQUIREMENTS FOR EQUITY METHOD INVESTMENTS

1. Name of each investee and percentage of common stock owned.
2. Accounting policies of investor with respect to investments in common stock.
3. The investments (as a single amount) in the investor's balance sheet, with earnings and losses from applying the equity method generally disclosed as a single amount in the income statement.

4. Difference, if any, between amount at which carried in the balance sheet of the investor and amount of underlying equity in net assets in the separate financial statements of the investee, and accounting treatment of the difference.

5. Aggregate value of each investment (except subsidiaries), based on quoted market price, if available.

6. The investor's share of extraordinary items and prior-period adjustments classified in a manner similar to the investee's classification as extraordinary items or prior-period adjustments, unless they are immaterial.

7. Material effects of possible conversions, exercises, or other contingent issuances of investee.

8. Names of significant investees in which less than 20% of voting stock and common stock is held and the reason for using the equity method if the equity method is used.

9. If income taxes are not accrued on undistributed earnings of subsidiaries or permanent-type corporate joint venture:

   a. Intention to reinvest undistributed earnings or remit them in the form of a tax-free liquidation.

   b. Cumulative amount of undistributed earnings on which the investor has not recognized taxes.

10. Material subsequent events and transactions, labeled as unaudited information.

11. Summarized financial information for unconsolidated subsidiaries and for 50% or less owned persons, including assets, liabilities, and results of operations (may be wholly or partly combined).

12. For investments not accounted for under the equity method in which 20% or more of voting stock is held, provide the names of the significant investees and the reason for not using the equity method.

9

CONSIDERATIONS OF THE PUBLIC
ACCOUNTING PROFESSION

This chapter is intended to address the special considerations of the CPA in an acquisition environment. This will be of use to both CPAs and those who work with CPAs in connection with acquisitions, including client company personnel, who sometimes engage CPAs for this purpose.

The references to AU sections relate to provisions included in the sections of *Codification of Statements on Auditing Standards Numbers 1 to 47* issued by the American Institute of Certified Public Accountants.

The special services rendered by outside CPAs in merger and acquisition situations will frequently center around confirming information about an acquisition candidate, providing additional information on which the client will rely in making the decision of whether or not to consummate the transaction, or in evaluating the proposed purchase price and terms of the acquisition. These services can include acquisition audits, reviews, or compilations of financial statements and special services, including services frequently referred to as pre-acquisition reviews.

Other special services that the CPA may provide include assisting the client in structuring and planning transactions, advising the client in negotiations, and assuming a consulting role in assisting clients in developing and commencing acquisition programs, in searching for acquisition candidates, or in referring acquisition candidates to clients.

The last section of this chapter covers auditing considerations regarding the financial statements of an acquirer after an acquisition has occurred.

PREACQUISITION REVIEWS AND OTHER SPECIAL SERVICES

Preacquisition Reviews

Preacquisition reviews performed by an independent CPA for a client typically follow the pattern of the preacquisition reviews previously discussed in Chapter 2.

It is important to note that there are no authoritative professional standards for the conduct of a preacquisition review by an independent CPA, or regarding what procedures should be employed. Such procedures must be established based upon agreement between the CPA and the client, and through use of professional judgment.

Many preacquisition review engagements will fall under the category of applying agreed upon procedures to specified elements, accounts or items of a financial statement, as described in AU Section 622. In performing this type of service, the CPA applies specified procedures to specified elements, accounts, or items which are not sufficient to enable expressing an opinion on the elements, accounts, or items. AU Section 622.02 permits this form of service and reporting provided that:

(a) the parties involved have a clear understanding of the procedures to be performed and

(b) distribution of the report is to be restricted to named parties involved.

AU 622.02 contains guidance on how a CPA may ensure that the parties have a clear understanding of the procedures. One of the procedures suggested is the distribution of a draft of the report or a copy of the engagement letter to the parties involved with a request for their comments prior to issuance of the report. This implies that CPAs have some degree of responsibility to all parties involved (and not just to their clients). Careful judgment is required in this area, particularly where full disclosure of the procedures and findings to certain parties (the seller, for example, where the client is the buyer) could be detrimental to the CPA's client.

It should be noted that standards of reporting (including the third standard regarding adequacy of informative disclosure) do not apply to special reports on applying agreed-upon procedures to specified elements, accounts or items of a financial statement. Even if the third standard did apply, the requirements for adequate disclosure under the third standard of reporting is not intended to require publicizing information that would be detrimental to the CPA's client. If a CPA becomes involved in a difficult reporting situation where significant issues and questions of disclosure regarding findings related to the carrying out of agreed-upon procedures are involved, the CPA should carefully evaluate his or her actions, giving consideration to all professional standards and ethics, and should consider consulting with his own legal counsel.

Other Special Services

Additional services performed by CPAs related to mergers and acquisitions include:

1. Assisting clients in developing and commencing acquisition programs.
2. Searching for acquisition candidates or referring companies wishing to be acquired to clients who may be prospective acquirers.
3. Assisting clients in structuring and planning acquisition transactions to meet desired objectives.
4. Providing advice to clients in negotiating the terms of an acquisition.
5. Review of controls and procedures of the acquired company, or providing consulting services connected with integrating the financial and accounting systems of the acquired company with those of the client.

Some public accounting firms maintain separate departments with staffs of specialists in merger and acquisition work who are especially qualified to provide special services in this area. These specialists may also provide services to clients on divestitures.

In rendering special services in mergers and acquisitions, CPAs should be careful to coordinate their services with those of other professionals, such as financial consultants, investment bankers, and lawyers, and to ensure that the client understands the limitations of expertise of the CPA. For example, it would not be appropriate for CPAs to allow clients to believe that they can definitively determine a proper amount for the stock or assets of an acquisition candidate, although they may assist clients in analyzing data contributing to such a valuation.

Normally, CPAs consider it appropriate to provide advice to clients in setting up acquisition programs, but do not consider it appropriate to be responsible for carrying out specific programs and actions. For example, an independent CPA would not normally consider it appropriate to negotiate on behalf of the client with the owner of the acquisition candidate, although he or she may provide advice to the client or the client's representatives during the negotiation process.

CPAs generally consider it acceptable to search for acquisition candidates on behalf of clients, or to refer companies seeking to be acquired to prospective acquirers. Some CPAs are reluctant to provide this assistance to companies requesting only this service, who are not already clients. CPAs receiving this type of request should carefully review the circumstances before accepting such an engagement.

ACQUISITION AUDITS, COMPILATIONS AND REVIEWS

Acquisition Audits

Audits of the separate financial statements of companies that may be acquired or have been acquired should in some cases be viewed differently than recurring annual audits. The essential difference is that an examination of the financial statements of an acquisition candidate or recently acquired company may require a relatively low materiality measurement when compared with the materiality considerations in a recurring annual examination of financial statements related to continuing operations and financial position on a going concern basis. The CPA's report on a preacquisition audit can have a bearing on whether or not the acquisition is completed, or may have a bearing on the final determination of purchase price. Even a postacquisition audit performed as part of an annual audit of the acquirer may have an effect on the final purchase price, if it is subject to adjustment based on the ultimate realizability of assets or liabilities, or the resolution of other contingencies.

With these considerations in mind, the CPA may very likely deem it appropriate, or may be requested by the client, to perform more searching audit procedures or establish a lower materiality level in making audit tests and judgments. More detailed procedures and precise estimates of accounts dependent on the impacts of future business events, such as valuation reserves, may be required.

In addition, CPAs may supplement their normal auditing procedures with greater emphasis on more operationally oriented areas to provide greater assurance that all matters of significance have been brought to their attention, or they may be specifically requested to perform additional procedures similar to those discussed in Chapter 2.

Additional reasons for extended audit procedures may be present if the audit is the CPA's initial audit of the financial statements of the company, or if it is the first audit ever of the company's financial statements (which is sometimes the case in acquisition audits). In such situations, extended procedures will probably be required to establish beginning balances, especially for those accounts having historical accumulations. Several specific areas where extended procedures may be required are:

1. Historical costs of fixed assets and accumulated depreciation.
2. If the income statement is being reported on, beginning balances of inventories and receivables, and investigation for any income or expense items that may have been recognized in prior periods, which should have been recognized in different periods.
3. Deferred tax balances, giving consideration to the use of proper rates from prior years in establishing the deferred tax liability.

Many acquisition agreements call for separate audited financial statements for several years after the acquisition of the acquired company for purposes of providing information needed in finalizing the purchase price. Alternatively, the client may desire audits of the separate financial statements, especially in cases where former management has continued to manage the acquired company. Even if a separate audit is not required, a CPA may be engaged to perform procedures to evaluate the ultimate realization of represented values of assets and liabilities, or to evaluate compliance with other covenants or representations in the purchase agreement.

Compilations and Reviews

A CPA may compile or review financial statements for a client that is a nonpublic entity, in accordance with Statement of Standards for Accounting and Review Services (SSARS) No. 1. These services may be provided to a client in connection with an acquisition. A seller will usually engage its own CPA for this purpose, rather than use the acquirer's CPA. It is possible, however, that an acquirer might engage its accountant to perform a review of the financial statements of another company it is considering acquiring.

Where compilations or reviews are performed, the standards and procedures required for such services, set forth in SSARS No. 1, should be followed. In an acquisition, the most difficult standard to comply with may be the required understanding of the industry accounting principles and practices and the required understanding of the entity's accounting records, practices, and personnel. This is because the engagement regarding the financial statements of an acquisition candidate may represent the CPA's first experience with the entity and its personnel.

With respect to a public entity required to have audited annual financial statements, the compilation and review standards of SSARS No. 1 do not apply. In the rare cases where the public entity is not required to have its annual financial statements audited, the CPA may perform a review and give negative assurance on the financial statements of the acquisition candidate in accordance with SSARS No. 1.

For a public entity that is required to have its annual financial statements audited, limited procedures may be performed, leading to giving negative assurance on the financial statements of a proposed acquisition candidate provided that the applicable requirements for a letter for underwriters, set forth in AU Section 631, are met.

REPORTING ON ACQUISITION ENGAGEMENTS

Careful judgment is required in communication regarding work performed by a CPA related to an acquisition. The form and content of the communication should be determined by the nature and extent of work performed, and in some cases should be expanded due to the sensitivity of merger and acquisition situations and the degree of reliance that may be placed on the report.

If a full audit of separate company financial statements has been performed, a standard audit report should be furnished. However, because an audit performed in an acquisition situation may involve more in-depth procedures than is normal, and is often expected to provide more precise reliance than is normally associated with recurring audits, consideration should be given to whether a supplemental communication is necessary to communicate the nature and extent of the procedures adequately, the assurances that are being given, and the degree of responsibility the CPA is assuming.

Many situations where a CPA performs less than a full audit, including some preacquisition reviews, can fall under the classification of applying agreed-upon procedures to specified elements, accounts, or items of a financial statement. Where the procedures specifically focus on confirming information with respect to expected or actual realizability of specific assets and liabilities for use in finalizing the purchase price, or in verifying representations made by either the purchaser or seller in the agreement, the standards for special reports on applying agreed-upon procedures to specified elements, accounts, or items of a financial statement should be referred to.

Where a CPA is asked to give negative assurance on financial statements of an acquisition candidate which have been reviewed, special reporting rules apply.

Reporting on Preacquisition Reviews and Other Special Services

Agreed-Upon Procedures.   AU 622.04 specifies the content of a CPA's report on applying agreed-upon procedures to specified elements, accounts, or items of a financial statement, which will be applicable in many cases to special acquisition review procedures. The report should:

(a) indicate the specified elements, accounts or items to which the agreed-upon procedures were applied,

(b) indicate the intended distribution of the report,

(c) enumerate the procedures performed,

(d) state the accountant's findings,

(e) disclaim an opinion with respect to the specified elements, accounts, or items,

(f) state that the report relates only to the elements, accounts or items specified, and does not extend to the entity's financial statements taken as a whole.

The following is a partial quotation of a report on agreed-upon procedures rendered in connection with a proposed acquisition which is contained in AU Section 622.06:

REPORT IN CONNECTION WITH A PROPOSED ACQUISITION
BOARD OF TRUSTEES
X COMPANY

We have applied certain agreed-upon procedures, as discussed below, to accounting records of Y Company, Inc., as of December 31, 19XX, solely to assist you in connection with the proposed acquisition of Y Company, Inc. It is understood that this report is solely for your information and is not to be referred to or distributed for any purpose to anyone who is not a member of management of X Company, Inc. Our procedures and findings are as follows:

(DESCRIBE PROCEDURES AND FINDINGS)

Because the above procedures do not constitute an examination made in accordance with generally accepted auditing standards, we do not express an opinion on any of the accounts or items referred to above. In connection with the procedures referred to above, no matters came to our attention that caused us to believe that the specified accounts or items should be adjusted. Had we performed additional procedures or had we made an examination of the financial statements in accordance with generally accepted auditing standards, matters might have come to our attention that would have been reported to you. This report relates only to the accounts and items specified above and does not extend to any financial statements of Y Company, Inc. taken as a whole.

Reporting on More General Procedures. Where the scope of a preacquisition review engagement is more general in nature than applying agreed-upon procedures to specified elements, accounts, or items of a financial statement, a form of communication suitable in the circumstances should be rendered. For example, in a preacquisition review covering more general business and investigative matters, the following is a suggested list of items to consider in a communication on the preacquisition review. The structure of the report may be similar to a report on agreed upon procedures.

1. Identification of the proposed transaction, and drafts of major agreements reviewed.
2. Description of areas reviewed, nature and extent of procedures performed, and reference to the engagement letter.
3. Officials of the company and acquisition candidate and other specialists (investment bankers, lawyers, etc.) met with and areas discussed, and information provided by each.
4. Disclaimer of opinion and denial of audit responsibility.
5. Key financial data and information, and where it was obtained.
6. An indication of with whom the report has been reviewed and to whom the report may be distributed.
7. Discussion of findings and matters of an accounting, financial, or operational nature that may be of interest to the client, together with any additional information or schedules that are pertinent to the acquisition candidate and might be helpful to the client.

Reporting on Complete Acquisition Audits

Reports on audits of the separate financial statements of companies that may be acquired or have been acquired may in some cases be relied on more precisely than audit reports for recurring annual audits. The possibility of the performance of more searching audit procedures, the materiality considerations, the effect the report could have on whether or not the acquisition is completed, or the possible effect on the determination of purchase price present important judgmental factors to be considered by the CPA in rendering the audit report.

Depending upon the auditor's evaluation of the above considerations, and the degree to which he or she believes reliance will be placed on the report, the auditor may consider describing in a supplemental communication to the client the procedures applied to specific items in the financial statements to avoid any possible misunderstanding regarding the nature and scope of the audit testing, and the assurances that are being given. Although this information would generally be included in the engagement letter, in particularly sensitive situations the auditor may consider it appropriate to communicate this in report form as well. Such communications of more in-depth description of procedures should be made in conformity with AU Section 551.20. This section refers to situations where an auditor is requested to describe the procedures applied to specific items in the financial statements. This expanded form of reporting on the procedures in an acquisition could arise from the auditor concluding that the expanded commentary is necessary, as well as from a client request. In any event, the auditor would be well-advised to review with the client the logic and form of an expanded report mode in advance, whether the report is expanded pursuant to a client request or based on the auditor's suggestion.

Additional commentary concerning an audit in an acquisition environment could include:

1. Discussion of significant procedures, audit issues, and how they were resolved.
2. Findings of matters that could affect measurement of the purchase price based on terms of the purchase agreement.
3. Discussion of assets and liabilities as to which the ultimate valuation remains uncertain. This may be desirable where the accountant wishes to emphasize that while the financial statements may be fairly stated in all material respects there are likely to be minor adjustments to assets and liabilities as a result of future experience.
4. Statistical data, explanatory comments, or other informative material, some of which may be of a non-accounting nature, which the CPA believes is important enough for formal communication.

The reporting guidelines of AU Section 551.20 require that additional commentary concerning the audit should not detract from or contradict the description of the scope of examination in the standard audit report, and that they be set forth separately from the information accompanying the basic financial statements.

The communication of an auditor's discussion of such matters as audit procedures, issues, or findings on matters which could affect the purchase price or otherwise be important to the acquirer in conjunction with rendering an audit report could be communicated in various ways depending on the importance and extent of the information. For example, communication could be in the form of:

1. Addition of a middle paragraph in the audit report to emphasize a matter.
2. A supplemental letter to the client in form similar to a special report on the performance of agreed-upon procedures to specified elements, accounts, or items of a financial statement.

Reporting on Compilations and Reviews

If the work performed by a CPA constitutes a compilation or review of financial statements of an acquisition candidate or recently acquired company, the standards applicable to reporting on a review or compilation would apply. The CPA should, however, be certain that the compilation and review report is adequate for use considering all the circumstances, and that its use complies with professional requirements.

Giving Negative Assurance

It is possible that a preacquisition review may include, in addition to other procedures, all the required procedures for a review of financial statements. Furthermore, the CPA may be asked to give negative assurance regarding the financial statements taken as a whole, in addition to reporting on the additional procedures. AU Section 504.20 provides that in connection with an acquisition of a public company, where a CPA is requested to describe limited procedures performed with respect to unaudited financial statements, and to give negative assurance regarding the financial statements taken as a whole, he may so report provided that the applicable requirements for a letter for underwriters, which are specified in AU Section 631, are met.

Professional standards do not require that a CPA must have audited the prior financial statements in order to perform a review of financial statements or limited procedures performed in accordance with the requirements for letters for underwriters. However, in both cases, there is a need and requirement for understanding of the entity's accounting and financial reporting practices. The CPA should take adequate steps to ensure that he or she will acquire sufficient knowledge of these matters to perform and report properly.

Following is a suggested form of report:

We have reviewed the accompanying balance sheet of ABC, Inc. as of December 31, 19XX, and the related statements of income and retained earnings and changes in financial position for the year then ended, in accordance with standards established by the American Institute of Certified Public Accountants.

All information included in the aforementioned financial statements is the representation of ABC, Inc.

A review consists principally of inquiries of company personnel and analytical procedures applied to financial data. It is substantially less in scope than an examination in accordance with generally accepted auditing standards, the objective of which is the expression of an opinion regarding the financial statements taken as a whole. Accordingly, we do not express such an opinion.

Based on our review, we are not aware of any material modifications that should be made to the accompanying financial statements in order for them to be in conformity with generally accepted accounting principles.

We have also applied certain agreed-upon procedures, as discussed below, to the accounting records of ABC, Inc. as of December 31, 19XX, solely to assist you in connection with the proposed acquisition of ABC, Inc. Our procedures and findings are as follows:

(Describe procedures and findings.)

The foregoing procedures do not constitute an examination made in accordance with generally accepted auditing standards. Also, they would not necessarily reveal matters of significance with respect to the comments in the preceding paragraph. Accordingly, we make no representations regarding the sufficiency of the foregoing procedures for your purposes.

This letter is solely for the information of, and assistance to, the (client company) in conducting its investigation in connection with the proposed acquisition of ABC, Inc. and is not to be used, circulated, quoted, or otherwise referred to without our prior written consent for any purpose other than review by company officials in evaluating the proposed acquisition of ABC, Inc., or review by officials of XYZ Bank pursuant to an application by (client company) for financing related to the proposed acquisition of ABC, Inc.

Professional standards do not specifically recognize the use of reporting formats permitted in letters for underwriters where the acquisition candidate is a nonpublic company. Accordingly, it would appear professional basis exists for giving both negative assurance regarding the financial statements of a nonpublic acquisition candidate taken as a whole, together with a description of requested additional procedures and comments on related findings in a single report. To be in technical compliance, therefore, in such circumstances where a nonpublic entity is concerned, it appears the CPA would be required to issue a report on a review which may give the requested negative assurance but may not make mention of the additional procedures. The additional procedures and findings would have to be covered in a separate special report on applying agreed-upon procedures to specified elements, accounts, or items of a financial statement, or in another suitable form of report for the procedures.

AU Section 622.04 (footnote 4) permits the inclusion of reports containing results of applying agreed upon procedures with the entity's financial statements. Appropriate standards, including AU Section 504 entitled "Association With Financial Statements," should be referred to. Also, when negative assurance is given, the standards of SSARS No. 1 entitled "Compilation and Review of Financial Statements" should be referred to.

Reporting on Financial Statements Prepared in Accordance with Accounting Practices Specified in an Agreement

AU Sections 9621.17-25 address the CPA's reporting concerns where an acquisition of financial statements with valuation bases other than generally accepted accounting principles specified for certain assets, such as receivables, inventories, and properties. These cases do not constitute a "comprehensive basis of accounting other than generally accepted accounting principles" in accordance with the provisions of AU Section 621.04d.

A CPA is permitted to express an opinion on the fair presentation of such financial statements in a manner similar to reports issued on the financial statements of regulated companies, provided that the report is modified as to the conformity of the special-purpose financial statements with generally accepted accounting principles. The basis of accounting and reason for the basis should be described in the report and in a note to the financial statements, and the report should comment on consistency with any similar reports which have been issued for previous periods.

The requirement for disclosing the principal effects of the departures from generally accepted accounting principles on financial position, results of operations, and changes in financial position may be complied with in a separate paragraph of the report, by referring to a note to the financial statements which provides the information, or by referring to coexisting audited financial statements which are in accordance with generally accepted accounting principles.

In preparing the report, the CPA should evaluate whether the effects of departures from generally accepted accounting principles, based on their significance, require a qualified, adverse, or disclaimer of opinion as to conformity with generally accepted accounting principles.

Any significant interpretations of provisions related to the agreement made by the client should be described in a paragraph in the report, or a note to the financial statements which is referred to in the report.

AU Section 9621.25 contains an example of the form of such a report, as follows:

> Report on Financial Statements Prepared Pursuant to an Acquisition Agreement (Effects of Departures from Generally Accepted Accounting Principles Have Not Been Determined).
>
> We have examined the special-purpose balance sheet of ABC Company as of June 30, 19XX, and the related special purpose financial statements of income, retained earnings, and changes in financial position for the year then ended. Our examination was made in accordance with generally accepted auditing standards and, accordingly, included such tests of the accounting records and such other auditing procedures as we considered necessary in the circumstances.
>
> The accompanying special-purpose financial statements have been prepared for the purpose of complying with, and on the basis of accounting practices specified in, an acquisition agreement dated May 15, 19XX, between ABC Company and DEF Company. These practices differ, as described in Note X, from generally accepted accounting principles; the

monetary effects on the accompanying financial statements of such differences have not been determined. Accordingly, we are unable to and
do not express an opinion on whether the accompanying special-purpose financial statements fairly present the financial position, results of
operations and changes in financial position of ABC Company in conformity with generally accepted accounting principles.

In our opinion, however, the accompanying special-purpose financial
statements of ABC Company are presented fairly on the basis of accounting described in Note X.

Reporting on Special Purpose Financial Presentations

AU Sections 9621.26-30 discuss reporting considerations where special-purpose financial presentations not presenting a complete presentation of financial position or results of operations are given, such
as a schedule of assets to be sold and liabilities to be transferred
pursuant to a buy-sell agreement. Such presentations are considered
to be financial statements for reporting purposes, and a CPA may
express an opinion on the fairness of the presentation of the information in conformity with generally accepted accounting principles. In
expressing the opinion, materiality should be measured based on the
presentation taken as a whole. The report should state what the presentation is intended to represent, and a suitable title for the presentation should be used. Generally accepted accounting principles, including informative disclosures, should be followed.

AU Section 9621.31 contains the following example of such a special-purpose report:

Report on a Statement of Assets Sold and Liabilities Transferred.

We have examined the statement of net assets of ABC Company as of
June 8, 19XX, sold pursuant to the Purchase Agreement as described in
Note X, between ABC Company and XYZ Corporation dated May 8,
19XX. Our examination was made in accordance with generally accepted auditing standards and, accordingly, included such tests of the
accounting records and such other auditing procedures as we considered necessary in the circumstances.

In our opinion, the accompanying statement presents fairly the net
assets of ABC Company as of June 8, 19XX, sold pursuant to the purchase agreement referred to above, in conformity with generally accepted accounting principles.

AUDITING CONSIDERATIONS REGARDING THE FINANCIAL STATEMENTS OF AN ACQUIRER

After an acquisition, an auditor will need to evaluate the significance of the acquired company to the consolidated financial statements of the client. Based upon the results of this evaluation, the CPA will decide the nature and extent of audit procedures necessary with respect to the acquired operation in regard to the recurring annual audit of the client's financial statements. Major areas for the CPA to be concerned with are:

1. The client's accounting for the acquisition, including selection of the applicable accounting method (purchase or pooling), application of the method, and verification of data.
2. Where the purchase method is applicable:
    a. Results of operations and changes in financial position of the acquired company after the acquisition date, which are included in the client's reported results.
    b. Operations of the acquired company prior to the acquisition date needed for combining with results of operations of the acquirer for pro forma disclosure purposes, if the acquirer is a public company.
3. Where the pooling-of-interests method is applicable, results of operations and changes in financial position of the combined companies after the transaction, and before the transaction, which are reported on a restated basis.
4. Possible reporting implications regarding the auditor's opinion where other independent auditors have audited prior or current financial statements of the acquired company.

Auditing Independent Appraisals

Because the independent appraisal is a key element in the accounting for an acquisition accounted for under the purchase method, audit procedures in this area should be carefully planned. Such procedures normally include a review of the appraisers' qualifications, a review of his or her procedures, and tests and verifications of the data included in the appraisal.

Auditing Operations of an Acquired Company

Various auditing and reporting concerns relate to the financial statements of an acquired company in the context of an acquirer's consolidated financial statements.

Where other CPAs have previously audited the financial statements of the acquired company, and continue to do so after the acquisition, the acquirer's CPA must consider the professional standards applicable where part of an examination was made by another independent auditor.

Frequently, where other CPAs have audited the financial statements of the acquired company prior to the acquisition, the CPAs of the acquirer will be engaged to audit the financial statements of the acquired company after the acquisition. In this case, considerations present when part of an examination is made by other independent auditors will apply to portions of the prior period restated financial statements for a pooling of interests, and to pro forma data to be disclosed for a purchase acquisition, where the acquirer is a public company.

Audit Reports Following an Acquisition

Pooling of Interests.   A business combination accounted for as a pooling of interests represents a change in the reporting entity for which prior year financial statements must be restated in comparative financial reports. Reference is required in the auditor's report as to consistency.

In a report on comparative financial statements, reference to the restatement of the prior year's financial statements can be made by revising the last segment of the standard auditor's report on comparative financial statements to read:

> in conformity with generally accepted accounting principles applied on
> a consistent basis as restated.

When a single year report is presented for the year in which a pooling of interests was consummated, footnote disclosures should set forth the revenues, extraordinary items, and net income of the previously separate companies for the preceding year on a combined basis.

Failure to make these disclosures would require the auditor's report to be qualified for lack of disclosure and consistency. This area is discussed in AU Sections 546.12-13.

In a report on single year financial statements, the reference to restatement may be made by modifying the last segment of the standard report to read:

> in conformity with generally accepted accounting principles applied on a basis consistent with that of the restated preceding year.

Where a pooling of interests has occurred, special reporting considerations are present if some of the financial statements included in the new combined entity for the current and/or prior year were examined by other auditors. The first decision an auditor must make is whether he has examined a sufficient portion of the combined financial statements to serve as principal auditor.

Following is an example of an appropriate audit report where the auditor is satisfied he can properly express an opinion as principal auditor, but has decided to make reference to the examination of the other auditor:

> We have examined the consolidated balance sheets of Company A and Subsidiaries as of December 31, 19X3 and 19X2, and the restated consolidated statements of income and retained earnings and changes in financial position for the years then ended. Our examinations were made in accordance with generally accepted auditing standards, and, accordingly, included such tests of the accounting records and such other auditing procedures as we considered necessary in the circumstances. We did not examine the financial statements of Company B which underlie the restatement of the consolidated financial statements for the year ended December 31, 19X2 (see Note 2), and which reflect total assets, sales and net income constituting 25%, 30% and 24%, of the respective 19X2 totals. These statements were examined by other auditors whose opinion thereon have been furnished to us, and our opinion expressed herein, insofar as it relates to the amounts included for Company B for 19X2 is based solely upon the opinions of the other auditors.
>
> In our opinion, based upon our examination and the opinions of other auditors, the aforementioned consolidated financial statements present fairly the financial position of Company A and Subsidiaries at December 31, 19X3 and 19X2, and the results of their operations and changes in their financial position for the years then ended, in conformity with generally accepted accounting principles on a basis consistent with that of the restated preceding year.

In some situations after a pooling of interests an auditor may conclude that he has not examined a sufficient portion of the restated prior year's financial statements to serve as principal auditor, or it may not be possible, or there may be no reason for the auditor to satisfy himself regarding the restated financial statements. AU Sections 543.16-17 provide for a form of reporting wherein the auditor does not assume responsibility for the work of other auditors, nor for expressing an opinion on the restated financial statements taken as a whole. Instead, the auditor may express an opinion on the current year financial statements taken as a whole and an opinion only as to the proper combination of the restated financial statements of the prior year. In order to report this way the auditor must test the clerical accuracy of the restatement and the methods of combination for conformity with generally accepted accounting principles, including intercompany eliminations, combining adjustments and reclassifications, adjustments to make the accounting policies of the entities consistent, and the manner and extent of presentation of required disclosures.

After the satisfactory carrying out of such procedures, AU Section 543.16 provides that a paragraph similar to the following may follow the standard audit report for the current year:

> We previously examined and reported on the consolidated statements of income and retained earnings and changes in financial position of XYZ Company and Subsidiaries for the year ended December 31, 19X1, prior to their restatement for the 19X2 pooling-of-interests. The contribution of XYZ Company and Subsidiaries to revenues and net income represented ___ percent and ___ percent of the respective restated totals. Separate financial statements of the other companies included in the 19X1 restated consolidated statements of income and changes in financial position were examined and reported upon separately by other auditors. We also have reviewed, as to compilation, applied procedures to the combination of the accompanying consolidated statements of income and changes in financial position for the year ended December 31, 19X1, after restatement for the 19X2 pooling of interests; in our opinion, such consolidated statements have been properly combined on the basis described in Note A of notes to consolidated financial statements.

Purchase Acquisitions. Following a purchase acquisition, the standard auditor's report will apply, and no reference to consistency is required, since there is no restatement of prior periods. However, consideration should be given to appropriate presentation of the operations of the acquired company prior to the acquisition required in supplemental disclosures where the acquirer is a public company which may have been audited by other accountants, or which may be unaudited.

Audit Reports Where an Acquisition has Occurred After the Balance Sheet Date. AU Sections 9509.21-24 contain guidelines for the auditor in rendering reports where significant subsequent events, such as a business combination, have occurred. In such cases, if a significant business combination has occurred after the completion of fieldwork but before the issuance of the report, the report should be dual dated, or the procedures for review of subsequent events should be extended to the date of the subsequent event and the report should be dated as of that date.

Unaudited pro forma information may be presented in a footnote if the business combination subsequent to the balance sheet date is significant. The note itself regarding the subsequent event should be an audited footnote; the pro forma information may be unaudited.

In reissuing a previously issued report at a later date, an unaudited note may be presented when a significant business combination occurred between the date of issuance of the original auditor's report and reissuance of the auditor's report.

Unaudited Information. AU 509.31 provides that footnotes to financial statements which contain unaudited information, pro forma calculations, or other unaudited information should be identified as unaudited information. If this identification is made, the auditor need not refer to the information in his report.

PLANNING AND ARRANGEMENTS WITH CLIENTS

In view of the many sensitive considerations the CPA faces when planning an acquisition engagement, it is important that a specific program of procedures be prepared for the engagement. The written program of procedures will present a basis for discussion with the client of the specific scope of the procedures to be performed, and what can be expected from the procedures.

Because of the inherently sensitive nature of work performed by a CPA in a merger or acquisition situation, and the variety of levels of procedures and responsibility that can be present, the CPA should issue an engagement letter, in addition to discussing the procedures and role to be assumed. The letter should clearly communicate the scope of the engagement to prevent any subsequent misunderstandings, and in addition, may describe the form of report that will be furnished. The engagement letter is also a good opportunity to communicate the CPA's understanding of any additional role he or she may take in providing advice to the client in the acquisition negotiations, and the limitations of responsibility with respect to that role.

The reduction in the possibility of a misunderstanding of the CPA's role, which should be achieved by the engagement letter, can reduce the risk of the CPA being subjected to legal liability from an acquisition engagement. In especially difficult or sensitive situations, the CPA should consider reviewing a draft of his or her engagement letter for work to be performed in connection with a merger or acquisition with his attorney.

APPENDIX 9-1: PROGRAM FOR AUDITING PURCHASE METHOD ACCOUNTING

GENERAL

1. Review the purchase agreement, contracts assumed or related to the acquisition (leases, employment agreement, etc.) for items of accounting significance. Be alert for any commitments that appear to be at other than current market rates, or do not provide future benefits to the client commensurate with the amounts of commitments.

2. Identify any contingent consideration and ensure such are properly reflected in the acquisition accounting.

3. Ascertain whether acquisition adjustments will be recorded in consolidation entries or pushed down into the accounts of the acquired company, and plan audit procedures accordingly.

4. Review subsequent results of operations of the acquired company for information having an impact on the acquisition accounting (e.g., disposal of an acquired asset at a loss).

INDEPENDENT APPRAISALS

1. Review the professional qualifications of the appraiser. Not all of the following procedures may be required where the appraiser has strong professional qualifications and is known to use sound procedures.
2. Ascertain that the basis upon which fair value is being determined is in conformity with the requirements of APB Opinion No. 16.
3. Review the appraiser's procedures to ensure all acquired assets will be included in the appraisal and that conversions and summarizations will be accurately performed.
4. Observe the appraiser while in the process of carrying out the appraisal to ensure established procedures are followed.
5. Verify information and data provided to the appraiser by the client company.
6. Review the appraisal report and verify for accuracy and theoretical correctness.

COMPUTING COST AND ALLOCATION

1. Review the list of items included in total acquisition cost and ascertain such items are properly includable in cost under APB Opinion No. 16.
2. Examine evidence for significant elements of cost, considering propriety of approach where subjective valuation considerations are present (e.g., stock given in consideration for purchase where a market price for the stock is not readily available).
3. Compare the book and tax bases of individual assets acquired and liabilities assumed, and ascertain that the tax effects of any differences in basis have been properly reflected in the carrying values established for book purposes.
4. Identify any contingencies and ascertain possible effects on acquisition accounting (e.g., possible need for future restatement for contingency resolution within one year in certain cases, or realization of a net operating loss carry-forward).

5. Ensure imputation of premium or discount has been performed wherever required.

TAX MATTERS

1. Determine if the structure of the transaction is consistent with the tax treatment recognized by the client.
2. Review propriety of items allocated to cost for tax purposes and consider whether any expenses incurred in connection with the acquisition that the client intends to deduct currently should be capitalized.
3. Where the acquisition is a taxable transaction, review the allocation of cost to individual assets and liabilities for tax purposes.

DISCLOSURES AND AUDIT REPORT

1. Review and verify data for disclosure of pro forma results prior to acquisition.
2. Where periods prior to acquisition have been audited by other accountants, or not subjected to complete audits, consider ramification on accountant's report as to whether opinion should make reference to audits by other accountants, whether any should be marked unaudited, or whether any data is so unreliable that no disclosure should be made because such could be misleading.
3. Review the financial statements to ensure the following required disclosures are made (information related to more than one relatively insignificant acquisition may be aggregated):
    a. Name and brief description of acquired company.
    b. Cost, number of shares issued or issuable, and amount assigned to stock.
    c. Period for which results of operations are included in income statement.
    d. Contingent payments, options, or commitments with proposed accounting teatment.

10

SECURITIES AND EXCHANGE COMMISSION AND OTHER REGULATORY REQUIREMENTS

Various regulatory agencies may have jurisdiction over acquisitions or other forms of business combinations, depending upon the specifics of the transaction. These areas should be carefully considered by the financial professional working on an acquisition. The interpretation of the applicability of laws and regulatory bodies will require legal counsel.

For public companies, registration statements may be required to be filed with the Securities and Exchange Commission (SEC) when securities are to be issued or exchanged in a business combination and a proxy statement must be prepared in cases where a solicitation is required from the shareholders of the company to vote on the possible acquisition or merger. Even where no securities are exchanged, a Form 8-K Current Report may be required.

Where public shares are issued or issuable in an acquisition or merger, a stock listing application must be filed with the stock exchange on which the company is listed.

Another important SEC requirement in the acquisition area relates to the requirement to make certain filings when a tender offer is made to acquire shares of another company.

If certain conditions are met, contemplated mergers and acquisitions must be reported to the Federal Trade Commission and the U.S.

Department of Justice prior to consummation, and the parties must wait at least 30 days after reporting before completing the transaction to allow these bodies to consider the antitrust implications of the transaction.

This chapter is intended to provide a general awareness of the major considerations in these areas, but is by no means a complete treatment, nor a complete presentation of the form or content of the various filings referred to.

SECURITIES LAW REQUIREMENTS

Various filings can be required with the SEC when a public company engages in an acquisition or other business combination.

The Securities Act of 1933 provides for use of the following forms when securities are offered in an "exchange offer":

Form S-1:   The general registration statement used when no other form is prescribed

Form S-7:   May be used where securities are being offered in exchange for assets or securities of another company.

Form S-14: May be used in certain cases when securities are to be issued in circumstances set forth in Rule 145(a) of the 1933 Act in a merger or acquisition and where a proxy statement is also used.

Form S-15: An optional form used for certain business combinations where the relative size of the acquired company and the total purchase price are "nonmaterial" to the acquirer, based on income, asset and equity tests contained in the Form S-15 instructions.

If a stockholder vote is required for approval of the acquisition or merger, proxies must be solicited by the registrant (see the following section on proxy statements). Form S-14 is organized to use the proxy statement as the prospectus portion of the registration statement, thereby eliminating the duplication of disclosures made in both the proxy statement and the registration statement.

The SEC has proposed a new registration statement, Form S-4, that may be used when registering securities associated with business combinations. Form S-4 would replace Forms S-14 and S-15 and extend the principle of the integrated disclosure system to business combinations. Form S-4 will reduce the distinction between cash transactions and exchange offers by expediting exchange offers.

The Securities Exchange Act of 1934, requires that a Form 8-K Current Report be filed with the SEC when a significant acquisition or divestiture has been consummated.

In some circumstances, the management of the target company may not cooperate by supplying all of the necessary information for the preparation of the registration statement. In this case, only information about the offeree company that is available from public sources, such as annual reports to stockholders and SEC reports, need be included in the registration statement. This is covered by the Securities Act of 1933, Section 7, Rule 409, which states:

Information required need be given only insofar as it is known or reasonably available to the registrant. If any required information is unknown and not reasonably available to the registrant, either because the obtaining thereof would involve unreasonable effort or expense, or because it rests peculiarly within the knowledge of another person not affiliated with the registrant, the information may be omitted, subject to the following conditions:

1. The registrant shall give such information on the subject as it possesses or can acquire without unreasonable effort or expense, together with the sources thereof.

2. The registrant shall include a statement either showing that unreasonable effort or expense would be involved or indicating the absence of any affiliation with the person within whose knowledge the information rests and stating the result of a request made to such person for the information.

Proxy Statements

SEC regulations do not require the solicitation of proxies, but do govern procedures for solicitation of proxies through Regulation 14A, promulgated by the 1934 Act. This regulation sets forth SEC requirements for form and content if it is determined that a proxy is required. A proxy can be required by:

1. Regulations of the stock exchange on which the company's shares are listed.
2. Statutory provisions of the jurisdiction under which a corporation is organized.
3. The company's bylaws.
4. Provisions contained in a company's certificate of incorporation or similar controlling instruments.

Both the New York Stock Exchange and the American Stock Exchange require that stockholder approval be obtained through a proxy solicitation if a business is acquired from an "insider" or the number of shares to be issued in the acquisition or the market value thereof would exceed 20% of the respective amounts related to presently outstanding shares.

Even though companies may not be required to obtain stockholder approval for a merger or acquisition because of stock exchange regulation, requirements of state law, or provisions of a corporate charter, they sometimes obtain such approval to avoid potential legal difficulties and criticism in the future.

In all cases, competent legal counsel should be consulted for a determination of whether a proxy statement is required.

When filing a proxy statement and proxy with the SEC, five preliminary copies must be filed at least 10 days before the material is delivered to stockholders. The SEC has the right to comment on the preliminary proxy statement, but it must notify the issuer that it will have comments within the 10-day period. If the issuer is not notified by the SEC within the 10-day period that it will have comments, the issuer may mail its proxy material to stockholders. At the same time that the definitive proxy is distributed, eight copies of the proxy statement must be sent to the SEC and at least three copies to stock exchanges on which the issuer is listed. The New York Stock Exchange requires four definitive copies and recommends that the preliminary information also be submitted.

Information required in a proxy statement concerning acquisitions and mergers is governed by Item 14 of Regulation 14A, "Mergers,

Consolidations, Acquisitions and Similar Matters." The following out-lines information required by Item 14 as to any companies involved in the merger or acquisition:

1. A brief description of the plan for merger, consolidation, or acqui-sition.
2. A brief description of the business, including the nature of the prod-ucts or services, methods of production and markets.
3. A brief description of the plants and other physical properties.
4. A statement as to dividend arrearages or defaults in principal or interest on outstanding securities.
5. A capitalization table for each company and a pro forma capitali-zation.
6. Selected financial information for five years including per share data for earnings, dividends and net assets for each company and on a pro forma basis.
7. A combined pro forma summary of earnings for five years indicating the aggregate and per share earnings, and the pro forma book value per share at the end of the latest period.
8. Financial information relating to the issuer's industry segments.
9. A Management's Discussion and Analysis of Financial Condition and Results of Operations as required by Item 11 of Regulation S-K.

When the acquiring company cannot obtain all the necessary infor-mation from the target company to be included in the proxy statement, the acquiring company may rely on Rule 409. However, copies of correspondence between the two companies evidencing the request for and the refusal to furnish the financial statements must be submit-ted to the SEC.

Tender Offers

Special disclosure and distribution of information requirements per-tain to tender offers to acquire shares of public companies if certain conditions are met. The major compliance requirement is the filing with the SEC of a Schedule 14D-1 which is required if the entity making the tender offer would control 5% of the class of security of the target company which is being acquired.

The nature of the entity making the bid (domestic corporation, for-eign corporation, etc.), the specifics of the tender offer, and other factors will impact the nature and extent of financial information which must be furnished. This is clearly an area in which the financial professional should seek competent legal counsel.

Other State and Federal Laws

Sales or exchanges of stock or other securities are regulated by various state and federal laws. Generally, it is illegal to sell or exchange unregistered securities, unless they meet specific exemptions. The burden of proof as to qualifying under the various exemptions lies with the issuer of the security.

Exemptions to the federal laws prohibiting transactions in unregistered securities generally apply to limited sales or exchanges of securities by corporations if:

1.   The company is incorporated or doing business in one state and the security is offered or sold only to residents of that state, or

2.   The issue is a private placement. A private placement is where the offer to acquire securities is made to no more than 35 persons. In addition, the purchaser of securities in a private placement must represent that he or she has purchased the securities for investment and not for secondary distribution.

SEC ACCOUNTING AND FINANCIAL STATEMENT REQUIREMENTS

SEC Accounting Requirements

The SEC generally enforces the provisions of APB Opinions No. 16 and 17. In addition, the SEC has issued interpretations and expanded on the requirements of these opinions in specific areas, especially those concerning pooling of interests accounting.

APB Opinion No. 16 states that all acquisitions of treasury stock during a two-year period prior to the consummation of a business combination would preclude the pooling of interests method from being used unless the "treasury stock acquired (is) for purposes other than business combinations includ(ing) shares for stock option and compensation plans and other recurring distributions . . . "

Accounting Series Release (ASR) No. 146 states the following:

The Commission concludes that treasury shares acquired in the restricted period for recurring distributions should be considered "tainted" unless they are acquired in a systematic pattern of reacquisitions established at least two years before the plan of combination is initiated (or coincidentally with the adoption of a new stock option or compensation plan) and there is reasonable expectation that shares will be issued for such purposes.

If an equal number of shares are sold prior to the date of consummation, however, the Commission believes that the treasury shares were not purchased in contemplation of a business combination. ASR No. 146A states that reacquisition of shares to fulfill contractual obligations or settle outstanding claims does not "taint" shares reacquired.

ASR No. 130 requires that securities received in a combination accounted for as a pooling of interests cannot be sold until financial results covering at least 30 days have been published.

In most circumstances, the SEC believes in the application of the "push-down" basis of accounting for separate financial statements of subsidiaries acquired and recorded by the purchase method. In Staff Accounting Bulletin No. 54, the SEC states that when an entity has become substantially wholly owned, the entire cost of the acquisition should be "pushed down" to the subsidiary's financial statements, thereby creating a new basis of accounting for the purchased assets and liabilities. However, if the subsidiary had publicly held debt or preferred stock that had been registered by the SEC, then the application of "push-down" accounting is not required.

Financial Statement Requirements

Historical Financial Statements Required for Registrations. For filings related to business combinations, Form S-1, Form S-7, and proxy statements must include the financial statements required by Regulation S-X and the supplementary financial information requirements of Item 12 of Regulation S-K. Depending upon the date of the filing of Form S-1, Form S-7, and proxy statement, interim financial statements may also be required.

Regulation S-X requires filing of audited balance sheets as of the end of each of the two most recent fiscal years, and audited statements of income and changes in financial position for each of the three fiscal years preceding the date of the most recent audited balance sheet.

Interim financial statements that are required by Regulation S-X may be unaudited. Information on other stockholders' equity must be given in a separate statement or in a note for the same periods as required for statements of income (and audited to the same extent). Appropriate notes to financial statements must be presented for the same periods, and audited to the same extent as the financial statements.

Form S-14 requires the financial statements that would be required for an initial registration of securities of each company participating in a business combination. The Form S-14 prospectus normally consists of the proxy statement combined with supplemental pages.

Form S-15 is an abbreviated prospectus that is filed together with a copy of the registrant's latest annual report to shareholders, and a copy of the latest annual report of the acquiree. The financial statements in the annual report may be incorporated by reference.

Financial statements of an acquiree are required in Form 8-K if the acquiree would constitute a significant subsidiary under the SEC rules, or if the acquiree's net book value (or price paid by the acquirer), total assets, or pretax income from continuing operations exceeds 10% of the respective amounts of the acquirer and its consolidated subsidiaries for the latest fiscal year. The specific periods for which statements must be filed vary depending on additional measurements of significance that are made after the above initial tests.

Generally, the financial statements required include a balance sheet as of a date reasonably close to the acquisition date and statements of income and of changes in financial position for each of the last three fiscal years. The balance sheet does not need to be audited. But if it is unaudited, then an audited balance sheet as of the close of the preceding fiscal year and unaudited statements of income and changes in financial condition for the period between the audited balance sheet and the unaudited balance sheet must be included. The registrant may omit, with written approval from the SEC, one or more of the financial statements if they are not reasonably available.

The financial statements required by Regulation S-X should be certified to the extent practicable for both the acquirer and the company being acquired. The certification of financial statements is governed by Article 2 of Regulation S-X. Any relief from the certification requirements of financial statements must be obtained by informal written request to the SEC. The Securities Act of 1933 Release No. 4950 states:

> When a representation is made that certification of financial statements of acquired companies for a full three-year period cannot be obtained and compelling and satisfactory evidence in support of such representation is furnished, the Commission considers the relationship of the following items of the acquired companies to those of the registrant (on a consolidated basis without inclusion of such companies) in determining whether relief from the three-year certification requirement should be granted:
>
> 1. gross sales and operating revenues;
> 2. net income;
> 3. total assets;
> 4. total stockholder equity; and
> 5. total purchase price compared to total assets of registrant.

The above items are evaluated as follows:

A. If none of the items exceed 10 percent, certified statements will not be required;

B. If any of the items exceed 10 percent but none exceed 25 percent, certification of the balance sheet and the income statement for not less than six months will be required;

C. If any of the items exceed 25 percent but none exceed 45 percent, certification of the balance sheet and the income statement for at least twelve months will be required;

D. If any of the items exceed 45 percent, certification of the balance sheet and the income statement for three years will be required, consistent with similar requirements as to the registrant.

Stock Exchange Requirements. There are some requirements in the financial statement area that are set forth by the individual stock exchanges.

If securities are to be issued in connection with an acquisition and listed on the New York or American Stock Exchange, the latest available balance sheet and related statements of income, changes in financial position, and retained earnings (including supplemental interim statements) are required to be audited by independent accountants or certified by the company's principal accounting officer.

Another such requirement is that if shares are to be issued in a pooling and listed on the New York Stock Exchange, an independent accountant's letter is required, stating that the use of the pooling of interests method for the transaction is in compliance with APB Opinion No. 16.

Historical Financial Statements of Acquirees Required in Ongoing Registrations. Separate financial statements or summarized financial data of an acquired entity may be required in ongoing periodic registrations filed with the SEC, such as the Form 10-K Annual Report. These will be required where the acquired entity is an unconsolidated subsidiary or a 50% or less owned entity accounted for by the equity method (as in a corporate joint venture), which meets the requirements of the SEC significant subsidiary tests.

The significant subsidiary tests compare the assets and income of the unconsolidated entity with those of the registrant, and may require separate financial statements or disclosure of summarized financial data, depending on the results of a secondary level of testing.

Significant subsidiary as defined by Regulation S-X is a subsidiary that meets one or more of three tests—two asset tests and an income test. The following outlines these tests:

1. The registrant's and its other subsidiaries' investments in and advances to the subsidiary exceed 10% of the registrant's consolidated total assets as of the end of the most recently completed fiscal year. (If a business combination has been or is to be accounted for as a pooling of interests, this test is also met when the number of common shares exchanged by the registrant exceeds 10% of its total outstanding common shares at the date the combination is initiated.)

2. The registrant's and its other subsidiaries' proportionate share of the total assets (after intercompany eliminations) of the subsidiary exceeds 10% of the registrant's consolidated total assets as of the end of the most recently completed fiscal year.

3. The registrant's and its other subsidiaries' equity in income from continuing operations before income taxes, extraordinary items, and cumulative effect of a change in accounting principle of the subsidiary exceeds 10% of such income of the regis-

trant on a consolidated basis for the most recently completed fiscal year.

Pro Forma Financial Statements. Pro forma financial statements are required in SEC registration statements and proxy statements where business combinations have occurred, are in progress or probable, or proposed by the acquirer for shareholder approval where the acquiree or proposed acquiree constitutes a significant subsidiary under Rule 1-02 of Regulation S-X. Pro forma financial statements show the results of operations and financial position on an "as if" basis, which assumes the separate entities had always been combined.

In the case of an SEC registration presenting financial statements, including a period for which a purchase method acquisition was made, the pro forma financial statements will present an historical "as if" combining of the previously separate entities prior to the date of the business combination. Where a combination accounted for as a pooling has already occurred, pro forma financial statements are not necessary, because the historical financial statements will have been restated.

In the case of proxies and SEC registration statements involving a proposed acquisition, the pro forma financial statements will present an "as if" combined presentation of the separate financial statements of the entities, even though the combination has not yet occurred.

When pro forma statements are prepared for a registration statement concerning a proposed acquisition, sometimes several alternative sets of pro forma statements are needed to show the effects of the combination based upon various levels of acceptance from an "exchange offer."

SEC Financial Reporting Release (SECFRR) No. 2 sets forth the requirements for preparing and presenting pro forma financial statements. SECFRR No. 2 also includes a provision whereby a financial forecast may be substituted for certain pro forma financial statements.

ANTITRUST REGULATIONS

The Hart-Scott-Rodino Antitrust Improvement Act of 1976 requires that certain mergers and acquisitions be reported to the Federal Trade

Commission (FTC) and the U.S. Department of Justice prior to consummation. The parties involved must wait at least 30 days before completing the acquisition to allow the governmental agencies time to consider the antitrust implications of the proposed transaction. Premerger notification is made on "Notification and Report Form for Certain Mergers and Acquisitions", and must be made when:

1. Either of the acquiring or acquired companies is involved in commerce or in any activity affecting commerce;
2. The annual net sales or total assets of one company are $10 million or more and of the other company are $100 million or more; and
3. The acquiring company would gain one of the following:
    a. 15% or more of the voting securities or assets of the acquired company or more than $15 million worth of both the assets and the voting securities of the acquired company;
    b. 15% or more of the issuer's outstanding voting securities which are valued in excess of $15 million;
    c. 25% of the issuer's outstanding voting securities; or
    d. 50% of the issuer's outstanding voting securities.

Additional notifications must be filed when 15%, 25%, and 50% of the outstanding voting securities of an issuer are about to be acquired. Smaller acquisitions are exempt if the acquiring company will not hold voting securities and assets aggregating more than $15 million.

Information included in the Premerger Notification Form applies only to operations conducted within the United States, including its commonwealths, territories, possessions, and the District of Columbia. Information requested includes a description of the acquisition, assets to be acquired, voting securities to be acquired, and dollar revenues by Standard Industrial Classification (SIC) Code for 1977 and the most recent year. The primary objective of the FTC is to determine if the acquisition or merger violates any antitrust laws.

If the FTC believes the merger or acquisition violates antitrust laws, the Commission must file for an injunction requiring the parties to "cease and desist" from consummation of the merger or acquisition. The FTC itself does not have the power to stop the merger or acquisition. Only a court of law can render a decision on whether or not antitrust laws would be violated.

Appendix 10-1: Significant SEC and Regulatory Pronouncements

THE SECURITIES EXCHANGE ACT OF 1933

Rule 409	Exemption from Requirements for Information Unknown or Not Reasonably Available
Rule 145	Mergers and Acquisitions
Release 4950	Certified Financial Statements of Companies Acquired or to be Acquired

THE SECURITIES EXCHANGE ACT OF 1934

Regulation 14A	Solicitation of Proxies
Schedule 14A	Information Required in Proxy Statements
Schedule 14B	Information Required in Statements

SEC ACCOUNTING SERIES RELEASES (ASR'S)

No.	Date	Title
130	9/29/72	Pooling-of-Interests Accounting
135	1/ 5/73	Revised Guidelines for the Application of ASR No. 130
146	8/24/73	Effect of Treasury Stock Transactions on Accounting for Business Combinations
146-A	4/11/74	Statement of Policy and Interpretations in Regard to ASR No. 146

APPENDIX A

SAMPLE OF LETTER OF INTENT

July 1, 19xx

Mr. Seller, President
Company B

Dear Mr. Seller:

This letter is to commit to writing the terms of a proposed transaction for the sale of all of the common stock of Company B to Company A which we have discussed and which Company A and Company B intend to enter into. In our discussions, we arrived at the following as the major terms of the transaction:

1. On November 15, 19xx (the "Closing Date"), Company A will purchase all the outstanding common stock of Company B from Mr. Seller, its sole shareholder for a total price of $100,000. Mr. Seller shall agree to indemnify Company A and hold it harmless from any liabilities or claims related to the business of Company B not included on the balance sheet of Company B as of the Closing Date.

2. At the closing, Company A will deliver to Mr. Seller, its certified check for $100,000, and Mr. Seller will convey to Company A, free of any and all liens and encumbrances, all the outstanding common stock of Company B.

3. Prior to or concurrent with the drafting of a formal agreement with respect to this transaction, Company A or its representatives may at reasonable times visit the premises of Company B and have full access to all its books and records for the purpose of examination. If, as a result of any information derived from these examinations, Company A believes that proceeding with this transaction is not in the best interest of Company A, then Company A shall so inform Mr. Seller in writing, and all activities with respect to this proposed transaction shall terminate.

4. Company A shall endeavor to carry out the investigations referred to in paragraph 3 during the months of August and September, 19xx. Counsel for Company A shall draft a proposed Stock Purchase Agreement for submission to Company B and its counsel by October 1, 19xx. The Stock Purchase Agreement shall include such terms, conditions, warranties, and representations as the parties may reasonably request. Company A and Mr. Seller will plan to execute the Stock Purchase Agreement on or about November 1, 19xx, and the Closing Date will be planned for November 15, 19xx.

While the above correctly sets forth the understandings and intents of Company A and Mr. Seller, this Letter of Intent is not to be construed as a legally binding instrument in any way. It is requested that Mr. Seller evidence the correctness of this understanding by signing in the space provided below.

Sincerely,
COMPANY A

by _____
    Vice President

The above correctly reflects my understanding and intent.

_____
Mr. Seller

_____
Date

SAMPLE CONTRACT—STOCK PURCHASE AGREEMENT

STOCK PURCHASE AGREEMENT made as of November 1, 19XX, by and among COMPANY A, a (name of state) corporation (hereinafter referred to as "Buyer"), and Mr. Seller, (hereinafter referred to as "Stockholder"), the owner of all of the outstanding capital stock of COMPANY B, a corporation organized and existing under the laws of the State of (name of state) (hereinafter called the "Corporation," or the "Company"),

WITNESSETH:

WHEREAS, upon and subject to the terms and conditions hereinafter set forth, the Stockholder desires to sell to Buyer and Buyer desires to purchase from Stockholder all of the issued and outstanding shares of stock of the Company,

NOW, THEREFORE, the parties hereto agree as follows:

Section 1. Terms of Transaction

Upon the terms and subject to the conditions hereinafter provided, and in reliance upon the representations and warranties contained or provided for herein, it is mutually agreed as follows:

1.1. *Sale and Transfer of Shares of the Company.* At Closing, Stockholder will sell, assign, and transfer to Buyer 100 shares of common stock of the Company, such shares to consitute all of the outstanding stock of the Company.

1.2. At any time or from time to time after the Closing, Stockholder shall execute and deliver to Buyer such other instruments and take such other action as Buyer may reasonably require to more effectively vest title to the shares of the Company being sold hereunder in Buyer and, to the full extent permitted by law, to put Buyer in actual possession and operating control of the Company, its assets, properties, business, and goodwill, together with all of the Company's contracts and commitments and all books, records, and other data relating to its assets, business, and operations, including all corporate minutes and stock record books and other corporate records.

1.3. *Purchase Price for Shares of the Company.* Buyer will pay to the Stockholder, as and for the purchase price all of the issued and outstanding shares of the Company the aggregate amount of One Hundred Thousand Dollars ($100,000.00) by certified check at closing.

Section 2. Closing

Consummation of the transactions contemplated by Section 1 shall be effected at 7:00 P.M. on November 15, 19XX, or as soon thereafter as practicable after all of the conditions herein have been satisfied. The Closing shall be held at (address), or at such other place as the parties may agree. The time and date of Closing is herein called the "Closing Date" or "Closing."

Section 3. Representations and Warranties by Stockholder

Stockholder represents and warrants to Buyer that:

3.1. *Ownership and Validity of Shares of the Company.* Stockholder is the owner, free and clear of any options, liens, claims, charges, or other encumbrances, of all of the outstanding shares of capital stock of the Company, as set forth on Exhibit A hereto; such shares are validly issued, fully paid, and nonassessable; Stockholder has full power and authority to make and enter into this Agreement and to transfer good and valid title to such shares free and clear of any options, liens, claims, charges, or other encumbrances; and on consummation of the transactions contemplated by this Agreement in accordance with the terms hereof Buyer will acquire valid and marketable title to the shares being sold hereby free and clear of any options, liens, claims, charges, or other encumbrances.

3.2.   *Capitalization of the Company.* The entire authorized and issued and outstanding stock of the Company is as set forth on Exhibit A hereto. There are no outstanding obligations, options, or rights entitling others to acquire shares of stock of any class of the Company or any outstanding securities or other instruments convertible into shares of stock of any class of the Company.

3.3.   *Organization and Qualification of the Company.* The Company is duly organized, validly existing, and in good standing under the laws of the jurisdiction of its incorporation, has full power to own all of its properties and to carry on its business as it is now being conducted, and is duly qualified to do business and is in good standing in all jurisdictions where its ownership of property or the conduct of its business requires it to be so qualified.

3.4.   *No Violation of Other Instruments.* The execution and delivery of this Agreement do not, and the consummation of the transactions contemplated hereby will not (a) violate any provision of the Articles of Incorporation or Bylaws of the Company, (b) violate any provision of, or result in the termination of, or the acceleration of, any obligation under any mortgage, lien, lease, franchise, license, permit, agreement, instrument, order, arbitration award, judgment, or decree to which the Company or Stockholder is a party or by which the Company or Stockholder is bound, or (c) violate or conflict with any other restriction of any kind or character to which the Company or Stockholder is subject.

3.5.   *Outstanding Interests.* There are no outstanding warrants, options, or other rights to subscribe for or purchase from the Company, or other plans, contracts, or commitments providing for the issuance of, or the granting of, rights to acquire (i) any stock or other ownership interest in the Company, or (ii) any securities convertible into or interchangeable for any stock or other ownership interest in the Company or to repurchase, redeem, or otherwise acquire any outstanding shares of stock or other ownership interest in the Company.

3.6. *Financial Statements of the Company.* The financial statements of the Company annexed hereto as Exhibit B (the "Balance Sheet" and "Income Statement") fairly present the financial position of the Company as of the date of the Balance Sheet (the "Balance Sheet Date"), and the results of operations of the Company for the period indicated, and all of said financial statements have been prepared in accordance with generally accepted accounting principles applied on a basis consistent with that of preceding years.

3.7. *Compliance with Laws.* The Company is not in violation of any law, regulation, or ordinance (including, without limitation, laws, regulations, or ordinances relating to zoning, protection of the environment, municipal or county planning, or similar matters) relating to its properties or its business which could have a material adverse effect upon the conduct of its business. There are no known developments affecting any of such properties pending or threatened which might curtail the present or future use of such property for the purpose for which it is used or which could have a material adverse effect upon the business of the Company.

3.8. *Events Since the Balance Sheet Date.* There has not been since the Balance Sheet Date and will not be between the date hereof and Closing:

(a) any change in the business, results of operations, assets, financial condition or the manner of conducting the business of the Company, which has or may be reasonably expected to have a material adverse effect on such business, results of operations, assets, or financial condition;

(b) any damage, destruction, or loss (whether or not covered by insurance) which has or may reasonably be expected to have a material adverse effect upon any material asset or the business or operations of the Company;

(c) any direct or indirect redemption or other acquisition by the Company of any shares of stock of the Company of any class, or any declaration, setting aside or payment of any dividend or other distribution in respect of stock of the Company of any class;

(d) any increase in the compensation payable or to become payable by the Company to any of its officers, employees, or agents;

(e) any option to purchase, or other right to acquire, stock of any class of the Company granted by the Company to any person;

(f) any employment, bonus, or deferred compensation agreement entered into between the Company and any of its directors, officers, or other employees or consultants;

(g) any issuance of shares of stock of any class by the Company;

(h) any entering into, amendment, or termination by the Company of any material contract, agreement, franchise, permit, or license;

(i) any indebtedness incurred by the Company for borrowed money or any commitment to borrow money entered into by the Company or any guarantee given by the Company;

(j) any amendment of the Articles of Incorporation of the Company.

3.9. *Undisclosed Liabilities.* At Closing Date there will be no liabilities of the Company of any kind whatsoever, whether or not accrued and whether or not contingent or absolute, determined or determinable, including, without limitation, any tax liabilities due or to become due, whether incurred in respect of or measured by income for any period prior to the Balance Sheet Date, and no existing condition, situation, or set of circumstances which could reasonably result in such a liability, other than liabilities shown on the Balance Sheet and those incurred in the ordinary course of business since the Balance Sheet Date, none of which has had or may reasonably be expected to have a material adverse effect on the business of the Company.

3.10. *Proceedings.* There are no private or governmental proceedings against the Company pending or to the knowledge of Stockholder threatened, which if determined adversely to the Company could have a material adverse effect on the business of the Company or which involve a potential material liability of the Company, nor are there any judgments, decrees, or orders against the Company enjoining it in respect of, or the effect of which is to prohibit, restrict, or affect any business practice or the acquisition of any property or the conduct of business in any area.

3.11. *Condition of Assets.* All machinery, equipment, and other facilities that are presently used in connection with the operation of the business of the Company are presently owned or leased by the

Company, are in good operating condition and repair, reasonable wear and tear excepted, and are adequate and sufficient for all operations presently conducted by the Company.

3.12. *Books and Records.* The books of account of the Company have been regularly kept and maintained, and fairly reflect all of the transactions of the Company to which it is a party or by which its properties are bound. The Company has filed all reports required by law or regulation to be filed and has fully paid, or accrued on its books of account, all duties and charges due or assessed against it.

3.13. *Contracts.* Except as set forth in Exhibit D, the Company is not a party to or subject to:

(a)   any employment contract or agreement, oral or written, with any officer, consultant, director, or employee;

(b)   any plan or contract or agreement, oral or written providing for bonuses, pensions, options, deferred compensation, retirement payments, profit sharing, or the like.

(c)   any contract or agreement with any labor union;

(d)   any lease of machinery, equipment, or other personal property involving payment of annual rentals;

(e)   any contract or agreement for the purchase of any materials or supplies;

(f)   any contract for the purchase of equipment or any construction or other agreement not otherwise listed in Exhibit D;

(g)   any instrument evidencing or related to indebtedness for borrowed money, or pursuant to which the Company is obligated or entitled to borrow money, or any instrument of guarantee;

(h)   any license or franchise agreement either as licensor or licensee or as franchisor or franchisee or any permit relating to the conduct of its business;

(i)   any joint venture contract or arrangement or any other agreement involving a sharing of profits;

(j)   any contract or agreement for the sale or lease of its products or the furnishing of its services or any sales agency, broker, distribution or similar contract, other than contracts made in the ordinary course of business on standard forms (copies of which standard forms are attached as a part of Exhibit D);

(k)   any contract containing covenants limiting the freedom of the Company to compete in any line of business or with any person;

(l)   any contract or agreement for or relating to the purchase or acquisition by merger or otherwise of the business, assets, or shares of any other corporation or of any partnership or sole proprietorship, which imposes continuing obligations on, or grants continuing rights or benefits to, the Company regardless of whether the purchase or acquisition has been consummated.

3.14. *Tax Returns.*   The Company has filed all required Federal, state and local tax returns, and is current with respect to payments of all income, franchise, property, sales, payroll or other taxes. The accruals for taxes in the Balance Sheet are adequate for all taxes payable as of the Balance Sheet Date, whether disputed or undisputed. The Company's Federal income tax returns have been audited by the Internal Revenue Service through (date). Copies of the Company's Federal income tax returns for the last 3 years are attached to this Agreement as Exhibit C.

3.15. *Important Customers and Suppliers.*   Annexed hereto as Exhibit E is a complete and accurate list of the names and addresses of the ten largest suppliers of products and services to the Company during its last three fiscal years, with a description of the existing contractual agreements, if any, for continued supply from each such firm.

Section 4.   Investigation and Indemnity

Prior to the Closing Date, Buyer may, directly or through its representatives, make such investigation of the assets, business, and records, including tax returns, of the Company (including, without limitation, investigation of titles to property and the condition of property and equipment, and the confirmation of cash, inventories, accounts receivable, and liabilities) as Buyer deems necessary or advisable, but such investigation shall not affect the representations and warranties of Stockholder contained or provided for herein or Buyer's rights to terminate this Agreement as provided in this Section 4 and in Section 9. Buyer and its representatives shall have, at reasonable times after the date of execution hereof, full access to the premises and to all the books and records of the Company, and the officers of the Company will furnish to Buyer such financial and operating data and other information with respect to the business and properties of the Company as Buyer shall from time to time reasonably request. As soon as practicable and in any event within 30 days after the date of this Agreement, Buyer shall give Stockholder notice if, on the basis of any material information contained in any of the Exhibits annexed hereto or of any material information obtained during the course of its investigation pursuant to this Section 4, it has decided that it wishes to terminate this Agreement. Such notice shall specify the information contained in such Exhibits or obtained during such investigation which is the basis for such decision. Stockholder shall have 10 days after the receipt of such notice to review with Buyer such information, and if Buyer does not withdraw such notice within said 10-day period, then all further obligations of Buyer to Stockholder and of Stockholder to Buyer shall terminate, subject, however, to the obligations of Buyer under Section 9.3. If Buyer does not advise Stockholder within such 30-day period that it wishes to terminate this Agreement, Buyer shall be deemed to have been satisfied with the information relating to the Company contained in such Exhibits or obtained during the course of its investigation.

Notwithstanding any investigation of the business and assets of the Company made by or on behalf of Buyer prior to the Closing Date, Stockholder agrees to indemnify Buyer and hold it harmless from and against all damages, losses and expenses caused by or arising out of (a) any breach of warranty or inaccurate or erroneous representation of Stockholder contained herein or in any Exhibit hereto or certificate delivered pursuant hereto or (b) any liabilities of the Company (other than liabilities shown on the Balance Sheet annexed hereto as part of Exhibit B and liabilities permitted hereunder to be incurred subsequent to the Balance Sheet Date in the ordinary course of the Company's business).

Section 5. Covenants of Stockholder

Stockholder hereby covenants and agrees that (except as herein otherwise specifically provided) between the date hereof and Closing:

5.1. The business of the Company will be operated in the ordinary course consistent with past practice.

5.2. No changes shall be made in the Certificate of Articles of Incorporation or Bylaws of the Company.

5.3. No stock of the Company shall be issued or sold by the Company and that no plan, contracts, or commitments providing for the issuance of, or the granting of, rights to acquire any capital stock or other ownership interest in the Company, and that no securities convertible into or interchangeable for any stock or other ownership interest in the Company will be granted, issued, or entered into by the Company and no shares of stock of the Company shall be redeemed, purchased, or otherwise acquired by the Company for any consideration.

5.4. No guarantees shall be made by the Company and no borrowing or mortgaging or pledging of any of the properties or assets of the Company shall be made without the prior written consent of Buyer.

5.5. No bonus, stock option, profit sharing, pension, retirement, or other similar arrangement or plan shall be instituted or changed by the Company, and no increase in the compensation payable or to become payable by the Company to any officer, employee, or agent shall be made (except, with respect to employees other than officers or agents, increases granted in the ordinary course of business based upon merit or cost of living), and no bonus, percentage of compensation, or other like benefit shall be accrued to or for the credit of any officer, employee, or agent of the Company, and no bonus, pension, retirement, or similar benefit or arrangement shall be made or agreed to by the Company.

5.6. No change shall be made in the banking arrangements of the Company.

5.7. Stockholder and the Company shall use their best efforts to preserve the Company's business organization. Stockholder and the Company shall use their best efforts to preserve the goodwill of the Company's suppliers.

5.8. The Company will duly comply with the laws applicable to it and to the conduct of its business, the violation of which laws could have an adverse effect upon the financial condition or results of operations of the business to be transferred hereby.

5.9. The Company shall not enter into any agreement with Stockholder (other than this Agreement) without the prior written consent of Buyer.

5.10. To the extent any representation or warranty made under this Agreement shall be or hereafter become untrue or incorrect in any material respect, Stockholder shall immediately cause to be provided to Buyer a written statement setting forth in full detail the substance of the event or facts giving rise to such untrue or incorrect representation or warranty.

Section 6.   Survival of Representations and Warranties and Indemnities

The representations, warranties, and indemnities included or provided herein, or certificate or other document delivered pursuant hereto, shall survive the Closing.

Section 7.   Conditions of Buyer's Obligation to Close

The obligation of Buyer to acquire the stock of the Corporation is subject to the satisfaction on or prior to the Closing of the following conditions:

7.1. *Performance of Acts and Undertakings of Stockholder.* Each of the covenants, acts, and undertakings of Stockholder to be performed or caused to be performed on or before Closing, pursuant to the terms hereof, shall have been duly performed.

7.2. *Continued Accuracy of Representations and Warranties of Stockholders.* The representations and warranties of Stockholder contained in this Agreement shall be true in every material respect on and as of the Closing with the same effect as though such representations and warranties have been made on and as of such date, and Buyer shall have received at the Closing a certificate, dated the Closing Date and executed by Stockholder, containing a representation and warranty of Stockholder to that effect.

7.3. *Approvals from Authorities.* Buyer shall have received, or shall have satisfied itself that it will receive, from all Authorities having any jurisdiction over the business of the Company all approvals of the transactions contemplated hereby in form satisfactory to Buyer, so that the Company may continue to carry on its business as presently conducted after consummation of such transactions, and no such approval (or any license or permit granted to the Company) shall have been withdrawn or suspended.

7.4.   *Consents.* All consents or other parties to the mortgages, notes, leases, franchises, agreements, licenses, and permits of the Company necessary to permit consummation of the transactions contemplated hereby shall have been obtained.

7.5.   *Delivery of Shares of the Corporation.* All of the shares of capital stock of the Company being purchased hereby shall have been delivered to Buyer in accordance with Section 1.1.

7.6.   *Adverse Developments.* There shall be no developments affecting any of the Company's properties pending which might curtail the present or future use of such property for the purposes for which it is used which would have a material adverse affect upon the business of the Company.

Section 8.   Conditions to Stockholder's Obligation to Close

The obligation of Stockholder to transfer to Buyer the shares of capital stock of the Company pursuant to this Agreement is subject to the satisfaction on or prior to the Closing Date of the Following conditions:

8.1.   *Performance of Acts and Undertakings by Buyer.* Each of the undertakings of Buyer to be performed at or before Closing pursuant to the terms hereof shall have been performed.

Section 9.   Termination of Agreement

9.1.   *Grounds for Termination.* In addition to the termination rights provided for in Section 4, this Agreement and the transactions contemplated hereby may be terminated at any time prior to Closing:

(a)   By mutual consent of Buyer and Stockholder;

(b)   by Buyer if: (i) there has been a material misrepresentation or breach of warranty in the representations and warranties of Stockholder set forth herein (or in any certificate delivered pursuant hereto); or (ii) any of the conditions specified in Section 7 hereof have not been satisfied; or (iii) Buyer shall have determined in its sole discretion that the transactions contemplated by this Agreement have become inadvisable or impracticable by reason of the institution or threat by government authorities or by any other person of material litigation or proceedings against the Company or against Stockholder or against Buyer; or (iv) Buyer shall have determined in its sole discretion that the business or assets or financial condition of the Company has been materially and adversely affected, whether by reason of changes, developments or operations in the ordinary course of business or otherwise.

(c)   by Stockholder if any of the conditions specified in Section 8 hereof have not been satisfied.

9.2.   *Effect of Termination—Right to Proceed.* In the event that this Agreement shall be terminated pursuant to Section 4 or Section 9.1, all further obligations of Buyer, except for the obligations of Buyer under Section 9.3, shall be terminated. Nevertheless, anything in this Agreement to the contrary notwithstanding, if any of the conditions specified in Section 7 have not been satisfied, Buyer, in addition to any other rights which may be available to it, shall have the right to proceed with the transactions contemplated hereby, and if any of the conditions specified in Section 8 have not been satisfied, Stockholder, in addition to any other rights which may be available to him, shall have the right to proceed with the transactions contemplated hereby.

9.3.   *Return of Company's Documents in Event of Termination.* In the event of the termination of this Agreement for any reason, Buyer will deliver to the Company all documents, work papers, and other material obtained from the Company relating to the transactions contemplated hereby along with any copies thereof in Buyer's possession, whether obtained before or after the execution hereof, and will take all practicable steps to have any information so obtained kept confidential.

Section 10.   Brokers

Stockholder represents and warrants to Buyer that no broker or finder has been employed by the Company or by Stockholder with respect to this Agreement or the transaction contemplated hereby. Buyer represents and warrants to Stockholder that no broker or finder has been employed by it with respect to this Agreement or the transactions contemplated hereby.

Section 11. Governing Law; Successors and Assigns; Counterparts; Entire Agreement

This Agreement (a) shall be construed under and in accordance with the laws of the State of (name of state), (b) shall be binding upon and shall inure to the benefit of the parties hereto and their respective successors and assigns; (c) embodies the entire Agreement and understanding, and supersedes all prior Agreements and understandings between Stockholder and Buyer relating to the subject matter hereof.

Section 12. Effect of Captions

The captions in this Agreement are included for convenience only and shall not in any way affect interpretation of any of the provisions hereof.

Section 13. Notices

Any notice or other communications required or permitted hereunder shall be sufficiently given if sent by certified or registered mail, postage prepaid, return requested, addressed as follows:

> To Buyer: Company A
>   (Address)
> To Stockholder: Mr. Seller
>   (Address)

or such other addresses as shall be furnished in writing by either party to the other party. Any such notice or communication shall be deemed to have been given as of the date so mailed.

IN WITNESS HEREOF, Buyer and Stockholder have caused this Agreement to be executed all as of the date and year first written above.

> Stockholder: Buyer:
>   Company A
> _____   By: _____
> Mr. Seller   Its: _____

Exhibits

Exhibit A	Capitalization and Stock Outstanding
Exhibit B	Financial Statements
Exhibit C	Federal Income Tax Returns
Exhibit D	Contracts
Exhibit E	Important Customers and Suppliers
Exhibit F	Leases
Exhibit G	Certificate of Incorporation and Bylaws
Exhibit H	Permits and Licenses
Exhibit I	Insurance Policies

SAMPLE CONTRACT—AGREEMENT OF SALE AND PURCHASE OF ASSETS

THIS AGREEMENT made as of November 1, 19XX, by and between Company A, a (name of state) corporation (hereinafter referred to as "Purchaser"), and Company B, a (name of state) corporation (hereinafter sometimes called "Seller").

WITNESSETH:

WHEREAS, Seller desires to sell to Buyer all of the assets of its business (describe business) and Buyer is willing to acquire such assets, all upon and subject to the terms and conditions hereinafter set forth,

NOW, THEREFORE, in consideration of the mutual convenants and agreements herein contained, the parties hereto agree as follows:

1. Sale and Purchase

1.1. *Assets to be Sold to and Purchased by Buyer.* Upon the terms and subject to the conditions set forth in this Agreement, Buyer hereby purchases from Seller, and Seller hereby sells, assigns, conveys, transfers, and delivers to Buyer, as of the date hereof, all the assets and properties (said properties and assets to be purchased being hereinafter called, collectively, the "Purchased Assets"), including, but not limited to the following:

(a)   all of the real estate and leases described on Schedule A hereto, the improvements thereon and easements appurtenant thereto.

(b)   all furniture and fixtures, tools, equipment, and machinery, including the major items of equipment listed on Schedule B hereto.

(c)   all inventories of raw materials, supplies, and finished goods, accounts receivable, and items of prepaid expenses.

(d)   all licenses, certificates of title, documents, and all warranties, service agreements, and such claims against third parties as are reflected on the Closing Balance Sheet (as hereinafter defined) of Seller's business.

Without limiting the generality of the forgoing, the Purchased Assets shall include all assets reflected on the September 30, 19XX financial statements of Seller's Business with only such charges therein as shall have occurred in the ordinary course of Seller's business, or as are provided for in this Agreement, between September 30, 19XX, and the date hereof.

1.2.   *Assignments.* Seller agrees to assign sales orders or other agreements included in the Purchased Assets, to the extent they are material to the business of Seller, and to obtain wherever necessary, the consent or waiver of any other party thereto.

1.3.   *Excluded Liabilities of Seller.* Except as otherwise expressly provided in this Agreement, Buyer does not in any way assume or accept any of Seller's liabilities or obligations except the liabilities reflected on the Closing Balance Sheet of Seller's business. Seller shall hold harmless and indemnify Buyer against all claims, liabilities, costs, and expenses (including reasonable attorney's fees) arising out of or resulting from obligations of the business of Seller not assumed by Buyer and Buyer shall hold harmless and indemnify Seller against all claims, liabilities, costs, and expenses (including reasonable attorney's fees) arising out of or resulting from the obligations of Seller's business assumed by Buyer hereunder or the business operations of the Business from and after the date hereof.

2.   Consideration for the Purchased Assets

2.1.   *Payment by Buyer* Buyer hereby delivers to Seller its certified check in the amount of $650,000.

2.2.   Seller shall prepare a balance sheet of the business as of the date hereof (the "Closing Balance Sheet") and shall afford representatives of Buyer the opportunity to observe the taking of inventory in connection therewith. Said inventory shall be valued at the lower of cost or market, taking into account obsolete items. The Closing Balance Sheet shall be prepared in accordance with generally accepted accounting principles on a basis consistent with prior periods and consistent with Seller's audited financial statements. Not later than December 15, 19XX, the Closing Balance Sheet shall be furnished to Buyer and Buyer shall pay to Seller (by certified check) not later than 20 business days after receipt of the Closing Balance Sheet the amount (if any) by which the net book value of Seller's Business as reflected on the Closing Balance Sheet is in excess of $650,000. Should the net book value of Seller's business as determined on the Closing Balance Sheet be less than $650,000, Seller shall, on the date of its delivery to Buyer of the Closing Balance Sheet, pay to Buyer, by Seller's certified check, the amount by which net book value is less than $650,000.

2.3.   *Settlement of Disputes.*   If Buyer does not agree with the Closing Balance Sheet, it shall so notify the Seller not later than 10 business days after the receipt thereof specifying the item or items with respect to which it is not in agreement. Seller and Buyer shall endeavor to reach agreement with respect to the disputed items within 10 business days of Purchaser's written notification to Seller as aforesaid and, should such agreement be reached, payment shall be forthwith made by Buyer to Seller or by seller to Buyer, as appropriate, in the manner specified in Section 2.2. hereof. Should the parties fail to reach agreement, the matter shall be referred to arbitration to be conducted by an independent arbitration firm, whose decision will be binding and conclusive on the parties hereto.

3.   Representations and Warranties by Seller

For purposes of inducing Buyer to undertake the obligations undertaken by it pursuant to this Agreement, Seller represents and warrants to Buyer as follows:

3.1.   *Authority of Seller.*   Seller is a corporation duly organized, validly existing, and in good standing under the laws of the state of its incorporation, and has the corporate power and authority to enter into and carry out its obligations under this Agreement, and neither the execution nor the carrying out of the terms of this Agreement will be in violation of the provisions of its Certificate of Incorporation or its By-Laws, or constitute a breach of any agreement to which Seller is a party.

3.2.   *Title to Purchased Assets.*   Seller has good and marketable title to the Purchased Assets, none of which is encumbered by any mortgage, pledge, lease, lien, or encumbrance, except for such minor restrictions and easements as are not substantial in amount and which do not and will not materially affect the present use of such properties or materially impair the business or operations presently conducted thereon. The Purchased Assets constitute all of the assets used by Seller's business in the operation of the facilities situated on the properties described in the Schedules to this Agreement.

3.3.   *Condition of Purchased Assets.*   The Purchased Assets taken as a whole are in good operating condition and repair and constitute all of the assets necessary for the conduct of Seller's business as presently conducted.

3.4.   *Regulations.*   To the knowledge of Seller, all buildings and other structures sold to Buyer under this Agreement and all operations conducted by Seller's business on the properties described in the Schedules to this Agreement comply in all material respects with all applicable zoning laws and other ordinances, laws, orders, regulations of OSHA and those regarding protection of the environment, health, and safety, deed restrictions, and contractual obligations. No notice has been received by Seller as to any uncorrected violations of any zoning laws and other ordinances, laws, orders, regulations, and requirements as aforesaid, deed restrictions or contractual obligations. All required permits, licenses, franchises, and other authorizations necessary to the conduct of the business which is presently being conducted, have been duly issued and are valid and in full force and effect except in each case to the extent that the failure to obtain and maintain same in full force and effect does not materially adversely affect the business of Seller. Seller has not engaged in any activity which Seller reasonably believes would cause revocation or suspension of any such permits, licenses, franchises, or authorizations, and no action of proceeding looking to or contemplating the revocation or suspension of any thereof is pending or, to the knowledge of Seller, threatened; and since the date Seller acquired its business, Seller has not been charged by any governmental authority or agency with any material violation of any federal, state, or local law relating to its operations.

3.5. *Contracts and Leases.* All contracts and leases referred to herein or in the Schedules hereto are in full force and effect in accordance with their terms and Seller is not in default thereunder. To the best knowledge of Seller, no condition presently exists which would give any party thereto the right to terminate any of such contracts or leases. To the knowledge of Seller, the performance by Seller of the obligations to be performed by it hereafter under any such contract or other commitment in accordance with the terms thereof would not have a material adverse effect upon the business or operations of Seller.

3.6. *Pending Litigation.* There is no known suit, action, arbitration, or legal, administrative, or other proceeding or governmental investigation, pending or, to the knowledge of Seller, threatened against Seller which might adversely affect any of the assets of Seller being transferred to Buyer hereunder, nor is there presently known to Seller any event or condition of any character pertaining to such assets that occurred prior to the date hereof which might give rise to any such proceeding or investigation that may adversely affect such assets or the title thereto.

3.7. *Financial Statements.* Schedule C to this Agreement consists of Balance Sheets of Seller's business as of September 30, 19XX, and Statements of Income of Seller's business for the 9-month period then ended. Each of said statements has been prepared in accordance with generally accepted accounting principles on a basis consistent with prior periods. The Balance Sheet presents fairly, as of September 30, 19XX, the financial condition and assets and liabilities of Seller's business; the Statement of Operations presents fairly the results of operations of Seller's business for the period indicated.

3.8. *Absence of Certain Changes or Events.* Since September 30, 19XX, except as disclosed herein or in any Schedule to this Agreement, there has not been with respect to Seller:

(a) Other than changes in the ordinary course of business, none of which has been materially adverse, any material adverse change in the financial condition, results of operations, manner of conducting business, assets, liabilities, properties, or business of Seller, including any damage or destruction of property by fire or other casualty, whether or not covered by insurance, any material labor dispute, or any taking of property by condemnation or eminent domain.

(b)   Any bonus, stock option, profit sharing, pension, retirement, or other similar arrangement or plan instituted by Seller or any change in any such plans or arrangements of Seller as in effect at September 30, 19XX that will affect Buyer or any increase in the compensation payable or to become payable to any officer, employee, or agent of the Seller's Business other than normal salary adjustments or any bonus, percentage of compensation, or other like benefits accrued to or for the credit of, any officer, employee, or agent of seller that will affect Buyer, or any bonus, pension, retirement, or similar payment or arrangement agreed to by Seller with respect to Seller's Business or the officers, agents, or employees thereof that will affect Buyer.

(c)   Any amendment of or modification to or entering into of any commitment:

> (i)   Involving aggregate payments by Seller in excess of $5,000; or
>
> (ii)   obligating Seller's business for longer than 90 days from the date thereof.

3.9.   *Delivery of Documents and Seller's Representations and Warranties in Connection Therewith.* Attached hereto are schedules containing the following items. Each such Schedule to be delivered by Seller hereunder shall be executed on behalf of Seller and shall be accompanied by a copy of each document referred to therein.

> (a)   A brief description of all real property owned of record or beneficially or leased by Seller's business and of all buildings, and structures located thereon; the original or true copies of the deeds, title insurance policies, and other title documents relating to such real property as is owned and of the leases relating to such real property as is leased.
>
> (b)   An accurate list of inventories of materials, merchandise, machinery, major items of equipment, furniture, and fixtures, included among the Purchased Assets, as recorded in the books of account and records of Seller's business as of September 30, 19XX.

(c)   An accurate list of each contract or other commitment of Seller's business (i) involving an aggregate payment by Seller's business of more than $5,000 or (ii) for continuous supplies of goods or services involving annual payments of more than $15,000 and not terminable on 30 days' notice by Seller. Seller represents that the aggregate amount of outstanding contracts and commitments for less than $5,000 do not in the aggregate exceed $40,000.

(d)   An accurate list of the names and current annual salary rates of all the present officers and employees of Seller whose current annual salary rate is $25,000 or more, together with a summary of the bonuses, additional compensation, and other like benefits, if any, paid or payable to such persons for the year ended December 31, 19XX.

(e)   An accurate list of all permits, licenses, franchises, and other authorizations necessary to the conduct of the business of Seller in the manner and in which such business is presently being conducted, except in each case where the failure to obtain and maintain said permits, licenses, franchises, and other authorizations does not materially adversely affect the business of Seller.

(f)   An accurate list of all leases, contracts, or other commitments of Seller to which any consent to assignment is required.

3.10.   *Extent of Representations and Warranties.*   No representation or warranty of Seller contained in this Agreement or any statement contained in any document referred to herein as being delivered by Seller, contains or will contain any statement of a material fact untrue at the time it is made, or willfully fails or will fail willfully to contain any material facts known to Seller necessary in order to make the statements therein not misleading. Except for the events or conditions set forth in this Agreement or otherwise disclosed to Buyer pursuant to this Agreement, Seller does not know of any event or condition or the threat of any event or condition specifically relating to Seller (including, without limitation, any event or condition relating to products of Seller) which will or could have a material adverse effect upon the business or operations to be transferred to Buyer hereby. Seller agrees to hold harmless, indemnify, and defend Buyer from and against all loss, damage, cost, and expense (including reasonable attorneys' fees) which are caused by or arise out of any misrepresentation or breach of warranty contained in this Section 3. Seller has made no representations or warranties, orally or in writing, except those expressly set forth in this Agreement or in any Schedule hereto, and Buyer acknowledges that it is not relying on any oral or written warranty or representation except those expressly stated herein or in any Exhibit or Schedule hereto.

4.   Representations and Warranties of Buyer

Buyer represents and warrants to Seller as follows:

4.1.   *Authority of Buyer.* Buyer is a corporation duly organized and validly existing and in good standing under the laws of the state of its incorporation, and has the corporate power and authority to enter into and carry out its obligations under this Agreement, and neither the execution nor the carrying out of the terms of this Agreement will be in violation of the provisions of its Certificate of Incorporation or its By-Laws, or constitute a breach of any agreement to which Buyer is a party.

4.2.   *Corporate Action.* Buyer has taken all necessary corporate action required by law, its Certificate of Incorporation, or its By-Laws to authorize the execution and delivery of this Agreement and to make the payments called for herein.

4.3.   *Extent of Representations and Warranties.* Buyer has made no representations or warranties, orally or in writing, except those expressly set forth in this Agreement and Seller acknowledges that it is not relying on any oral or written warranty or representation except those expressly stated herein. Buyer agrees to hold harmless, indemnify, and defend Seller from and against all loss, damage, cost, and expense (including reasonable attorneys' fees) which are caused by or arise out of any misrepresentation or breach of warranty contained in this Section 4.

5.   Investigation and Indemnity

Any investigation made by Buyer prior to the date hereof of the assets, business, and records, of Seller shall not affect the representations and warranties of Seller contained or provided for herein.

Notwithstanding any investigation of the business and assets of Seller made by or on behalf of Buyer prior to the date hereof, Seller agrees to indemnify Buyer and hold it harmless from and against all damages, losses, and expenses caused by or arising out of (a) any breach of warranty or inaccurate or erroneous representation of Seller contained herein or in any Schedule or information delivered pursuant hereto or (b) any liabilities of the Seller (other than liabilities specifically assumed by Buyer).

6. Certain Agreements of Seller and Buyer

6.1. *Bulk Transfer Law.* Buyer hereby waives compliance by Seller with the provisions of any applicable Bulk Transfer Law or Bulk Sales Law, and Seller shall hold Buyer harmless as to, and indemnify it against, any lien or claim of any creditor of Seller (and any cost or expense, including reasonable attorneys' fees in connection therewith) resulting from the failure of Seller and/or Buyer to comply with any provisions of any such law.

6.2. *Subrogation.* Seller hereby subrogates Buyer to all rights or actions which Seller may have against others in respect of the Purchased Assets, except for rights or actions against third parties arising pursuant to the provisions of antitrust or trade regulation, statute, or case law.

6.3. *Finders and Brokers.* Each party agrees to indemnify and hold the other harmless from and against any loss, liability, claim, or expense to which such other party may be subject in the event that any person, firm, or corporation shall assert any claim of entitlement by reason of an agreement with the indemnifying party, to be payable in connection with this Agreement or the trnsactions contemplated hereby, or because of any act, omission, or statement of the indemnifying party pertaining to any of the subjects set forth above.

6.4. *Employee Procedures and Benefits.*

(a)   Buyer shall offer employment to all of the employees of Seller employed on the date hereof at rates of salary no less favorable than those presently paid to such employees by Seller. If any such employee shall be terminated by Buyer (other than for cause) within 90 days after the date of this Agreement, Buyer shall pay to such employee termination and severance pay benefits in amounts equal to those which such employee would have received from Seller if the employment of such employee had been terminated by Seller as of the date of termination by Buyer.

(b) To the extent reasonably possible, Buyer shall provide all employees of Seller who are employed by it under this Section 6.4, vacation, sick pay, medical, hospitalization, disability, and life insurance benefits substantially equivalent to those presently provided by Buyer to its other employees.

(c) Seller shall retain all accrued pension benefit obligations, liabilities, and assets through the date hereof for all of the then active, vested former, and retired salaried employees of Seller covered under the Seller's Retirement Plan. Seller shall amend its Plan to recognize a participant's service with Buyer after the date hereof for purposes of fulfilling the vesting requirements for the accrued pensions up to the date hereof. After acquiring vesting, distribution of benefits shall be made to participants in accordance with the terms of the Plan.

7. Survival of Representations and Warranties

All covenants, representations, and warranties of Seller and of Buyer contained herein, and remedies for failure to perform any obligation, agreement, covenant, or provision to be performed by Seller or by Buyer hereunder, shall survive the closing of the transactions contemplated hereby, regardless of any investigation or inquiry made by Seller or by Buyer for a period of two years from the date hereof.

7.1. *Further Assurances.* At any time or from time to time after the date hereof, Seller shall, at the request of Buyer and without further consideration, execute and deliver any further instruments or documents and take all such further action as Buyer may reasonably request in order to more effectively vest Buyer with full and complete title to, and to place Buyer in actual possession and operating control of, the Purchased Assets, and to assist Buyer in exercising its rights with respect thereto or performing its obligations with respect to this Agreement, and more effectively to carry out the terms of this Agreement.

7.2. (a) Real and personal property taxes, rents, utilities, and other operating expenses shall be prorated as of the date hereof, and Seller and Buyer shall bear their respective pro rata share thereof.

(b) As soon as is reasonably practicable after the date hereof, there shall also be prorated as of the date hereof liabilities or credits to or for the benefit of Seller's employees who become employees of Buyer for salaries, wages, or allowances, bonuses, employment taxes, and union benefit contributions, and Seller and Buyer shall bear their respective pro rata shares thereof.

8. Miscellaneous Provisions

8.1. *Sales and Transfer Taxes.* All sales, transfer, or other taxes payable in connection with the sale herein provided shall be paid by the Buyer.

8.2. *Complete Agreement.* This Agreement constitutes the entire agreement between the parties hereto with respect to the transactions contemplated and supersedes all prior agreements and undertakings relating to the subject matter. This Agreement may be amended, modified, and supplemented only by a written instrument duly signed by the party against which such amendment, modification, or supplement is sought to be enforced.

8.3. *Successors and Assigns.* All of the covenants, representations, warranties, terms, and conditions of this Agreement shall inure to the benefit of, and be binding upon, the parties hereto and their respective successors and assigns. Nothing in this Agreement is intended, expressly or impliedly, to confer upon any party, other than the parties hereto and their successors and assigns, any rights or remedies under or by reason of this Agreement except as expressly provided herein.

8.4. *Notices.* All notices, requests, demands, and other communications required hereunder shall be in writing and shall be deemed to have been duly given or made if delivered personally or sent by registered or certified mail, postage prepaid, as follows:

A. To Buyer at:

(Buyer's name and address)

B.   To Seller at:

(Seller's name and address)

Either party may change the address to which such communications are to be sent to it by giving ten (10) days' written notice of such change of address to the other party in the manner above provided for giving notice. Notices will be considered delivered on the date of personal delivery or on the date of deposit in the United States mail in the manner above provided for giving notice by mail.

8.5.   *Sections and Other Headings.* The sections and other headings contained in this Agreement are for reference purposes only, and shall not affect in any way the meaning or interpretation of this Agreement.

IN WITNESS WHEREOF, the parties hereto have caused this Agreement to be duly executed as of the day and year above written.

SELLER: BUYER:

By _____   By _____

Its _____   Its _____

SAMPLE CONTRACT—CORPORATE JOINT VENTURE AGREEMENT

THIS AGREEMENT, made and entered into as of the first day of October, 19XX, among the shareholders (names) of Company A, a (name of state) corporation, and the Shareholders of Company B, a (name of state) corporation. The shareholders of Company A and Company B are hereinafter collectively referred to as the "Investors."

WITNESSETH:

The Investors desire to form a new company and to carry on and expand the businesses previously separately conducted by Company A and Company B.

NOW, THEREFORE, in consideration of the premises and the mutual covenants hereinafter set forth, the parties hereto agree as follows.

Section 1. Formation of NEWCO

1.1. As promptly as practicable, the Investors will cause a corporation to be organized under the laws of the State of (name of state) to be known as NEWCO.

1.2. As promptly as practicable after the formation of NEWCO, the Investors will cause NEWCO to become a party to this Agreement.

1.3. A. Venture shall have an initial capital consisting of two hundred (200) shares of capital stock classified as Common Stock, which shall have no par value.

B. On the Transfer Date (defined in Paragraph C of this Section 1.3) the Investors shall subscribe to and pay for said shares of capital stock as follows:

(i) Shareholders of Company A shall subscribe, pro rata, to one hundred (100) shares of Common Stock of NEWCO and in exchange for the issuance to them of such shares shall transfer to NEWCO all the issued and outstanding capital stock of Company A.

(ii) Shareholders of Company B shall subscribe, pro rata, to one hundred (100) shares of common stock of NEWCO and in exchange for the issuance to them of such shares shall transfer to NEWCO all the issued and outstanding capital stock of Company B.

C. The Transfer Date referred to in Paragraph B of this Section 1.3 shall be October 15, 19XX or, subject to Section 4 hereof, such earlier or later date as the parties hereto may agree to select, provided that the Transfer Date shall not occur prior to the satisfaction of the conditions set forth in Section 4 hereof:

D. The parties hereto may agree that shares of Common Stock to be issued in proportionate amounts to Investors, shall be issued initially for nominal consideration to permit them to cause NEWCO to implement certain provisions of this agreement prior to the Transfer Date and the number of shares of capital stock to be issued to Investors on the Transfer Date shall be decreased by the number of shares issued prior to the Transfer Date.

Section 2.   Business of NEWCO

The business of NEWCO shall be to continue and expand, subject to the limitations hereinafter set forth, the businesses presently conducted by Company A and Company B, which will be acquired by NEWCO as provided in this Agreement.

Section 3. Management of NEWCO

3.1. NEWCO shall be managed by (a) a Board of Directors of eight persons, four selected by each of the holders of shares of common stock of NEWCO, (b) by an Executive Committee of two persons, one selected by the present Stockholders of Company A and one selected by the stockholders of Company B, and (c) by other officers selected as provided in the By-Laws of NEWCO. NEWCO shall enter into appropriate employment or consulting agreements with members of the Executive Committee to properly define the responsibilities of each committee member.

3.2. Except as otherwise herein provided, or as provided in the Certificate of Incorporation or By-Laws of NEWCO, all matters relating to the conduct of the business and affairs of NEWCO which are not within the powers of the officers of NEWCO shall be decided by mutual agreement between Investors holding, on a combined basis, a majority of the Common Stock of NEWCO at the level of the Executive Committee, of the Board of Directors or of the shareholders of NEWCO, as may be appropriate.

3.3. The Board of Directors of NEWCO shall authorize its officers and employees, and shall cause Company A and Company B, (through their Boards of Directors) to authorize their respective officers and employees, to act for the respective corporations and may, from time to time, establish guidelines therefor including limitations on commitments which may be made without obtaining prior approval of the appropriate Board of Directors.

Section 4. Conditions Precedent

The Transfer Date shall not occur until the fulfillment of the following conditions (or waiver by the parties other than the party by whom action is required to fulfill and such condition):

(List conditions)

Section 5. Legend on Certificates, Dividends, and Transferability of Shares

5.1. The face of each certificate evidencing shares of Common Stock of NEWCO shall bear the following legend:

> The shares of stock represented by this Certificate are subject to the provisions of a Joint Venture Agreement dated as of October 1, 19XX, as the same may be amended from time to time, by and among the Shareholders of Company A and Company B. The holder of this certificate by his acceptance hereof, agrees to be bound by all of the provisions of such Joint Venture Agreement as amended from time to time, all of which the holder hereof should examine carefully before accepting this Certificate.

The Investors agree that prior to effecting any sale of shares of stock of NEWCO, the Seller will provide a copy of this Agreement, as amended from time to time, to the person to whom such sale is to be made and will advise such person that he will be bound by and must comply with all of the terms and conditions of this Agreement as if he had executed this Agreement. Any such person shall, after such sale, be deemed a successor to the person making such sale for purposes of this Agreement.

5.2.   The parties hereto agree that NEWCO will pay annual dividends to the holders of Common Stock, pro rata, in an amount equal to 20% of NEWCO consolidated net earnings after income taxes for each fiscal year during the term of this Agreement which earnings shall have been computed in accordance with generally accepted accounting principles.

5.3.   Among the Investors, the shares of Common Stock, and any additional shares of capital stock which may be issued, shall be freely transferable. Any transfer to a third party shall be submitted to a prior right of first refusal from the Investors other than the Investor wishing to withdraw from the joint venture. Each of the Investors wishing to acquire the shares being sold shall have the right to acquire an amount of the shares to be sold in proportion to the relative shareholding percentages of the Investors wishing to acquire such shares. The selling price will be, in the absence of an agreement between the parties, determined by independent valuers as defined in Section 5.4.

5.4.   In case of disagreement between Investors as to the selling price, each of the Investors wishing to sell or acquire shares shall have the right to nominate an independent expert valuer. If these valuers cannot reach a common value, such Investors will jointly nominate an additional independent expert valuer who will arbitrate the situation to enable the Investors and other independent valuers in arriving at a common value.

5.5. In the event of the death of any of the Investors, the shares of stock of NEWCO owned by the deceased Investor shall become subject to the provisions of paragraphs 5.3 and 5.4 and may be immediately acquired by the other Investors from the estate of the deceased, in accordance with the valuation procedures set forth in paragraph 5.4.

Section 6.   Miscellaneous

6.1. This Agreement shall inure to the benefit of and be binding upon the parties hereto and their respective legal representatives, successors, and assigns.

6.2. Except as otherwise provided in the Agreement, all notices and other communications which shall or may be given pursuant to this Agreement shall be in writing and shall be delivered in person or by prepaid registered or certified mail, return receipt requested, addressed to the intended recipient at the following address:

A. If to Shareholders of Company A:
(list names and addresses)

B. If to Shareholders of Company B:
(list names and addresses)

Any such notice or other communication shall be deemed received on the tenth day after mailing or on the day of actual receipt, whichever is earlier. Any party may change its address for purposes of this Section 6.2 by notice duly given to the other party as above provided.

6.3. This Agreement shall be governed by the laws of the state of (name of state).

6.4. Whenever an obligation, duty, or liability of Shareholders is referred to in this Agreement, such obligation, duty, or liability shall be the joint and several obligation, duty, or liability of each of the Shareholders of Company A or Company B, as the case may be.

IN WITNESS WHEREOF, the parties hereto have caused this Agreement to be executed as of the day and year first above written.

Shareholders of Company A:

_____ _____

_____

_____

_____

Shareholders of Company B:

_____

_____

_____

_____

NEWCO:

By _____

Its _____

APPENDIX **E** _____

OTHER AREAS FREQUENTLY COVERED IN BUSINESS COMBINATION AGREEMENTS

The sample contracts contained in Appendices B, C, and D embody the basic structure of these kinds of agreements, and are prepared on the basis of relatively straightforward transactions. This exhibit will indicate many of the additional clauses of importance to the financial professional which may appear in business combination agreements, depending on the specific transaction.

Financing of Purchase Price

1. A purchase agreement may provide for part of the purchase price in the form of notes receivable held by the seller. In such cases, the seller may require that stock, assets, and/or the business be pledged as collateral to secure the debt.
2. A purchase contract may contain a clause making the carrying out of the deal contingent on the buyer being able to obtain financing from banks or other outside sources.

Contingent Purchase Prices

1. Earn out clauses provide that the seller will receive additional payments adjusting the purchase price based on future performance. Such payments may be based on net income, stock prices, or other variables.

2. Sometimes purchase prices are based on specified amounts over or under net worth or net book value. For example, the purchase price might be net book value at the closing date plus $200,000. At the closing date, exact book value may not be known, in which case an estimated amount may be paid at the closing, with adjustment between the parties made upon the later finalization of net book values. In this situation, buyer and seller may develop different estimates of items subject to valuation adjustments, requiring sometimes difficult negotiation to finalize the purchase price.

3. In some cases, there will be a clause whereby the seller will not be paid the entire purchase price until certain identified contingencies are resolved.

Accounts Receivable

1. Sometimes the seller will warrant the net realizable value of accounts receivable being acquired by the buyer.

2. Other contracts may provide that the seller will retain title to the accounts receivable, but that the buyer will collect the receivables as part of the taking over of the business. In such cases the contract may include a clause stating that all cash receipts will be applied to the oldest outstanding invoices, unless the customer specifically indicates that other than the oldest invoices are being paid.

Inventories

1. Some contracts call for the taking of physical inventories on or about the transfer date. These physical inventories will often be observed and verified by representatives of both the buyer and seller.

2. Other clauses may provide that all inventory items are saleable and will be sold within a specified period of time.

Covenants Not to Compete

1. These may require the seller to agree not to compete with the buyer for a specified time period. Sometimes the covenant is

limited to geographic areas near the business which has been sold.

2. The specific assignment of a portion of the purchase price, or making this item the subject of a separate agreement will strengthen the case for deducting an amount in the future for tax purposes as amortization of a covenant not to compete.

Opinion of Counsel

1. Some purchase agreements will state that as a condition precedent to closing, attorneys for the buyer and seller must furnish a written legal opinion that the transactions to be entered into are legal, and certain other matters, such as the valid corporate existence of the entities entering into the agreement.

Officers and Employment Matters

1. Sometimes purchase contracts will include a provision that employment agreements will be executed with the former owners or officers.

2. The contract may have a requirement that the officers of the acquiree submit their resignations as officers, whether or not employment contracts are in existence.

3. A purchase agreement may address the continued employment of the seller's employees, although it may not be worded so as to be legally binding on the buyer. Provisions may be made for levels of employee benefits to be given to employees under the ownership of the buyer, and termination payments to be made to the employees if an employee is terminated.

Insurance Policies

1. Sometimes a purchase agreement will address the insurance practices of the seller, and require that the insurance policies, or details of the seller's insurance policies be attached to the purchase agreement.

INDEX